AN
UNGODLY
WAR

To the memory of
Lauren Jane

AN UNGODLY WAR

THE SACK OF CONSTANTINOPLE & THE FOURTH CRUSADE

W.B. BARTLETT

SUTTON PUBLISHING

First published in 2000 by
Sutton Publishing Limited · Phoenix Mill
Thrupp · Stroud · Gloucestershire · GL5 2BU

British Library Cataloguing in Publication Data
A catalogue record for this book is available from the British Library

ISBN 0-7509-2378-4

Typeset in 10/12 pt New Bastkerville.
Typesetting and origination by
Sutton Publishing Limited.
Printed in Great Britain by
Biddles Limited, Guildford, Surrey.

Contents

List of Plates

Between pp. 74 and 75

Between pp. 170 and 171

Picture Credits

The author and publisher wish to thank the following for permission to reproduce illustrations (references given are plate numbers):

AKG, London: 2, 4; Ronald Sheridan (photographer), Ancient Art and Architecture Collection: 5; Bodleian Library, University of Oxford: MS. Bodl. 264, f. 218r: 3; Bodleian Library, University of Oxford: MS Laud Misc 587, f. 1: 6a; British Library: MS Roy. 16. G. VI., f. 74: 6b; Burgerbibliothek Bern, cod. 120.II, f. 119r: 10; Corpus Christi College, Oxford, UK/Bridgeman Art Library: 12b; Hagia Sophia, Istanbul/Bridgeman Art Library: 1b; Katz Picture Agency: 12a; A.F. Kersting: 1a; Louvre, France/Giraudon/Bridgeman Art Library: 8; The Pierpont Morgan Library, New York: MS M. 638, f. 23v: 9; The Pierpont Morgan Library, New York: MS M. 638, f. 12: 11; The V&A Picture Library, London: 7.

Acknowledgements

Carrying out the necessary research for a book such as this makes one acutely aware of how much is owed to so many historians over the years. The principal credit for *An Ungodly War* must lie with those who have given so much of themselves in the pursuit of enlightenment. To the many great students of the Crusades, who have devoted themselves tirelessly to the subject that they love and have committed their thoughts to paper, we all owe our gratitude. More particularly, those who read and critiqued this book have been the source of both encouragement and assistance to me. Their comments have always been constructive and helpful, and to them I am especially grateful.

To my publishers I also owe my thanks, especially to Jane, whose help I always appreciate, and to Clare who continued to keep her good humour when modern technology appeared to be conspiring against us. A publication such as this, as anyone who has ever written will know, is a team effort, and in this respect I have been most fortunate.

Finally, but not least, perhaps my greatest debt is to my family, especially Angela and Deyna, who have uncomplainingly let me immerse myself in books, or lock myself away in the study, for hours on end. They must sometimes have been driven to distraction by it all but, if they were, they never let it show. Without them, above all others, this book would not have been possible.

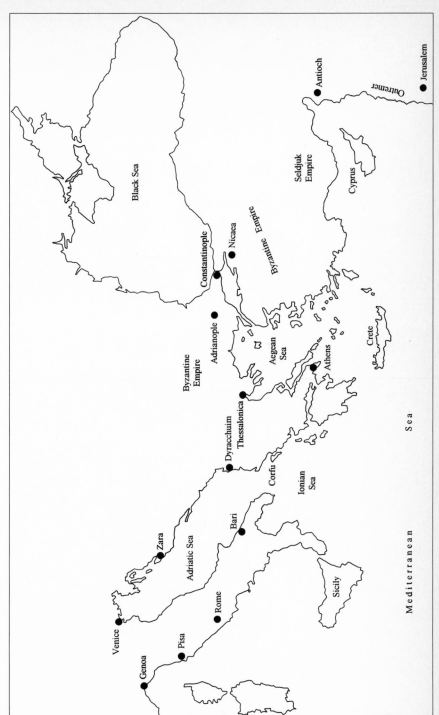

The Eastern Mediterranean on the eve of the Fourth Crusade

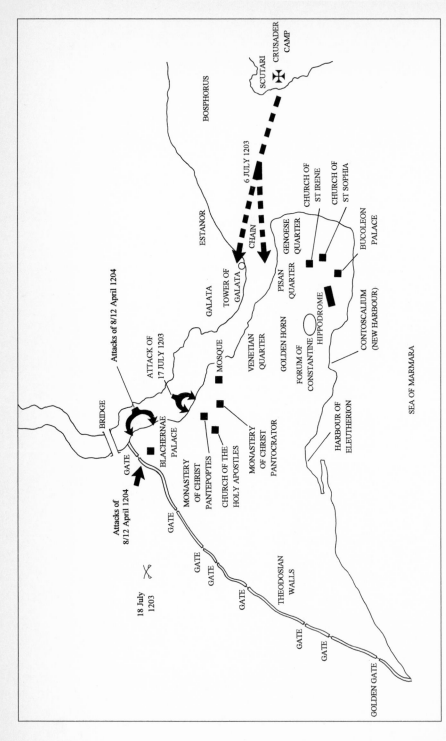

The assaults of the Franks on Constantinople

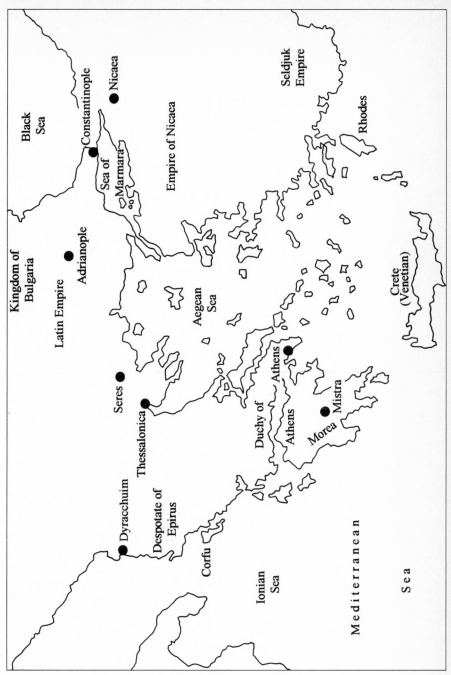

The division of the Byzantine Empire in the thirteenth century

Introduction

As the sun rose over Constantinople on the morning of 16 April 1204, it shone down on a city licking its wounds. For a millennium, the city had represented all that was best in Christian culture. Its artists produced masterpieces at which the rest of the world could only marvel, while its architects erected churches of such size and magnificence that when men came from the West to visit the city they could only stop and stare in awestruck wonder. The sheer scale of the place dwarfed anything that Western Christendom could offer. Truly, Constantinople held in its hands the heritage of much that was best in Greek and Roman civilisation.

For nearly one thousand years, the classical world had lived on within this city's massive walls. No Alaric had robbed it of its many treasures, as had happened to Rome 900 years previously. Constantinople had indeed faced many a crisis. On more than one occasion, the wolf had stood at the gates, in the form of Arab, Turk or Slav. Always the city had managed to survive, although not without sometimes superhuman effort.

Now the city had fallen. The blood of its innocents washed over the streets, while its violated womenfolk wept tears of shame and anger at the hideous fate that had befallen them. The proud conqueror strutted imperiously through a shattered city, a city that had for three days been handed over to the army of the invaders, for the soldiers to do with as they pleased. Of all the insults, the greatest was that offered to its Christian heritage. Its finest churches had been ravaged, stripped of their greatest treasures. Its people mourned not only the personal losses that they had suffered, but also the passing of a way of life.

In the bitterest of ironies, the city had suffered not at the hands of a Muslim or pagan invader. The enemy this time was a Christian one, an army that had been sent to the East with the objective of defending Christendom. In the cruellest of contradictions, it had just dealt Christendom in the Orient a hammer blow from which it would never recover.

The saga of the disagreements and misunderstandings between Byzantium and the West is one of the strongest themes of Medieval history, and the sack of Constantinople is one of the seminal events of the period. Yet this act, of such enormous significance, is still a mystery to many in the West. One modern commentator remarked that the battle between Eastern and Western Christendom was 'a conflict of major importance culminating in the event of 1204, a date of real importance in the history of Europe but one that has never been adequately expressed in Western books or classrooms'.[1]

What follows is an attempt to understand the apocalyptic events that took place in Constantinople in 1204, to explain how and why they happened, and to understand the context in which they occurred. It is the story of how an army that went forth in the name of God lost sight of its fundamental motivations. It is a tale that demonstrates how misguided idealism can often lead to disaster and which shows that, of all motivations, selfish gain can often be the strongest. And it is more than that. It is the story of how, in what was supposed to be an act of God, the classical world finally passed from reality to history.

CHAPTER ONE

A Clash of Cultures

On the afternoon of 16 July 1054, the leading churchmen of the ancient city of Constantinople were assembled in the holy church of St Sophia, in the same way that their predecessors had done for hundreds of years. They had come to hear Mass, to worship the Lord of Christendom. It appeared, at least on the surface, that this day was no different from any other in Byzantium. There was little to mark the occasion out from the many similar services that had been held in this revered and marvellously elegant building throughout the course of the year and the centuries.

Suddenly, the sanctity and spirituality of these sacred moments were disturbed by the arrival of three men, who marched imperiously down the aisle towards the High Altar. Oblivious to the Byzantine churchmen who watched, bewildered, the men approached the front of the church and flung something down on the altar. Then, their task completed, they turned around and retraced their steps through the ranks of the assembled Greeks and made their way out through the great doorway. In a last, deeply symbolic gesture they removed their footwear and wiped the dust from their feet. Then they left.

The three men were representatives of the Pope in Rome, and the object they had deposited on the altar was a Bill of Excommunication. Its target was Michael Cerularius, Patriarch of Constantinople. The leading churchmen of Western Christendom had just declared spiritual warfare on the leading churchman of the East.

Every story must start somewhere, and in any historical narrative the choice of a particular starting place is somewhat arbitrary. History is rarely made by any one event in isolation, and events are usually dictated by a combination of factors. However, the excommunication of Cerularius is as good a place as any to begin in considering the confused relationships of Byzantium and Western Europe at the time of the crusades. In the way that it epitomises the differences in attitudes and perceptions between Eastern and Western Christendom, it is the perfect symbolic moment.

The terrible events of 1204 were the culmination of a prolonged period of mistrust, a time when the eastern and western halves of Christendom moved closer to each other and, paradoxically, were forced further apart as a result. The events of the eleventh and twelfth centuries brought Byzantium and the West into closer contact than they had been for hundreds of years. Our story must begin, then, with an examination of the tangled web of events throughout this period of history, which led finally, tragically, one might almost say inexorably, to the destruction of Constantinople.

The three men who had placed the bill on the altar were representatives of Pope Leo IX, a man who, ironically, was dead by this time. In 1054 the Papacy was passing through a crucial phase in its development. For many years, the Pope had been appointed by a political master, firstly by the leading families in Rome and latterly by the Western (German) Emperor. However, in the decade leading up to the events described the Papacy had made a bid for independence. A succession of Popes had not only attempted to reform the Church – and it was an institution in great need of reform from all the abuses prevalent at this time – but they had also tried to assert their independence from secular rulers. More than this, they claimed that the spiritual authority of the Papacy was not only independent, but was actually superior to the secular authority of the Emperor.

Pope Leo IX was a man made in such a likeness, but tragically for him his attempts to increase his power had led to personal disaster. His position in Italy (a term that describes a geographical region and which had no political meaning in the eleventh century) had been extremely uncertain. He had been greatly threatened by the emergence of the Normans in the area. These adventurers had arrived from Normandy just after the turn of the millennium, and had quickly seized most of the many opportunities that had come their way to increase their power and landholdings in the peninsula. They were the great adventurers of their day, travelling widely in search of land and wealth. Close cousins of the Vikings, they had inherited many of that people's propensity for aggression and opportunism. This had caused them to clash with all of the major powers in Italy; namely, the Western Emperor, the Muslims and, most importantly for our story, the Byzantines who had held a significant portion of the southern part of the peninsula. They quickly swept all before them, and in the space of four decades came to dominate much of the region.

Pope Leo was understandably nervous of their progress. The Western Emperor, Henry III, was equally perturbed but was distracted by conflict in Hungary. Leo therefore sought desperately for allies. The Byzantine lands in Italy were being overrun by the Normans. It was therefore natural that Leo should approach them for help. As a consequence, he sent a small delegation to Byzantium with just such a goal in mind.

Unfortunately, the enterprise was dogged with difficulties from the beginning. The head of the church in Byzantium was Michael Cerularius. He was a man who had some virtues and many faults. He was a good administrator, but he was a proud and tactless character. Worst of all from Leo's perspective, he was proud of the heritage of Byzantium and looked on the West with disdain.

There had been friction between the West and Constantinople since the latter was first made capital of the Roman Empire by Constantine the Great in the fourth century. The move was a tacit admission that the focal point of power within the Roman Empire had moved irrevocably to the East. It was a diminution of the importance of Rome itself. Subsequent developments proved such a move to be completely justified. The West was overrun by a succession of barbarian, pagan tribes. Only in the East did Rome live on, in the city given its name by the Emperor Constantine.

Despite a number of alarms over the centuries, Byzantium had prospered. Constantinople was without a doubt the greatest city in Christendom, both in terms of its size and its culture. However, over time, its links with the West had become ever less secure. It looked upon Western Europe, even now that its kings and emperors were Christians, as the home of barbarians.

The differences between Byzantium and the West were greatly marked in the spiritual sphere. Theology was a keenly debated subject in the East. Its intricacies seemed to appeal to the deep-thinking Byzantine mind. Religious debate had characterised Christian society for centuries, and it was at its most profound in Byzantium. Theologians had fought bitterly in the past over topics of great importance to the religious minds of the time, such as the nature and divinity of Christ. As a result of these spiritual battles, the Greek Church within the Byzantine Empire had developed its own stance on many issues to do with doctrine and dogma. Some of them brought the Eastern Church into conflict with the views of the Western Church, headed by the Pope. In contrast, the West had little place for the meditative other-worldliness of Byzantine theology. In common with the people whose faith it represented, Western Christianity was practical, pragmatic and uncomplicated.

In an era when religion, culture and society were inextricably linked, these differences were the cause of real friction between the two halves of Christendom. Churchmen from the West who attended church services in Constantinople might imagine that they had entered a different world. The services were different; for one thing those in the East lasted longer, and they were conducted in Greek rather than Latin. Even the clothes of the Eastern priests were different, as indeed was the style of their hair.

Some of the issues revolved around the place of unleavened bread in the Eucharist. There was also fierce division over whether priests should be allowed to marry, as they were in the East, or whether they should adopt the Western model, and stay celibate. One of the most intense sources of disagreement revolved around the role of the Pope. Despite the fact that the post had been dominated by secular powers for many years, the Pope was still regarded as head of the Christian Church in the West. However, there were fundamental differences between this perception, and that held within Byzantium. So intense did these differences become that, during the time of Cerularius, the Roman churches in Constantinople were closed by command of the Patriarch.

At the heart of these tensions was the very nature of the Church in East and West. The Eastern Church was unashamedly mystical in outlook, focusing very much on the affairs of the spiritual world to the exclusion of the physical. Theological debates were commonplace, keenly felt and entered into by many educated people, lay as well as spiritual. This contrasted markedly with Christian practice in the West, which was much more down to earth in its attitudes.

Most churchmen in the East would accept that the Pope was a very important Christian leader. Many would even accept that he was pre-eminent among his fellows, a first among equals. However, the absolute obedience that the Papacy demanded of the Christian Church was not recognised by many within the Greek world. The Papacy's stance was fundamentally rejected by a large number of prominent Byzantine churchmen. Indeed, while Cerularius was Patriarch in Constantinople, he castigated the Patriarch of Antioch for his followings of Western teachings, outlining in his letter, in terms of disbelief, that: 'Rumour has reached me that the patriarchs of Alexandria and Jerusalem [along with the patriarchs of Constantinople and Antioch and the Pope these were deemed the leading clerics in Christendom] are following the teachings of the Pope in Rome'.

Despite these very real differences, the emergence of the Normans in Italy forced Leo to seek an accommodation with Byzantium. However, he had chosen his delegation poorly. It was led by Humbert, Cardinal of Mourmoutiers, a man who seems to have shared many of the faults owned by Cerularius. With him were Cardinal Frederick of Lorraine and Peter, Archbishop of Amalfi, neither of whom had any love for the Byzantines. When Cerularius therefore met them with virtually open hostility, rather than attempting to win their arguments with tact they quickly became bombastic and threatening. This moved the Patriarch not one jot. It merely served to harden his attitude. When he heard that Leo had died he refused to continue with negotiations. His obstinacy infuriated Humbert. It was the last straw as far as the Cardinal was concerned, and it was following this act that he had made his dramatic gesture of excommunication in the church of St Sophia.

Was this so-called 'Great Schism' of 1054 a defining moment in history? In absolute terms, perhaps not. Relations had been bad before – a very serious breach had occurred two centuries previously between the Patriarch of Constantinople, a man named Photius, and Pope Nicholas I – and would be again. The excommunication of the Patriarch was just one event in an evolving tale of mistrust and misunderstanding between East and West. There would be many attempts to heal the rift in the future. Despite this, the symbolic significance of the act is irrefutable. It epitomised the fact that Byzantium and the West had different views on religion and on the place of the Papacy within it. The Greeks were prepared to concede a primacy of honour to Rome but regarded an Ecumenical Council as having final authority in matters spiritual. At this moment in history, this was of immense import. Religion and culture were completely enmeshed. Such differences were keenly felt; deep emotions would be stirred by them. From such disagreements, major conflagrations could be ignited.

Cerularius was not acting in consort with the Emperor of Constantinople. The latter could see the merit of an alliance with the Papacy. However, the Patriarch had many supporters in Byzantium, and the attempt to reach an accommodation with the West was stillborn. Even though the Patriarch overstepped the mark a few years later and was deposed, he was regarded by some as a virtual martyr.

In the meantime, the political situation in Italy changed dramatically. The Normans continued their conquests in the peninsula, threatening to rob the Byzantines of all their territories. As a result of the attempts by the Papacy to reform itself, the institution came into conflict with the Western Emperor. Because of this, the Papacy found itself virtually forced into an alliance with the Normans. Such a combination would be dangerous indeed for the Byzantines.

Something needs to be said of the position of the Western Emperor at this time. He ruled Germany, as well as parts of France and much of northern Italy. The fact that he was also known to historians as the Holy Roman Emperor hints at his close connections with the Papacy. For most of the first half of the eleventh century the Pope had in fact been his nominee. This gave him dominance over the institution. However, the attempts at reform of successive Popes had sown the seeds of confrontation. In 1059 Pope Nicholas II declared that no longer would the Papacy be the gift of the Emperor. In future, only the Church itself should be responsible for electing its leader.

Nicholas further exacerbated his differences with the Western Emperor by his alliance with the Norman leader Robert Guiscard. The Normans were great adventurers, and the greatest of them all was Robert Guiscard.[1] By the terms of the treaty made with the Pope, Guiscard recognised the supremacy of the Papacy over all his Italian possessions. This was a clever move on his part. His territories had been won by conquest, and by recognising the primacy of the Papacy he was hoping to make it more difficult for others to attempt to regain them. The Western Emperor saw through this transparent scheme, and declared that the Pope's edicts were invalid; he even suggested that he should be deposed. Before this could come to anything, Nicholas died. This did nothing to end the dispute; the Romans duly elected a new Pope but the Germans would not recognise him and elected one of their own. Western Christendom accelerated down a dangerous road that would lead to full-scale conflict between the secular and spiritual arms of society.

The Byzantine territories in Italy were swallowed up by the advancing Norman tide. The Normans closer relations with the Papacy were most unwelcome to the Greeks. However, there were other threats to distract the Byzantines. Their northern borders came under intense attack from Turkish and Slavic tribes during the eleventh century, which were only repulsed with difficulty. Dangerous as these attacks were, however, the greatest challenge was to come in the heartland of the Byzantine Empire, in Asia Minor.

For several centuries, the Turkish peoples of central Asia had been a threat. These people were especially adept at hit-and-run raids. They were well armed, brave and very mobile. Relatively recent converts to Islam, they were nevertheless committed to their religion, although many more traditional Muslims would find it difficult to understand every part of their theology (for a time many Turks retained their ancient shamanistic beliefs). They had struck at the Byzantines often in the past. However, throughout the early years of the eleventh century their raids became much more intense. The power of the Turks grew until, as the year 1071 arrived, they were a massive threat. In this year, a large number of Turks raided the east of Asia Minor. As this region provided both much of the manpower and much of the grain for the Byzantine Empire, the challenge could not possibly be ignored.

The raids had come at an inopportune time for Byzantium. The Emperor, Romanus Diogenes, was a man with many enemies. A conscientious man of unexceptional abilities, he was not blessed with the stamp of genius that Byzantium needed. A succession of mediocre rulers had done a great deal of harm to the Empire. Its politics were characterised by intrigue, plots and disloyalty. It would need a strong hand to protect Byzantium both from its enemies and from itself. Romanus was not such a man.

He was further distracted by events in Italy, where the news was all bad. Little of the peninsula remained in Greek hands by now. The Norman advance appeared to be unstoppable. So it proved. Even as Romanus prepared to leave his capital, dreadful tidings reached him. The Normans had captured Bari, the last Byzantine possession in Italy. To make matters worse, Romanus was forced to rely on a large proportion of mercenaries in his army. In a supreme irony, a significant number of them were Norman.

The fall of Bari proved to be an appropriate portent of the campaign ahead, which was a disaster for Romanus and for his Empire. Romanus divided his force, and when the Turkish enemy attacked, he was deserted at a critical phase in the battle. The defeat that followed, at Manzikert in the eastern extremities of Asia Minor, was cataclysmic. Romanus was captured. He was well treated by his enemies and returned home to Constantinople a short time after, following the payment of a large ransom.

Sadly, but entirely predictably, in Romanus' absence subversive elements had been plotting his downfall. Andronicus Ducas, a leading Byzantine noble whose despicable abandonment of Romanus at Manzikert had condemned him to defeat, returned in haste to Constantinople and intrigued for the overthrow of Romanus. Given the totality of the Byzantine defeat in Asia Minor, the downfall of the Emperor was an inevitability. So it was that a new Emperor, Michael VII, was proclaimed. Romanus wandered back towards his capital in a desultory manner with a small force accompanying him. He eventually handed himself over to his arch-enemy Andronicus on a promise of safe-conduct. Never did he make a graver error of judgement.

Andronicus quickly made his intentions clear. Romanus was taken back towards Constantinople on the back of a donkey. This was only the start of the deposed Emperor's humiliation. When he reached the city that had been so shortly before the capital of his Empire, he was thrown into prison. Soon after, he had his eyes gouged out, the traditional punishment of a civilisation that ironically prided itself on its superiority over the barbarian nations of the world. So badly botched was the job that within days Romanus died in agony.

The new Emperor, Michael, proved to be no better than the old in improving the fortunes of Byzantium. His unsuitability for the task that faced him was quickly evidenced. Among the mercenaries who had accompanied Romanus to Manzikert was a man named Roussel of Bailleul, who led the Norman contingent in the Byzantine force. Their part in the battle was less dishonourable than non-existent, as they had been divided from the main force before the battle and, whether by design or accident, did not arrive on the battlefield to assist their erstwhile paymasters.

If Roussel could not be accused of out-and-out treachery in the battle, no such benefit of the doubt can be awarded to his subsequent actions. A short time after the disaster at Manzikert, a force set out for Asia Minor with the hopelessly optimistic aim of limiting the damage being caused by Turkish insurgents. It included a number of Normans. Roussel at this stage decided to announce his intentions overtly. When far away in Asia Minor, he set up his own independent state.

There was an important message in his actions as far as Byzantium was concerned: mercenaries from the West could not be trusted. There was, of course, absolutely nothing new in this message. The actions of the Normans demonstrated quite clearly the motivations that underlay their support. It was a pertinent reminder that great care should be taken in dealing with such men. In reality, Roussel's actions were merely a precursor to a much greater danger that was to present itself to Byzantium several decades later.

Michael's response to the problem was wholly inappropriate. In an attempt to bring the errant Norman to book, he enlisted the help of Turkish mercenaries. This only exacerbated an already parlous situation. The Turks took advantage of Michael's difficulties to secure their position in Asia Minor further. Eventually, Roussel was bested by a Byzantine commander, Alexius Comnenus, who was to play more than a passing part in the future affairs of Byzantium. However, much damage had been done in the attempt.

If this was a mistake on the part of Michael, his dealings with the Normans in Italy were no more successful. In an attempt to better relations with them, he arranged that his son Constantine should marry Helena, daughter of Robert Guiscard. If William the Conqueror is perhaps the best known Norman to modern readers, there is very strong evidence that in his day the reputation of Robert Guiscard exceeded even his. Robert was a colossus of his time. Everything about him was larger than life. Even his wife, Sichelgaita, was an amazing woman. Renowned for her bulk, she routinely accompanied him into battle, her Amazon-like qualities terrifying her opponents.

Robert had swept through Italy like a whirlwind. His conquests included many Byzantine possessions. This, however, was not the limit of his ambition. He had designs on Sicily, which was then in Muslim hands but had been part of the Byzantine Empire and would still be considered by the Greeks as in their sphere of influence. Such considerations made no difference to him. His ambitions would not end in Italy. Given half a chance, he would stir up further trouble for Byzantium without compunction. Michael's gestures of friendship towards Robert were tantamount to inviting a cuckoo into the nest.

His opportunity did not arrive immediately, but when it did present itself Robert grasped it with both hands. The Emperor Michael VII was a poor ruler. He was incapable of fending off the intrigues that were inevitably launched with a view to deposing him. When riots broke out in Constantinople over the rampant inflation gripping the Empire, a noble named Nicephorus Botaneiates assumed the reins of power. Michael managed to retain his life, but little else.

This of course meant that the little princess, Helena, lost her opportunity of acceding to the throne with her husband-to-be. It might be thought that this had frustrated the plans of Robert Guiscard. Not a bit of it. It provided him with a ready-made excuse to stir up yet more trouble for Byzantium. Robert acted the part superbly. First of all, a strange Greek monk appeared in Salerno in Italy. He claimed to be the deposed Emperor, Michael. It is doubtful if anyone really believed him. Robert, however, was completely convinced – at least in public. The presence of the monk provided him with the opportunity to provide a focus for a military campaign to attack the Byzantine Empire.

The assault duly came in May 1081. The Norman fleet made its way in a leisurely fashion to the Byzantine island of Corfu. By the standards of the time, the force was fairly large. The backbone of it was made up of thirteen hundred Norman knights. They were among the most feared troops of their day. They were well armed and well disciplined, and they had great respect for Robert Guiscard. There were also some Muslim troops from Sicily, as well as several thousand infantry. Taken as a whole, the force presented a serious threat.

Certainly the governor of Corfu appears to have been in awe of the force. He surrendered to the Normans quickly and without real resistance. The fleet then made for a much sterner target; the Byzantine port of Dyracchium. This was a major port, on the coast of modern-day Albania. With important road-routes leading from it all the way to Constantinople, it was effectively one of the gateways to Byzantium. It was strongly fortified, as befitted a place of its importance.

By this time, the Emperor Nicephorus had himself been deposed. His replacement was a man of much greater worth than him. He was Alexius Comnenus, the same man who, a few years earlier, had brought an end to the exploits of the uncontrollable Roussel of Bailleul. In him, Robert was to find his greatest enemy. A very capable administrator and a master politician, Alexius was also a man of considerable martial prowess. The conflict between the two men would become long-standing and fascinating.

The people of the port of Dyracchium asked Robert why he had come. Disingenuously, he declaimed that his aim was to restore the deposed Emperor Michael to his rightful place as the ruler of Byzantium. The citizens said that they would not deny him access to the city if he would show them the Emperor. So Robert brought out the Greek monk impersonating him to show off to the citizens. When they saw the impostor, they broke out in spontaneous laughter, not believing that anyone could seriously credit the bogus clerk as the Emperor. Then they sent to Alexius for help.

Alexius in turn summoned aid from one of Byzantium's traditional allies. In the light of their inglorious part in the eventual dismantling of the Byzantine Empire it might seem surprising that the city of Venice would be a supporter of the Emperor. However, in fact there was a long and mostly mutually supportive relationship between the Byzantine Empire and the city of Venice. For many years, the latter had been part of the Byzantine Empire and, although now long independent, relations between the two had remained good.

Venice had made its name in the world by its ability to trade many different objects with many different people. The people of the city were not overly concerned at the race or creed of their customers; in 971, for example, we find the Byzantines castigating them for providing arms to their Muslim enemies. However, such disagreements were relatively rare. By 992 the Venetians had made an agreement with the Byzantines to export goods to Constantinople with the benefit of lower tariffs than those granted to their rivals. Throughout the course of the eleventh century, the Venetians consolidated their position in the Mediterranean, using their impressive merchant fleet as the basis of an ongoing process of successful economic expansionism.

The Venetians responded to Alexius' call for assistance. They despatched a fleet to attack the Normans. At the same time, Alexius set out to challenge the Normans from the land. He devised a plan whereby he would launch an offensive against the Normans while, simultaneously, the defenders of Dyracchium would sally forth and assault the rear of the distracted enemy forces. It was a simple plan, and apparently at first it worked well. According to the chronicler William of Apulia, the Normans were outnumbered. The Byzantine troops forced the Normans back, and panic quickly pervaded Robert's army.

However, Robert managed to rally his men. Inspired, according to the same chronicler, by the banner given to the Normans by the Pope as a mark of his support, they launched a ferocious counter-attack while the enemy were distracted by their attempts to plunder the Normans' possessions. Unable to resist their ferocity, the Greeks broke and then fled. It was claimed that thousands of them died in the defeat. Alexius was forced to give up his attempts to raise the siege and 'was compelled to return home inglorious, weeping'.[2]

The Venetians had been equally unsuccessful in their attempts to destroy the Normans by sea. Some ships were sunk when the fleets clashed, but the Venetians' superiority did not prove to be decisive. Alexius, however, had weapons other than military armaments in reserve. Dyracchium fell to Robert shortly afterward but as he pushed deeper into Byzantine territory he was forced to rush back to Italy. Disturbing tidings had reached him. The Western Emperor was discomfited by the increasing success of the Normans, which had seriously disturbed the balance of power in the Italian peninsula. Egged on by Alexius, he had attacked the Pope, causing Robert to postpone his campaign and hurry back to defend him.

Thus Robert, who had hoped to become the new Emperor in Constantinople, had been thwarted. He did not know it, and no one else at the time would have suspected it, but fortune had passed him by. This had been his greatest opportunity for success and it had gone, never to return. He duly rescued the Pope from his parlous situation and then set about returning to Byzantine lands. He planned to attack Cephalonia, in Greece, with his son Roger Borsa. While on board ship waiting to set sail for the area he was gripped with a fever. His wife, the awesome and terrifying Sichelgaita, was beside herself when she saw how serious his condition was: 'she tore her clothes, wept, and ran quickly to be with him; and seeing that her husband had all but succumbed, she slashed at her cheeks with her finger-nails, tore at her dishevelled hair, and lamented.'

In the midst of this appalling demonstration of grief, Robert Guiscard expired. He had been one of the foremost Normans of his own or any other time. Politically astute, militarily exceptional and capable of inspiring enormous devotion among his men, he would be a difficult, indeed an impossible, act to follow. He had held the greatest chance of achieving glory against the Byzantines. No other man of his time could hope to hold in his hands the same possibilities of success. Unfortunately, this would not stop others from trying.

For the time being, the scene shifted from the military to the religious arena. The schism of 1054 had naturally enough caused much difficulty between Eastern and Western Christendom. However, it had seemed, momentarily, that relations might improve. Following the Battle of Manzikert, the Emperor Michael had sought an accommodation with Rome. His timing was propitious. Shortly after, in 1073, a new Pope was elected, Gregory VII. Gregory was one of the greatest of Medieval Popes.

There had been a succession of reforming Popes who had actively sought to advance the interests of the Papacy. Gregory not only picked up the mantle (he had in fact been one of the powers behind the Papacy for many years before he was elected, and had been a key influence on Papal strategy), he would take it forward to undreamed of levels.

Soon after his election, the Emperor Michael sent an olive branch to Gregory in the form of a letter of congratulations. Seemingly delighted at the approach, Gregory sent his representative, the Patriarch of Venice, to Constantinople to assess the state of Byzantium at that time. It would seem that the Patriarch reported that Michael's attempts to improve relations were genuine for, soon after, Gregory introduced a radical change in Papal policy, the ramifications of which would, in the not too distant future, be enormous. He proposed to send an army of Christian knights to the aid of Byzantium who would be used in a counter-attack against the Turks. The scheme ultimately came to nothing; Gregory was distracted as he became increasingly involved in an escalating dispute with the Western Emperor, Henry IV. The dispute became so bitter that it drove Gregory into the arms of the Normans and eventually destroyed him personally. This meant that he could not pursue his plans for the East, but the seeds of an idea that would shortly seize the imagination of the West had been sown.

The immediate hopes of a thawing in relations between Rome and Constantinople were anyway dashed when Michael was deposed. Gregory instantly excommunicated his successor as Emperor, Nicephorus. The same fate befell Alexius Comnenus when he usurped the throne in 1081. Alexius did try to seek the support of Gregory in his affairs with the Normans but his requests fell on deaf ears. It seemed, not without reason, that the affairs of the Normans and the Papacy were hopelessly intertwined. Indeed, after this rejection, the relationship between Byzantium and the Papacy plummeted to one of its lowest points ever. The Latin churches in Constantinople were closed. The Byzantines openly supported the enemy of the Papacy, the Western Emperor, and the Pope increasingly looked like the mouthpiece of the Normans.

At this low point, the fickle hand of fate chose to deal a more favourable set of conditions. Alexius was to prove to be a great statesman and Emperor. At this moment in time, an equally great man was to become Pope. He was Odo de Lagery, who took the Papal name Urban II. He was convinced that the wounds between Rome and Constantinople needed to be healed in the interests of Christian unity. He became Pope in March 1088. Within eighteen months, he had held an audience with ambassadors from Byzantium at Amalfi, during which the excommunication on the Emperor was lifted. Alexius for his part responded in an equally positive fashion. The Latin churches in his capital were reopened, and the ecclesiastical hierarchy in the East were encouraged to accept the authority of Urban as Pope. Doctrinal differences still continued, but in a language that was noticeably less intolerant and antagonistic than had heretofore been the case.

It appeared that relations had improved enormously, which indeed in the short term they had. It is perhaps ironic that in this more conciliatory climate lay great danger for Byzantium. A chain of events had been started that would bring East and West into closer contact. As a result of this new proximity, the two cultures would be brought into closer liaison. Rather like two unstable chemical elements that together react to create an explosion, the effect would be deeply harmful to Byzantium.

But these religious differences, great and important though they were, provided only one of the causes of tension between East and West. Culturally, the differences were also massive. Byzantium was heir to much that was great in the world of Ancient Rome and Greece. Its architecture was magnificent, and its art without rival in the Christian realm. It had a wonderful heritage, which it had maintained and expanded over the course of centuries. The palaces of the Emperor and the nobles presented a quality of building that was far in excess of any that could be seen in the West, and its churches shone in a splendour that would dazzle all who visited them.

Within the walls of Constantinople was also to be found an immensely powerful commercial hub. For centuries the city had been the pivotal point in the trade routes between the West and Africa, Asia and the Levant (although Egypt had in recent times usurped this role to a large extent). Within its triple walls (which were 5 metres thick) was a huge assortment of craftsmen, artificers and tradesmen of all descriptions. The city was hugely wealthy, although its wealth was concentrated in the hands of the ruling classes and many of the population lived in squalor.

Its size was truly awesome, certainly by the standards of the time. It has been estimated that something approaching 400,000 people resided within the city boundaries. As such, it dwarfed any of the still evolving cities of Western Europe. Visitors from the West could not fail to be impressed, even overwhelmed, by its magnitude. They would also be astounded by its collection of relics. The worship of relics formed an integral part of religious observance within Christendom at this time, and indeed throughout much of the Medieval era. And nowhere were more relics to be found than in Constantinople, which held the largest collection of holy nails and bones in the Christian world until they were scattered throughout Christendom in the aftermath of the whirlwind that was to unleash itself on the city in 1204. As such, the city acted as an irresistible magnet to much of the busy pilgrim traffic that was to make its way to the East in the tenth and eleventh centuries.

Essentially, Byzantium was an Empire that, although still powerful, was approaching its decline. The past few centuries had seen a shift of power away from the great, overarching centralised bureaucracy in Constantinople and towards provincial government. Local governors became more autonomous and Imperial power as a result became less certain. There were, it is true, extreme contradictions in this situation: the position of Emperor was treated with almost reverential status, while poor and weak Emperors came and went with alarming frequency. The problems that this loss of Imperial power posed were exacerbated by intense external pressure from barbarian attacks, and the resultant loss of land – especially in Asia Minor – denuded the Empire of troops. Consequently, the Byzantine army began to rely increasingly on mercenaries, many of whom were from the West. The tenth century had been a period of great revival in Byzantine fortunes after several centuries of relative deterioration, but the effort that it had involved had weakened the Empire. A process of decline began which would eventually lead to the downfall of Byzantium.

If Byzantium to an extent represented the past, then Western Europe was the future. A vibrant feudal society was evolving in the West, one of the results of which would be a seemingly insatiable expansionist society. Charlemagne, who ruled in the early part of the ninth century, had formed a large empire which, largely through his personal authority, he managed to govern within a strong centralised system. His death, however, led to a diminution of central authority. In its place, local lords began to assert an ever-increasing level of autonomy. As their power grew, so did their desire for land. The age is notable for the degree of aggression and militarism that this group practised. They were, according to the chroniclers of the day, extraordinarily violent in their methods. This, combined with the extensive poverty of the poorer classes and the frequent natural disasters of plague and famine that decimated Western society at this time, made it in many ways an apocalyptic period of history.

Despite these frequent horrors, the expansionism of the West was an overt demonstration of the energy and ambition that were to transform the position of Western Europe from a region on the barbarian fringes of civilisation to the most dominant power bloc in the known world. That such expansionism was often violent must be admitted. However, there was also much progress in economic terms. As we have already touched upon, the Italian maritime states plied their trade extensively across regularised trade routes that criss-crossed the Mediterranean and forged a commercial link between East and West.

The Eastern and Western halves of Christendom were at very different stages in their historical cycles; in fact, the former was past its prime and heading into decline while the latter was very much in the ascendancy. Little of this would have been apparent to most people at the time; Byzantium still appeared to be massive and impregnable, although the attempts of the Normans on the Byzantine Empire demonstrates that even then some in the West detected signs of weakness. However, the differences did mean that if the two very different cultures were brought into closer contact, a very volatile element indeed would be introduced into the equation.

It is against this background that the decision of Alexius Comnenus to seek help from the West in reconquering at least some of the lost territories in Asia Minor must be seen. Alexius, who was a fine soldier, secured his northern frontiers by a decisive victory against the barbarian tribes who constantly attempted to penetrate the Empire's defences. He also made some progress against the Turks in Asia Minor. However, the relative paucity of military resource available to him forced him to seek help from the West. He therefore despatched his envoys to Urban II to ask for his help in raising an army of mercenaries to assist him.

The use of Western mercenaries by Byzantium was of course nothing new. Warriors from the West, although their loyalty was often suspect, were highly regarded both for their fighting skills and the quality of their armament. They were regularly used as part of the Byzantine army. What singled out this plea for help was the response to it. Unconsciously, Byzantium was to be partly responsible for the extraordinary events that followed. By making the request for help to the Pope – who was presiding over the Papacy at a time of increasing assertiveness, which led to a quite dramatic evolution of the institution – Alexius had shifted the motivation behind sending any expedition from the West. No longer was it a strictly secular affair; now there was a religious objective too. This was further stressed by the tone of his envoys when they put Alexius' case before Urban at Piacenza in 1095. They emphasised the fact that Infidels were now threatening the buffer of Christendom in the East, further encouraging a religious slant to the expedition.

Urban was not slow to respond. The proposal for help held a number of attractions. It increased the profile of the Papacy at this crucial time in its history, and helped to win support for it (the Germans were still antagonistic towards Urban, and the period was characterised by a number of rival 'anti-Popes' whom they installed in opposition to pontiffs such as Urban). It demonstrated the assertiveness and confidence of the institution. It also channelled aggression into outlets that would be less threatening to the Church (which had been the victim of the extreme violence of the age on many occasions).

Most importantly for our story, it also helped to rebuild bridges between East and West. Urban fervently desired a closer union between the two. A man of some vision, he appears to have realised that this could not be implemented by force if it was to be long lasting. Rather, the process needed to be one conducted with consideration and tact. By sending help to the East, Urban hoped to demonstrate that Byzantium and the West could co-habit together, and that the way forward was for closer cooperation between the two.

Laudable as this aim was, it was unrealistic in the context of the time. The warlords of the West, although they had deep spiritual motivations, also had other more earthly ambitions. The opportunity of obtaining land and plunder would prove very difficult to resist. Much as Urban would like to control their actions, it was a forlorn hope that he would succeed.

As it transpired, Urban's efforts to raise an army to help Byzantium, which were launched at a great convention in Clermont in the latter part of 1095, provoked an unexpected and quite amazing result. In the summer of 1096 Alexius was presented with alarming news from the garrison commander at the border town of Belgrade. Thousands of people had descended without warning on the town. It was an army from the West, but one that bore no resemblance to any that was anticipated. Instead of well-armed soldiers, the vast force was composed primarily of poorly armed peasants, and included in its number were many women, old men and children. Urban's appeal had touched a chord deep within the hearts of ordinary people, of whom great numbers had given up everything they owned in the West (which, in truth, was very little, if anything at all) and set out to face the Muslims.

Few, if any, cared if Byzantium was assisted by their presence. Their goal was Jerusalem, the Holy City, which had not been part of the Byzantine Empire for nearly five hundred years. Predictably, the rabble (for such it was) behaved poorly and robbed the local inhabitants of property and honour on more than one occasion. Eventually, they were confronted by Byzantine forces in battle, which was unsurprisingly a one-sided affair in which the peasants were routed. A large number still made it to Constantinople where, fortunately, they were not punished for their poor behaviour. However, this army was shipped over the Bosphorus to the mainland of Asia Minor as quickly as possible in case they should try to make more trouble for the Empire. Here they were soon joined by other peasant forces. Their influence on Asia Minor, which was mainly evidenced by loutish behaviour and violence against the local inhabitants (who, incidentally, were fellow Christians, though not of the Roman persuasion), was ended soon after when Turkish forces attacked and massacred them at Civetot.

Although these early forces were a concern to the Empire and did on occasion exhibit anti-Byzantine tendencies, they were not likely to undermine the structure of Byzantium. Though their lack of self-discipline was a great threat to the public order, this was not just a demonstration of xenophobic reaction against the Greeks (later peasant forces that followed the first wave caused almost as much damage in the West as they did within the borders of Byzantium). Far more dangerous to the fabric of Byzantine society were the genuine military forces that were to follow.

There was a considerable response to the request for a Christian army from many classes of society. A number of properly armed forces were raised in the West to help in the fight against Islam. Of course, this was to an extent what Alexius had asked for. However, he would certainly have been concerned at the size of the response, which was so great that the forces making their way through his Empire would be very hard to control. And he would have been horrified to learn the identity of some of the leaders.

Clearly, Alexius had in his own mind a very clear agenda of what was expected from such help. The fact that most of the force stated that their ultimate aim was Jerusalem would have been of little significance to him. The city held no strategic importance for Byzantium. Far more relevant was the reconquest of Asia Minor, an area that was integral to the survival of the Byzantine Empire. It was important, indeed vital, to the interests of Alexius and his Empire that the Western armies acted in a way that would further his interests; most fundamentally of all, any land that they conquered in territories that were traditionally part of the Byzantine Empire must be handed back to him.

Accordingly, Alexius devised a scheme that he hoped would protect his interests. He would ask the leaders of the Western armies to take an oath of allegiance to him. He knew that an oath of fealty held a great place in the practices of the West, although it was of far less meaning within the Byzantine world. He therefore insisted that, when the leaders of the crusader armies passed through Constantinople on their way east, they each took such an oath to him.

The first leader to arrive, Hugh of Vermandois, brother of the French king, was a weak and easily influenced man who took the oath without compunction. It was unfortunately a misleadingly easy victory for Alexius. Subsequent leaders would be far less compliant. The next to arrive was Godfrey of Bouillon, a prominent noble from the Low Countries. He refused point blank to take any oath, saying (not without justification) that he had already sworn allegiance to the Western Emperor and he could not serve two masters. Alexius increased the pressure on him by cutting off food supplies to his force, which was encamped outside the city walls of Byzantium. This was an enormous threat to Godfrey. Armies of this period were completely incapable of transporting enough food with them and were totally at the mercy of the inhabitants of the country that they were in. They would therefore quickly starve.

Godfrey was infuriated. Without warning, he attacked the city. Well armed though his men were, they were not numerous enough to take such a strong city and were beaten back. Alexius was enraged at Godfrey's actions, although he perhaps protested too much; a hungry army is not likely to act rationally. He attempted to negotiate further. When this failed, he openly threatened Godfrey with force, at which the Western leader was forced to capitulate.

Alexius was desperate that he do so. He had received not long before the most chilling news of all. Another army was on its way. This time it was a Norman force, and at its head was Bohemond, son of Robert Guiscard and a man who had openly made war on the Byzantine Empire for years. The Norman troops were in fact surprisingly well behaved during their progress to Constantinople. Bohemond, when he reached the city, was amazingly compliant, and reverentially took the oath to Alexius without demur. Alexius well understood why. He would have known that Bohemond had no intention of keeping such a vow. Indeed, Bohemond soon made clear his reasons for such respect. He wished to be made overall commander of all the Christian armies in Asia Minor. Alexius would have reasoned that once Bohemond had conquered any territories in the region he would never have meekly handed them back to Alexius, and he would of course have been absolutely correct in his thinking. He therefore fobbed him off with a weak promise that he would be duly considered for overall command when the moment was right. Bohemond knew that he could hope for little more at this stage and accepted the situation for the time being.

There was anyway another leader on his way who also wished for supreme command. He was Raymond, Count of Toulouse, one of the first to say he would leave for the East and one of the last actually to do so. Raymond resisted all attempts to force him to take the oath, and for a time open confrontation seemed unavoidable. Eventually, a watered down oath was taken. Ironically, despite his initial resistance, Raymond would prove to be the most supportive of the leaders of this First Crusade to Byzantine interests.

The last group to arrive was led by Robert of Normandy (brother of King William II of England), Count Stephen of Blois and Robert, Duke of Flanders. This last group, which behaved well, took the required oath without protest. In return, their men were allowed to enter

Constantinople in small groups. Here, they were amazed at what they saw. The city was a sight unlike any they had ever seen before. Its splendour and size overwhelmed them. In a metaphorical sense, it seemed to have streets that were paved with gold. This all added to the mystique of the city, a mystique that was eventually to reach almost fabled status. Constantinople would become a byword in the West for wealth, for ostentation and for luxury, a combination that, to a Western culture that prized the thought of plunder above most other attractions, would make it a dangerously attractive target.

Thoughts of future difficulties would not have been high in the minds of the crusader army that stood on the threshold of the expedition into enemy territory. An objective and dispassionate mind would have noted, however, that already relations with Byzantium had been difficult. The open confrontation between Godfrey and Alexius, and the prevarication of Raymond of Toulouse, demonstrated that the leaders of the Western armies would not meekly acquiesce to become pawns of the Byzantine Empire. The presence of Bohemond and his past record as far as the Greeks were concerned were equally worrying. Alexius had generated a much greater response than he had anticipated in his request for help. But he had done something more. He had started the process that would lead to the death of the Empire that he held so dear.

CHAPTER TWO

Danger Signals

The eleventh century saw a dangerous development in the relationship between Eastern and Western Christendom. By bringing the two power blocs into closer contact, tensions that had existed for some time were greatly exacerbated. The annihilation of the Byzantine territories in the Italian peninsula by the Normans naturally enough created much resentment in Byzantium, as did the subsequent attempts of Robert Guiscard and then Bohemond to conquer the Byzantine Empire for themselves. The dangerous process by which the affairs of Byzantium and the West were enmeshed continued with the incredible events of the First Crusade and its immediate aftermath. However, if the latter part of the eleventh century saw sinister shadows clouding the relationship between Byzantium and the West, then the next century was to see those spectres become much more real. Now that Byzantium was brought more closely into the orbit of the Western world, its riches, accompanied by its evident weakness as the century progressed, would increasingly excite the jealousy of the West. The balance of power in Christendom would start to shift, slowly but inexorably, westwards.

The crusades played a vital role in this process, although the expansion of commerce and the increasing confidence of rising powers, especially the Italian maritime states, meant that closer contact was inevitable anyway. That the increasing contacts between the two spheres of European Christendom would inflame tensions very quickly became apparent. Once the armies of the First Crusade made their way into Asia Minor, the first flash point was soon reached. Hardly had the expedition begun than, led by its Byzantine guides, it reached the city of Nicaea. The city had formed an integral part of the Byzantine Empire for centuries. It had a wonderful heritage, and some significant acts in the development of Christianity had been played out within its ancient walls. However, when Asia Minor imploded after the Byzantine defeat at Manzikert the city had been captured by the Turks. It was currently the capital of the leading Turkish chieftain in the West of Asia Minor, one Kilij Arslan.

Kilij Arslan was campaigning far to the east of the country when the Christian army laid siege to the city. He did not hurry back, possibly underestimating the situation because of the abysmal performance of the peasant army that had preceded this main force. When he did become fully aware of how great the danger was, he sent an army to raise the siege but it was beaten off. With the Turks defeated, it seemed that the city must fall and that great plunder would be available to the crusader armies.

The Western forces duly made preparations for their final assault on what they knew to be a city on the verge of defeat. However, on the morning that this attack was to be launched, it became obvious that it would not be needed. Over the city walls fluttered the banners of the Byzantine Empire. Without reference to the Western leaders, Alexius had been negotiating in secret with the garrison. In return for being spared the very real horrors of a sack, the Turks had agreed to surrender the city to the Emperor. The crusaders were bitterly disappointed. They had been robbed of great riches at the eleventh hour. They felt betrayed at what they saw to be the duplicity of Byzantium.

That sense of betrayal was soon magnified. Within the city was the family of Kilij Arslan. Alexius took them back to Constantinople, not as prisoners but as honoured guests. In the Byzantine capital, they were treated in a manner befitting their elevated status. They were then released to the care of Kilij Arslan without any ransom. The Westerners were aghast at the treatment meted out to people they regarded as Infidels. To them, this could be nothing less than a plot by the Byzantines against the armies of the West. The *Gesta Francorum*, an anonymous work that chronicles the progress of the First Crusade, leaves little doubt of the writer's view of Byzantine politics: 'the Emperor, who was a fool as well as a knave told them [the family of Kilij Arslan] to go away unhurt and without fear. He had them brought to him at Constantinople under safe conduct, and kept them carefully so that he could have them ready to injure the Franks and obstruct their Crusade.'

These words exemplify the chasm that existed between the views of Eastern and Western Christendom as far as Asia Minor was concerned. Diplomacy was an integral, and extremely effective, part of the Byzantine approach towards its enemies. There were deemed to be many ways to attain the objectives of the Empire, of which warfare was only one. Indeed, warfare was costly, in terms of finance as well as human life. Therefore it was used typically as a last resort. Diplomacy offered a much less expensive alternative. But such subtle reasoning would be lost on the armies of the West. They came from a society that thrived on conflict. Further, the crusader armies were driven by religious motives, urged on by unsophisticated propaganda that portrayed the Turks as the enemies of Christ. They could not understand how Alexius, Emperor of Christendom's oldest power, could stoop so low as to treat with the Muslims. This difference in perspectives was to taint the relationship between Greek and Westerner throughout the crusading period.

Alexius placated the disappointed crusaders with generous gifts. The improvement in understanding that followed was to be short-lived. As the Western armies advanced further into Asia Minor, they inevitably moved further away from the influence of Alexius in Constantinople. The crusaders suffered appalling hardships, and were assailed by malnutrition, disease and dreadful extremes in climate as well as by a determined Turkish enemy. Eventually, however, they crossed the Taurus Mountains and descended onto the Syrian coastal plain. Here they were to face their greatest challenge in the venture so far.

Astride their line of advance stood the ancient city of Antioch. It had a hallowed place in the history of their faith; the word 'Christian' had been coined here for the first time. It had also been one of the leading cities in the Byzantine Empire and its Roman predecessor for over a thousand years. It had been lost to the Turks only twenty years previously. It was massive, surrounded by walls that climbed mountains and plunged into valleys. It was large and wealthy, and strategically important. In short, it was a city that Alexius Comnenus would demand back if it were to fall to the crusader army.

The siege of the city began on 21 October 1098. The city resisted the attacks of the crusaders. Failing to take it quickly, the Western armies soon began to suffer from the effects of the harsh winter and the shortage of food. Large numbers of the besieging troops began to die. Decimated by disease and hunger, still worse news was to come. The crusader army received terrible tidings; Kerbogha, Emir of Mosul, one of the strongest Muslim warlords, was on his way to relieve the siege at the head of a vast army.

It seemed that the First Crusade was doomed to meet its nemesis here, outside of the walls of Antioch. Certainly, it appeared so to Count Stephen of Blois, one of the leaders of the crusade. He was a man who had never been fully committed to the crusade (gossip had it that he had been bullied to take part by his wife), and he was of a timid nature. Terrified by what he saw as his imminent destruction, he fled the crusader army and started to make his way homewards. As he made his way back through Asia Minor he met the Emperor Alexius with the large force with which he intended to assist the crusade. Stephen told Alexius it was useless; by now, the crusaders must have been annihilated. Seeing little point in continuing his journey, and aware that anyway the onset of winter shortly would make further progress very difficult, Alexius abandoned his expedition. It was a momentous decision.

News of the destruction of the crusade was decidedly premature. Stephen and Alexius had reckoned without the resilience of the crusaders, the hand of fate and, most of all, the cunning of Bohemond.

The latter had made contact with dissentient elements within Antioch. With their help, he had arranged that the crusaders should be let into the city in the dead of night. The plan worked spectacularly. The gates were opened to the Western hordes by the few knights who had climbed into the city over a ladder. The city fell, its Muslim inhabitants massacred so terribly that its streets ran red with rivers of blood. Then, in a decisive battle outside of the city where the troops were once again inspired by Bohemond, the relieving army of Kerbogha was beaten back. Against insuperable odds, the city had been captured and then held. The Muslims had been beaten. Now it was time for the reckoning with the Greeks.

It was very easy for Bohemond to argue that Alexius had abandoned the crusaders. The Imperial representative with the crusade, one Taticius, had left the army shortly before the city was captured. Although he said that he intended to return and indeed left many of his entourage with the army, it was not difficult for someone with Bohemond's silky tongue to convince an already sceptical Western audience that he had betrayed them. The oaths of allegiance taken to Alexius counted for naught; and indeed it was straightforward enough to justify any refutation of them by the Emperor's perceived abandonment. There would be no Greek lord in this city. To prove the point, a new Patriarch of Antioch was appointed; conspicuously he was a Latin churchman. The Patriarchate, one of the most revered appointments in the Christian world, had always previously been held by a Greek cleric. It was a deeply symbolic act, evidencing as it did the mood of the West, which sought to impose Western perceptions of Christendom on a largely unconvinced Eastern world.

It was also a decisive moment in a political sense. The city was far enough away from Constantinople to assert its independence from the Byzantine Empire. It was separated from the strong hand of the Greek Emperor by hundreds of miles of arid plains and enormous chains of hostile mountains. Between the western areas of Asia Minor that were held by the Emperor and the city were large parties of mobile, aggressive Turks. Now that the city had fallen to the West, it would be very difficult for Alexius to take it back into his sphere of influence. Few can have believed that the leaders of the crusade would meekly hand all their conquests over into the hands of their traditional owner, the Emperor in Constantinople. After this open declaration of defiance nobody can have been in any doubt as to the intention of the crusaders to keep their conquests for themselves.

The crusaders, however, did argue among themselves on the delicate subject of who should rule the city. Raymond of Toulouse was the only man to argue in the Emperor's interests, but he was outmanoeuvred by

Bohemond. The Norman desired the city for himself and he was to get his way. Little good it did him though. He had a reckless streak in his character that quickly led him into trouble when he went raiding into Turkish lands in Asia Minor. He rushed headlong into a trap and was captured. He was locked away in a dark, inaccessible mountain castle for several years before he was ransomed.

On Bohemond's return, several difficulties awaited him. Much had changed since he left. The First Crusade had pushed on and, miraculously as it seemed, had captured Jerusalem. A new Christian kingdom had been created in Palestine. However, it was faced with great danger. Its major weakness was its shortage of manpower. Several expeditions of reinforcements that had followed in its wake had been slashed to pieces by a Turkish enemy in Asia Minor that was far more organised than the one that had faced the earlier armies. Ironically, the resurgent Turkish threat helped the crusader leaders of Antioch; it meant that Alexius was too pre-occupied to reassert his rights in the city. However, Bohemond was well aware that new blood from the West was needed to consolidate the recently formed crusader territories. It was also some years since he had left his lands in Italy, and it was not unreasonable to assume that he wished to see that his affairs were still in order. Accordingly, he decided to return to the West.

Whether Bohemond intended his return to be temporary we can only surmise. In any event, he would never see the East again. On his return to the West, he quickly reverted to type. There was by this time a new Pope, Paschal II, a man of much weaker mettle than his predecessor Urban. Bohemond explained to the Pope all the difficulties faced by the new crusader territories. Greatest of all, he told the pontiff, was the threat from the Greek Emperor. Paschal was easily convinced. Accordingly, in 1105, he called for a new Crusader army to be raised; this time its enemy would be Alexius. The enterprise was stillborn; other more immediate problems had to be faced and the crusade simply never happened. Nevertheless, the fact that it had even been considered illustrated the fragility of the understanding between Eastern and Western Christendom.

Bohemond took the opportunity of his return to resurrect Robert Guiscard's old, unfounded, claims to the Byzantine Empire. He launched another assault on Dyracchium. This time, however, Alexius was ready for him. With the help of Turkish mercenaries, his initial attack was repulsed. Then a Greek fleet severed his lines of communication with Italy. Finally, Alexius brought up a large army. The odds against Bohemond were hopeless. He was forced to agree to humiliating surrender terms. He was to recognise all his conquests in Byzantine territories as rightly belonging to Alexius. The agreement that confirmed these arrangements, the Treaty of Devol (signed in 1108), must have been a moment of sweet revenge for Alexius. It was not, however, to make any practical difference at this stage; Antioch was ruled in Bohemond's absence by his nephew, Tancred, who refused to recognise Alexius' claims to his city. Bohemond returned to Italy, where he died a few years later.

Alexius was unable to press home his claim to sovereignty in Antioch. There were too many distractions elsewhere to occupy his attentions. For example, in 1111 warships from Genoa and Pisa threatened the Ionian coast. Alexius used diplomacy to cancel out this threat. He let the Pisans set up a permanent trading colony in Constantinople. This suited their purpose splendidly, as their primary interest was in strengthening their commercial presence in the eastern Mediterranean. This removed the immediate threat but introduced dangerous new elements into the politics of the time. Venice had initially been slow to react to the opportunities offered by the crusader kingdom of Outremer and, although they now had a presence on the Palestine coast, both the Genoese and the Pisans had stolen a march on them. Now the special relationship between Venice and Byzantium had been threatened by a new Genoese presence in the capital of the Empire.

Worse was to follow as far as Venice was concerned. Alexius died and was replaced by his son, John Comnenus. Venice approached him in 1122 for a renewal of the special trading privileges that the Venetians had enjoyed from his father. The new Emperor, however, wished to stamp his mark on affairs quickly. Venice was already seriously undermining the commercial strength of the Byzantine Empire, and Greek merchants were seeing their livelihoods threatened by the rapacious Venetian traders. The Venetians were not popular in Byzantium. Accordingly, John felt strong enough to refuse their requests.

Venice was understandably enraged. The city had one of the most powerful fleets in the world. Although the Venetians were renowned primarily for their skill in obtaining maximum commercial advantage for their city, they were also excellent naval warriors. They responded with calculated fury. Their ships attacked the Byzantine island of Corfu, which managed to beat off the assault. However, the islands of Rhodes, Chios, Samos, Lesbos and Andros fell to them. These were in a magnificent position to allow the Venetians to create havoc along the Byzantine sea-lanes in the Eastern Mediterranean. The threat to the commercial viability of Byzantine trade in the area was enormous. John decided that he should withdraw his objections to the Venetian claims for special privileges and formally approved them in 1126. Despite the eventual reconciliation between Byzantium and Venice, this was still a serious affair and Venice could no longer assume that the 'special relationship' would continue. In fact, the incident marked the acceleration of tensions in political relations between Byzantium and the West. The Empire would, throughout the course of the twelfth century, try to play off the interests of Venice and other trading nations, particularly the Genoese, against each other. 'Divide and conquer' was a time-honoured tactic in the Byzantine diplomatic armoury, and had worked well in the past. This time, however, the policy would have serious adverse consequences. The Venetians would lose confidence in their relations with Byzantium, and, as a result, they would become openly hostile to the Empire. They would prove dangerous enemies.

At this point, however, a permanent break between Venice and Constantinople was still some way off. John proved to be an outstanding warrior. He sought to consolidate the much-improved position that Alexius had left as his legacy. For a while, this meant that the crusaders who had refused to recognise Byzantine suzerainty were left in peace. But the insult offered to his Empire by the continued Frankish occupation of lands that he thought to be his own continued to rankle with the Byzantine Emperor. The calm that the crusader territories enjoyed during the early years of John's reign proved to be merely temporary. It lasted only as long as it took for the Emperor to assert his authority both within his Empire (his succession, not unusually, was opposed by several cliques, which continued to plot against him after he succeeded to the throne) and also against his external enemies. As it happened, this took a long time. Antioch, however, was not forgotten. On 29 August 1137 the Western rulers of Antioch were shaken from their apathy by shattering tidings. Without warning, John had appeared before the walls of the city.

This put the Western rulers in a great quandary. Although they had consistently ignored the long-distance requests of the Emperor for recognition, open hostility had so far been avoided. Initially, they resisted John's demands that he be admitted. In the delay that followed, they sent to their King, Fulk, in Jerusalem asking him what they should do. Fulk advised that, on legal grounds, they had no choice but to adhere both to the oaths taken by the first crusader leaders in Constantinople forty years before and the terms of the Treaty of Devol. They had to recognise the rights of the Emperor. Accordingly, they paid homage to the Emperor.

Of course, it was nothing more than a token gesture. The Western leaders still occupied the citadel in Antioch and as such effectively controlled the city. John demanded that they hand it over to him. The Franks engineered a riot to avoid doing so. In mock panic, they frantically advised the Emperor that they could not guarantee his safety; it would therefore be in his best interests if he left Antioch. He did so.

He returned again to Antioch in 1142 and demanded that the city admit him. This time, he was openly refused. He withdrew, planning to come back later and assert his rights by force. Events elsewhere intervened and he died before he could do so.

John Comnenus was succeeded by his son, Manuel. Although his reign had not been without its successes, he left as a legacy a set of conditions that were to lead to the destruction of the Byzantine Empire. Manuel was incensed by the way that Antioch had treated his father. To chastise the crusaders, he despatched a fleet to attack the city, although he did not take it. Further difficulties arose during the Second Crusade, which was sent from the West to Outremer after the fall of the important city of Edessa in 1144. Once again, the crusader armies took the land route through Byzantine territories and onwards into Asia Minor. There were two major armies involved, one led by the Emperor Conrad of Germany, and the other by King Louis of France.

When the leaders reached Constantinople, Manuel insisted that they take an oath of allegiance to him. This they were most loath to do, although eventually they were forced to accede. The two armies then made their way into Asia Minor. The German army arrived in the East before the French force, and consequently was first to set out across Asia Minor. Manuel advised them to stay close to the coast, as they could be more easily re-provisioned there by using the Greek fleet. This sound advice was ignored. Oblivious to the dangers they faced, the German army walked straight into a Turkish ambush. A large number of them were killed in the massacre that followed. Conrad himself barely escaped with his life.

Louis' force was slightly more successful, although it still suffered much at the hands of both the Turks and from the effects of disease and fatigue in the debilitating Anatolian sun. However, Louis' men were genuinely shocked when a Turkish force that they beat off during their advance retreated into a Greek city for protection. They felt that Manuel had betrayed their cause by offering protection to the enemies of the crusade. It mattered little that Manuel had not invited the crusade to the East; few Byzantine Emperors were likely to do so after the confrontations of the First Crusade and the political difficulties that followed. To the men from the West, Manuel was a traitor to the Christian cause. There was little room in their vision of the world for compromise or dissimulation, both of which had been an integral part of Byzantine tactics for centuries.

The German Emperor Conrad was taken ill and stopped at Ephesus to recover. Here he was joined by Manuel, who had a keen interest in medicine. Under his guidance, Conrad was nursed back to health. As a result, the two men became close friends. The same could not be said for

Louis and Manuel. The French king made his way to Outremer. Here the crusade quickly disintegrated into farce. Rumours abounded that Louis had been cuckolded by his beautiful wife, Eleanor of Aquitaine. Personal embarrassment quickly became military fiasco when the Crusaders decided to attack the city of Damascus, at that time ruled by the crusaders' only important Muslim ally in the region. The city was far too strong to take and the attack on it was abandoned after only three days. Louis returned to Jerusalem, bitter at the humiliation. For a huge investment of time and money, nothing had been achieved. He returned home to France soon after. In his heart, he carried an irrational and pathological hatred for the Emperor of Byzantium, whom he felt (for no very good reason) had betrayed him and the Christian cause. He was approached by Roger, the Count of Sicily, who suggested that they jointly launch an attack on Byzantium. The opposition of Conrad, however, meant that the plan came to nothing.

Shortly after, Manuel's attention was drawn to Italy. The Empire had never recovered its lost lands in the peninsula. During the past few decades, Italy had become the centre of an enormous power struggle on the European mainland. The armies of the German Emperor and the Count of Sicily had ranged back and forth over it in a constant battle for supremacy. In the midst of it all, tossed about like flotsam on a stormy sea, the Papacy desperately attempted to maintain some form of independence. The increasing power of the Normans in Sicily, which continued to grow under Count Roger's successor, William I, had disconcerted Manuel. Accordingly, he had formed an alliance with the Papacy and the German Emperor against the Sicilians. A campaign was launched in Italy. The Sicilians were relentlessly forced back. Then, seemingly on the verge of total defeat, William launched a counter-attack and won a miraculous, and ultimately decisive, victory. The campaign was abandoned with no lasting results obtained.

His ambitions in Italy frustrated,[1] Manuel was forced to return to the persistent problem of Antioch. The current ruler in the city was a noble who had arrived from the West a few years before. His name was Reynald of Chatillon, undoubtedly one of the most self-serving and duplicitous men of all crusading leaders. Without warning, he had invaded the peaceful Greek island of Cyprus in 1156. The attack was totally unprovoked. The island was subjected to rape and pillage on an unprecedented scale. Reynald may have reckoned that Manuel had too many problems elsewhere to retaliate. Manuel was indeed slow to respond, but when he did it was on a huge scale.

In 1158 Reynald received the awful tidings that Manuel was on his way towards Antioch at the head of a huge army. Resistance would have been futile, and Reynald therefore adopted the only approach that was likely to save his skin – abject humiliation. He made his way barefoot to the camp of Manuel and prostrated himself at the Emperor's feet. It required a huge loss of face on Reynald's part but the approach was effective. Manuel forgave Reynald his stupidity and, on the surface at least, relations returned to normal.

In the aftermath of this meeting, Manuel met the King of Jerusalem, Baldwin. The two men, who shared a common love of life, instantly empathised with each other, and a close friendship quickly formed. There was much merry-making in the two camps. Manuel even took part in a tournament. In itself this may not appear surprising. However, the tournament was very much a West European phenomenon. To Manuel's Byzantine subjects, it was clearly part of the pattern that was emerging, and indicated that their Emperor was openly adopting Western customs. To a deeply conservative society like Byzantium, a society that had indeed often regarded the men from the West as barbarians, it was a betrayal of Greek traditions.

This was not a trivial issue. Many within Byzantium observed Manuel's predilection with Western customs and felt deeply uncomfortable about his attitudes. Byzantine commerce had already suffered greatly as the Italian city-states swallowed up ever more in the way of traditional Byzantine markets. In addition, the Empire had been regularly exposed to the unwelcome attentions of crusading armies from the West. Because of this, and because of Byzantium's deep conservatism, there was much anti-Western feeling in the Empire. It was a feeling that was not always mirrored in the actions of Manuel, and because of that he lost the respect of many of his subjects.

However, even a superficial examination of events clearly demonstrates that there were certainly ambiguities in the attitude of Manuel towards the West. This was particularly so with regard to Venice. The city's fortunes continued to prosper as the twelfth century progressed, inevitably taking custom away from Byzantine commerce and giving rise to a great deal of Greek envy as a result. Manuel may well have felt threatened by this. Certainly, the wealth and influence of Venice continued to increase, and it was most marked within or close to traditional Byzantine spheres of influence. On several occasions, the relationship between Byzantium and Venice reached a critical point. Counterbalanced against the increasing assertiveness of a confident Venetian state, the Byzantines in return posed their own kind of threat to the West. Manuel's influence extended well beyond the traditional boundaries of Byzantium, and regions as far afield as Hungary and Kiev would come within the influence of his Empire. Venice particularly felt threatened when the King of Hungary, Geza II, died and the Byzantines subsequently assumed significant control over the affairs of his kingdom. This gave the Byzantines a stranglehold on parts of the East Adriatic coast, opposite the city of Venice.

In 1171 an open break occurred. Manuel had continued with the policy of playing off the interests of other Italian states, especially Genoa, Pisa and Amalfi, against those of Venice. Consequently, there were deep tensions between the rival Italian states. These usually bubbled away beneath the surface, but in 1171 they erupted spectacularly. Incensed at the increasing influence of the Genoese, the Venetians in Constantinople attacked their trading quarter in the city at Galata. Manuel's response was decisive but draconian. In a wonderfully coordinated operation, all the Venetians who could be found were seized by Manuel's men. In all, ten thousand Venetians were taken, and their goods were confiscated. Venice was outraged at the Emperor's actions. Furious, the Doge, Vitale Michiel, ordered every Venetian who was still abroad to return home. A substantial expeditionary force was raised with the goal of punishing Manuel severely for his actions. However, when the fleet set out Manuel sent ambassadors to intercept it. They explained disingenuously that Manuel's actions had been misinterpreted; the Emperor was desperately keen to restore peaceful relations.

The Doge, who had sailed with the fleet, accepted that Manuel was acting in good faith. Keeping his large force intact, he withdrew it to the island of Chios to spend the winter. While it was here, the fleet was ravaged by disease, and the Italian forces were decimated. It was now that Manuel showed his true colours. He was not interested in seeking peace; he had merely been buying time while he gathered his strength. Now that he had gained the upper hand, he had no intention whatsoever of giving in to the demands of the Venetians. Now powerless to enforce their claims for restitution, the fleet returned home. The citizens of Venice were infuriated that the time and money invested in the expedition had all been wasted. For this they blamed their Doge, Vitale Michiel. A mob caught him as he tried to escape retribution and murdered him. Because of the Doge's failure to attack Constantinople, the Venetians had been deprived of an opportunity for revenge. However, the wrongs that they felt Manuel had visited upon them were not forgotten. The immediate chance of vengeance had passed, but the Venetians would not be slow to seize the initiative should another chance for retribution present itself.

One cannot look at the actions of Manuel without gaining the impression that, as an Emperor, he attempted to be far too clever for his own good. He was always manoeuvring, plotting and scheming to find a situation from which he could gain political advantage. Having upset the

Venetians – a dangerous people to alienate – he now attempted to intervene once more in the politics of the West. The Western Emperor was a man named Frederick Barbarossa, a giant of his time. He was a man who believed absolutely in the divine right of emperors to rule as they saw fit, without hindrance from any quarter. From the moment of his accession, confrontation between him and the Papacy was inevitable. The struggle for Papal supremacy, which had caused so many problems during the previous century, continued to scar the political landscape of Western Europe.[2]

As devious as ever, Manuel hit on a scheme by which he hoped to profit from this situation. He made an approach to the Pope suggesting that he would accept the spiritual supremacy of the Pope if the pontiff would restore to Byzantium lands long lost to the Empire. He also wished to be crowned in Rome. The offer was not without its attractions; it would have given the Papacy the chance to end the schism between the Eastern and Western Churches. There was never any possibility that Manuel could have delivered on his promises though. Public opinion in Byzantium would have been outraged. Even though Manuel was powerful, such an act would have been regarded as betrayal, and it would not have been long before plots were hatched against him. Byzantium had suffered from vicious coups and counter-coups throughout its history. The stability given to the Empire by Manuel, his father and his grandfather (the three men ruled consecutively for nearly a century) may suggest that the Comnenii were a strong Imperial dynasty. Events shortly after Manuel's death would show all too clearly that such a perception was totally erroneous.

Manuel's approaches to the Papacy came to nothing (the excommunication placed on the Patriarch of Constantinople was not in fact formally lifted until 6 December 1965!), as indeed they were destined to from the outset. An old threat then took his attention once more. The Turks of Asia Minor were once more in the ascendant. Threatened by their growing successes in the region, Manuel raised a very large army to destroy them, which marched to the east of Asia Minor. Here it approached a valley near the fortress of Myriocephalum. At the far end, a few Turks were seen by Manuel's scouts. Manuel resolved to move on this small band of the enemy. Some of his advisors warned him that the situation smelt strongly of a Turkish ambush, but Manuel knew better; urged on by other less cautious elements within his entourage, he launched a headlong assault on the Turks in the distance.

Sadly for him, the Turks were indeed waiting for him to commit such a rash and foolish act. As his army poured into the valley, it suddenly found itself attacked on all sides. Large numbers of Byzantine troops continued to stream into the valley; this added to the confusion, and made it impossible for the Greeks to extricate themselves. They were trapped and utterly defeated. For reasons that have never been fully understood, the Turkish leader, Kilij Arslan, allowed Manuel to withdraw subsequently on the offer of generous terms. He could have annihilated the Byzantines had he fully pushed home his advantage. Manuel returned to Constantinople with some of his army intact but it appears that his spirit was broken by the defeat.

Manuel died in 1180, leaving behind an Empire rocked to its foundations. He was a strange mix; he had all the attributes of greatness but any review of his reign must conclude that he never lived up to the promise that his many talents suggested. Crucially, his attempts to adopt Western customs were despised by his people. They were deeply resentful of the increasing influence of Western merchants within the Empire, and they were disgusted at Manuel's attempts to increase his influence with the West by the use of marriage treaties with some of the leading ladies of Western Europe.[3]

Yet any possibility of improving relations with the West was seriously compromised by Manuel's suppression of the Venetians within his Empire, and by his meddling – ultimately unsuccessfully – in the politics of Italy. During his reign, at some point he numbered among his allies the German Emperor, the Count of Sicily, the Pope and the Doge of Venice. At other times, he was at loggerheads with all of them. These were dangerous men to antagonise, men who were unlikely to be convinced by Manuel's protestations of friendship when he changed sides with such bewildering frequency. Indeed, Manuel's inconsistent policies only served to exaggerate the Western perception of Byzantine duplicity.

There were deep undercurrents within the Empire. Xenophobic emotions among the Byzantines had been barely subdued and were always ready to explode in a frenzy of violence against foreign elements. Worst of all, Manuel's death left a power vacuum. His successors would be weak and ineffectual. The defeat at Myriocephalum was also a major blow to Byzantine prestige. After Manzikert, it was a second hammer blow to the Byzantine Empire. To outsiders it appeared as if the Empire was in a state of serious decline, which was indeed the case. In the context of these violent, expansionist times, such signs of frailty could only serve to inflame the ambitions of opportunists in search of easy prey.

CHAPTER THREE

The Storm Clouds Gather

The illusion of stability created by the dynasty of Manuel and his immediate predecessors quickly disintegrated following his death. Certainly, he had been a brilliant man, but unfortunately as an Emperor he was an underachiever. Apart from his misadventures in foreign policy, he had also lived beyond his Empire's means. He left as his legacy a treasury that was denuded of funds. Worse than this, following his death all the anti-Western feelings pent up in Byzantium, particularly in Constantinople, erupted spectacularly and horrifically within a few years. Consequently, relations with the West, which had become increasingly strained as the century progressed, deteriorated alarmingly as the twelfth century neared its close.

Manuel left an eleven-year-old son, Alexius, as his successor. He had made no preparations as far as a succession policy was concerned, following the hopeful (and obviously completely erroneous) advice of his fortune-tellers that he could expect to live for much longer than he actually did. Therefore, the effective government of Byzantium passed into the hands of the late Emperor's wife, Maria, who became Regent.

Maria suffered from two major disadvantages. Firstly, she was a Frank (the name given collectively to the Westerners who had settled in Outremer, the crusader kingdom in the East). The people abhorred Manuel's policy towards the settlers in the kingdom which, after the initial difficulties over Antioch and the misbehaviour of Reynald of Chatillon, had evolved into one of mutual friendship and support. They were also alarmed by the increasing economic superiority of the West, which had led to a sharp decline in the fortunes of merchants within Byzantium who had lost ground in both domestic and foreign markets as a result. The prospect of being ruled by a Frank must have filled most of the population with nothing but horror.

Maria's second handicap was that there were obvious flaws in her character that served to inflame the situation. She appears to have been incapable of choosing her advisers carefully, which did nothing to improve a precarious state of affairs. As her main confidante, she chose the nephew of the late Emperor, a man also named Alexius (a confusing aspect for any historian of this period is the limited range of names that the Byzantine nobility used for their offspring). Rumours quickly spread that he offered Maria more than just advice, and vicious tongues soon questioned the morals of the Empress dowager and Regent. Her ally and rumoured lover was also a supporter of the Franks and was, in fact, the uncle of the Queen of Jerusalem. As such, he was unlikely to commend himself to the Byzantine people any more than Maria.

The government of Maria and Alexius proved completely ineffectual. It became very clear that, if anything, Latin influence in Byzantium was likely to increase under their rule. Predictably, within a very short time, plots were hatched against Maria and her coterie. The most serious of these was led by her own stepdaughter, Maria. The plotters planned to murder Alexius, but their scheme failed and the leading conspirators were forced to seek sanctuary in the holy church of St Sophia. Alexius attempted to ignore the sanctuary offered by the building, a sacrilegious act that further angered the Byzantine people. In the backlash that followed, the Empress was forced to pardon the conspirators. This, however, was merely a prelude to a much more dangerous coup attempt. Realising that her position was becoming increasingly insecure, the Empress sought for help from the King of Hungary. Unfortunately for Maria, before such aid was forthcoming full-scale rebellion broke out in the Empire.

Living in Asia Minor was a cousin of the late Emperor, a man named Andronicus Comnenus. He was a dazzling individual. Superficially, he had much of the romantic about him. Those that knew him wrote that although he was now in his sixties, he looked a good twenty years younger. Not only was he possessed of exceptional looks, he was also by the standards of the time a giant of a man, standing over six feet tall. His past was littered with tales – mostly true – of his romantic liaisons. On more than one occasion, he had inflamed the passions of the late Emperor because he had seduced a lady who held rather too prominent a position in society. His greatest scandal had been to elope with the widow of a previous King of Jerusalem. Not only was the lady much younger than he was (a problem of no significance whatsoever given the social mores of the time), much more seriously she was related to him. Given the choice of withdrawing from what was widely regarded as an incestuous relationship or giving up his position in society, Andronicus chose the latter. The couple were forced to flee into exile in the Islamic world, at Damascus.

Subsequently, Andronicus was forgiven. Apparently, he was possessed of immense charm and a generous smattering of good luck (a quality that would unfortunately desert him). After this pardon, he returned to Asia Minor. It was to him that the Byzantine people now looked for the prospect of salvation. Envoys from the people were despatched to

Andronicus, suggesting that he raise an army and march on the capital. This he duly did. As he approached the capital, many flocked to join him. It would be inaccurate to describe resistance as sporadic; it was to all intents and purposes non-existent. In triumph, Andronicus entered Constantinople as a conqueror. However, once he was safely ensconced within the city walls, another side of his character revealed itself. Unfortunately, there was a much blacker, almost barbaric side to this man who seemed, superficially at least, to be in possession of so many virtues. Andronicus was cruel, and the absolute power that he had won for himself would exaggerate this until it assumed a quality of viciousness.

Andronicus quickly demonstrated this cruelty, although the Byzantine people were, for the moment, too blind to recognise it. They blamed only one group for their troubles – the Latins. The twelfth century saw the ultimate flowering of an insular Byzantine culture that venerated all those things that were part of its own tradition and rejected the cultural traits of everyone else. It is no accident that scholars assert that this period coincides with the time during which the purest Greek was spoken.[1] This manifested itself in a fierce attachment by many of the people to those things that they perceived as being part of their heritage, and a bitter rejection of 'foreign' influences. Given the increasing economic penetration of the West and the effect that this had on the Byzantine economy, it perhaps symptomises a society suffering from a crisis of confidence.

Spurred on by their passionately felt xenophobia, the Byzantines in Constantinople turned on the Western inhabitants of the city with unbridled ferocity. The Latins had admittedly been arrogant in their attitudes towards the Byzantines, but this could not justify the outrage that followed. Every Latin who was caught – young, old, male, female, even those in hospitals – were butchered. Only a few who took to their ships managed to flee; no doubt, some of them returned to the West to add another chapter to the growing litany of accusations of Byzantine duplicity and treachery. The massacre was an appalling act, in its way every bit as heinous a crime against humanity as the sack of Constantinople by Western armies twenty years later. It was also widely supported by many of the inhabitants of Constantinople.

The aftermath of this bloodbath was equally horrific. There was a violent purge of the previous ruling caste in the city, perhaps predictable when judged by the ruling conventions of Byzantium but nonetheless disturbing for all that. The displaced dynasty was washed away in a torrent of blood. The first victims were Maria, the stepdaughter of the late Emperor, and her husband. The same woman who had conspired against the Empress and her advisers died in suspicious circumstances – it was widely assumed that poison was the cause. Close behind followed the Empress herself. In an act of particular cruelty (which, presumably, the Byzantines would have called barbarism if they had witnessed it happening in the West), her own son was forced to sign her death warrant. Soon after she was strangled in her prison cell.

Officially, the boy Emperor Alexius still governed. Even this shallow pretence was soon removed. Firstly, Andronicus had himself declared co-Emperor. Shortly afterwards, the boy Emperor was himself strangled. Andronicus now enjoyed absolute power. As if to emphasise it, he married Agnes of France, the twelve-year-old widow of the child he had just murdered. It is impossible even at this remove to read of the actions of Andronicus without grave concern. Murder and intrigue were of course hardly unknown to the Byzantine world, or for that matter any other part of the Medieval globe. Yet so extreme were the acts of Andronicus that they still retain the capacity to shock. They sit uncomfortably with the pious view of themselves that the Byzantines sometimes seem to present, or for that matter with the views of some modern historians who seem to think that barbarism was the sole reserve of Western Christendom.

At any event, it appears that Andronicus soon became aware of how perilous his grip on power was, despite his menace. There was of course extreme indignation in the West at the massacre of the Latins in Constantinople. The new Emperor quickly realised this, and sought to repair the damage with Venice particularly. How sincere the Venetians thought his attempts at reconciliation were must be a matter of conjecture. They had, after all, seen their citizens arrested en masse following Manuel's purge in 1171, and large numbers had been put to the sword without warning. Certainly, the West had long been critical at what they saw as the duplicity of the Byzantines; these two events on their own gave very solid evidence to support their case. For the time being, however, the Venetians agreed to accept the reparations that Andronicus offered them for their loss.

But this was not the end of Andronicus' troubles, merely a foretaste of what was to come. The Emperor ruled with a cruelty that was extreme even for the times. His actions were probably based on understandable paranoia on the part of the man himself. His claim to the throne, after all, was based on nothing but his violent arrogation of authority. There had been many plots against the late Empress Maria, and there was no reason to think that the environment would become any more stable now. Andronicus had become ruler by acclamation of the people, yet there were many in the corridors of power who would welcome a premature end to his reign. There was no doubt that he had more than a few enemies, but so insecure did Andronicus become that he regarded almost anyone as a potential threat. Accordingly, the atmosphere in Constantinople became extremely tense. It took on many of the trappings of what would now be termed a police state. Potential or perceived opponents were rounded up and thrown into jail, or summarily killed.

All of this might have been forgiven had Andronicus offered success to his subjects in return for his excesses. Such mitigation of his cruelty was not forthcoming, and events were about to take a rapid turn for the worse. Ever since the days of Robert Guiscard, the Normans of Sicily had posed an enormous threat to Byzantium with their seemingly insatiable ambition for expansion. The threat – which had never truly gone away – was about to resurrect itself with renewed vigour. The current ruler of Sicily, Count William II (known somewhat pretentiously as 'The Good'), decided that he would launch a fresh attack on Byzantium. To increase his chances of success, he put together the greatest expedition yet launched by the Normans. There were hundreds of ships in the fleet, carrying, according to some chroniclers, 80,000 men.

William's chances of achieving his objectives were greatly increased by the fact that Andronicus appears to have had no warning of the attack. The first target of the Normans was the port of Dyracchium. It surrendered without the pretence of a fight. Although the garrison was not provisioned for a siege, and therefore could not have lasted long anyway, the meek capitulation of the garrison augured badly for Andronicus and spoke volumes for the state of morale in the Empire at that time. From the port, the Normans struck out across the Balkans. There was no resistance to their advance until they reached the walls of Thessalonica on 6 August 1185. There they set up a tight siege of the city, with the Norman fleet effectively enclosing it in a vice-like blockade as they cut off the sea routes into its port. Resistance was short, sporadic and ultimately futile. It merely offered the invaders an excuse to sack the city when it was subsequently captured. It fell on 24 August, and its inhabitants were then subjected to a brutal outburst of rape and pillage which presaged the fall of Constantinople a few years later.

The Greek chroniclers were genuinely shocked by the way that the Normans defiled not only the Greek women but also the Greek churches. Undoubtedly, their stories lose nothing in the telling and there is an element of propaganda in their narrative. However, if the stories of the Normans supposedly sacrilegious acts are founded in some element of fact, it perhaps represents the regard in which the West held Byzantium. The Latins regarded the Byzantine form of Christianity as strange and even heretical, and might therefore have seen little contradiction or blasphemy in defiling their places of worship. The Sicilians had been closer to the Greek method of worship than many in the West (Sicily had itself been a part of the Byzantine Empire for some time and there were still elements of Byzantine tradition in the island). If the Sicilians regarded the Byzantine church with disdain, there was every reason to think that others in the West would share that view.

The reaction to the loss of Thessalonica – the greatest metropolis in the Empire after the city of Constantinople – was one of panic. Andronicus struck out more wildly than usual. In his capital at that time was his cousin, Isaac, a member of the Angelus family, one of the leading noble dynasties in the Empire. He had been an earlier target of the Emperor but had managed to flee, unlike one of his brothers, who was taken and suffered the loss of his eyes as a result. However, Isaac was in such poverty that he felt he had little choice other than to return to the city that he knew better than any other, and take his chances there.

Accordingly, he had surreptitiously returned, and had taken lodgings in a humble quarter of the city where he was given shelter by a widow. However, it seems that his secret was not as complete as he would have wished. News of his whereabouts had reached the Emperor's ears. Under the influence of his persistent and irresistible paranoia, Andronicus sent his most trusted steward to the house where Isaac was hidden. The widow, despite some attempts to deny the presence of her illustrious lodger, was compelled to admit the steward. He entered and told Isaac that he was under arrest and must come away with him.

Isaac stepped outside. He was, by what we can judge at this remove, placid and weak. But at this precise moment, he assumed a role that was completely out of character. Knowing that his life expectancy must now be very short indeed, it appears that Isaac decided that he would exit the stage with a grand gesture. He moved himself closer to the steward. Then he pulled out a sword that those who had arrested him had carelessly forgotten to remove, and with it 'struck the steward in the middle of the head and clove him through clear to the teeth'.[2]

The steward's entourage were evidently stunned by this unforeseen turn of events and Isaac managed to grab a horse, on which he charged through the streets of Constantinople. He made a fearful din as he did so, shouting to the amazed bystanders whom he passed in the streets that Andronicus was trying to murder him. He headed for the great church of St Sophia, in which he would try to take sanctuary. The people of Constantinople were clearly moved at his plight and rushed to the church to aid him. Isaac's headstrong actions acted as the catalyst that released much pent-up anger among the citizens at the high-handed manner in which Andronicus was behaving. Inspired by Isaac's resistance, the mob, without any pre-meditation, declared Andronicus deposed and Isaac Emperor.

Andronicus quickly became aware of the noise emanating from the church, which was connected to his palace. He made his way through his own special entrance to the balcony, where he looked down in rage on the usurper in the body of the great building below. He picked up a bow, with which he meant to despatch Isaac forthwith. There then occurred one of those miraculous divine interventions so beloved of Medieval chroniclers (an intervention so convenient and consistent with other examples from this 'age of miracles' that we should, perhaps, treat it as a rather good demonstration of poetic licence, that is, with a good deal of scepticism). As Andronicus drew back his bow to release the arrow, the bowstring snapped. Frustrated in his attempts to assassinate Isaac, the Emperor fled back to his palace.

However, this offered Andronicus only a temporary respite, as the mob hurried round to the palace gates. It quickly became apparent to Andronicus that his days were numbered. Not even his personal bodyguard moved to protect him. Seeing the only thing left to him was life itself, Andronicus attempted to save it. He took ship with his wife and started to sail away from Constantinople. Yet divine forces were to intervene once more. A storm whipped up and the ship was driven back to the city. Unable to make their escape, Andronicus and his party hid in an inn. His end was now inevitable. He was a conspicuous figure, well known and much hated by most of his former citizens. Sure enough, the innkeeper's wife spotted the now ex-Emperor hiding behind a cask of wine. She recognised him instantly, and word was quickly sent to the authorities concerning his whereabouts.

They hurried to arrest him. The first act of his jailers was to cut off his right hand; worse was to follow. He was deprived of food and water and, after a few days, he was blinded. Isaac was then asked to legislate on what should be done with Andronicus. If the chroniclers are to be believed, Andronicus must indeed have been a tyrant; the possibilities for eliminating him included burning him or boiling him to a slow and agonising death in a cauldron. But Isaac chose perhaps the cruellest option of all. He handed Andronicus over to the people to deal with as they wished. He was dragged from his prison and paraded through the streets of Constantinople atop a scrawny, flea-bitten camel. The sight of their old persecutor was more than they could bear. The mob, incensed at his previous excesses, dragged him from the camel. They pelted him with rocks and filth. A prostitute poured scalding water over him. Others slashed at him with knives. Then they hung Andronicus upside down. After a mercifully short time, he expired, a sad end to a spectacular but ultimately wasted life. Cruel as his death was, it maybe had an element of justice. Andronicus died as he had lived, by the sword.

The demise of Andronicus Comnenus, against all odds, saved Constantinople. Isaac Angelus was declared Emperor. He assembled an army that was despatched, more in hope than expectation, to beat back the Normans, now less than 200 miles from his capital. It appeared that the Normans were unprepared for a counter-attack and, when it came, they panicked. The Norman army broke and fled. In the rout that followed, the people of Thessalonica turned on them and exacted full revenge upon those who failed to escape their clutches. Downcast and bested, the remnants of the Norman army made its way homeward, its dreams, seemingly on the verge of fulfilment not long before, in tatters.

It was a dramatic and successful start for Isaac. Unfortunately, it proved completely unrepresentative of what was to follow. It quickly became apparent that Isaac was as inefficient as any of his predecessors. He ran a particularly corrupt administration. He also appeared to be incapable of acting tactfully towards the West. The Middle East was on the verge of massive upheavals. The Muslims in the region had found a new leader, one who was about to launch a stunning counter-attack on the crusader kingdom of Outremer. Fuelled by the political ineptitude of the crusader leaders – principally that same Reynald of Chatillon who had caused so much difficulty with the Emperor Manuel twenty years before – this leader, known to history as Saladin, launched a counter-crusade of his own. He gathered together a massive army, which in 1187 attacked the Christian kingdom of Jerusalem.

The crusaders responded by raising a huge army of their own. However, they were completely outthought and outfought by Saladin, who lured them into a virtual desert in the middle of summer. The resultant defeat of the Christian army at the Battle of Hattin was spectacular and, in every sense of the word, crushing. Once this army had been annihilated, there was simply no fighting force left to defend the kingdom.

Resistance crumbled with alarming rapidity. Most significantly of all, Jerusalem itself fell to the Muslims. The leaders of the East were quick to send their congratulations to Saladin on his triumph. Among such messages of praise was one from the Byzantine Emperor, Isaac Angelus. Isaac had strong political reasons for doing this. He would have noted how powerful Saladin was, and he would have had no desire whatsoever to antagonise such a strong ruler. The Greek Christians in Jerusalem – of whom there were a significant number – had suffered much loss of freedom at the hands of the Latin Christians, and ironically they would also have welcomed a return to Islamic rule, as in the past it had been a tolerant religion and Saladin was known, with good reason, as a beneficent master. As the traditional protector of the Greek Christians, Isaac would have been quick to recognise that their lot would actually improve with Muslim masters. However, such subtle diplomatic considerations would count for little with the peoples of the West. To them, the loss of the Holy City was an unmitigated disaster and its loss to the anti-Christ was a cause for shame. There would be much indignation and outrage, and a true sense of betrayal, when they heard of Isaac's congratulatory sentiments.

This resentment was to manifest itself openly during the crusade that followed. The reaction to the loss of Jerusalem led to the preparation of a major expedition, involving the King of England, the King of France and the Emperor of Germany. King Richard of England and King Philip of France both opted for the sea route to the East which, although more expensive, was much safer and would ensure that losses due to attrition en route would not be great. However, the Western Emperor, Frederick Barbarossa, decided that he would cross Asia Minor. This meant that he would have to pass through Byzantine territory.

This was worrying news for the Byzantines. Many of the Germans blamed the Greeks, with little foundation, for the vicissitudes of the Second Crusade. Frederick himself had been a member of that ill-starred expedition, and he probably would have had his own negative views on the contribution of the Byzantines to the disastrous events that befell the German army at that time. Further, his dealings with the Pope a few years previously spoke eloquently of his blunt and direct approach to dealing with difficult situations.[3] He was idolised by his men, and he was at the head of a vast force. The portents were certainly not good.

Hardly had Frederick crossed the Byzantine border, when problems began. The border areas in the north of the Byzantine Empire were awash with Bulgarian and Serbian brigands. They quickly began to cause trouble for the German army. Frederick was outraged by the attacks they launched against his troops. Unfairly, he blamed Isaac for encouraging them, failing to recognise that Isaac had no influence over these unruly tribesmen whatsoever. Frederick swallowed his pride and negotiated what amounted to a safe conduct with the brigands. When he heard of this arrangement, it was Isaac's turn to be perturbed. He assumed that Frederick was attempting to form an alliance with the Bulgarians and the Serbs, with a view undoubtedly to ousting him from his throne.

Therefore, the relationship between the two men was clouded from the start with mutual suspicion and antipathy, and a much more open breech soon occurred. Isaac sent some advisers to Frederick in order to try to smooth the passage of the German army and, most importantly, to ensure that Constantinople was left in peace. He was deeply disturbed when he heard strong rumours subsequently that the envoys that he had sent were in fact implacably opposed to Isaac and had spent much of their time suggesting to Frederick that he should depose the Emperor. Perhaps this explains Isaac's panic-stricken reaction. Frederick sent his own ambassadors to Constantinople. When they arrived, they were instantly arrested and clapped in irons. Surely Isaac never made a greater mistake. Presumably he believed that by his actions he could ensure the good behaviour of Frederick. If so, he completely underestimated the stamp of the man. Frederick's response was swift and, to any who really knew him, entirely predictable. He received tidings of Isaac's actions with unbridled anger, as apparently did the rest of his army. Enraged, he sent a missive to his son, Henry, who had remained in Germany:

> When we [the German army] heard this, the whole army of the cross was enraged, and did not cease from devastating and seizing cities, towns and castles . . . since the crossing of the Hellespont is impossible unless we obtain from the emperor of Constantinople the most important hostages and subject the whole of Romania [Byzantium] to our rule we urge you to send envoys to Genoa, Venice, Ancona and Pisa and elsewhere to get the help of knights and vassals to come by sea and meet us at Constantinople around the middle of March 1190 when we can ourselves attack the city from the landward side.[4]

Faced with this demonstration of strength, the terrified Isaac eventually backed down, and Frederick's envoys were released unharmed. In return, Isaac had to supply hostages of his own to guarantee the good behaviour of the Byzantines while the Germans carried on into Asia Minor. The only concession that Frederick would make was that his army would not cross the Bosphorus via Constantinople but would use a crossing some way from the city. It was a small concession, but it was the best that Isaac could hope for and it did help in small measure to increase the security of his capital.

The German threat on this occasion came to nothing. Frederick's army moved off into Asia Minor. There the expedition was to meet with sudden and shocking disaster. While crossing a river in Armenia, Frederick, who was by this time, quite elderly either fell or was thrown from his horse. He expired quickly in the cold waters of the river. Following his premature demise, the German expedition fell apart. So charismatic was Frederick as an Emperor that there was simply no one else with the expedition who could take his place. A few of the Germans pushed on towards Palestine but most of the force decided that they should return home to protect their interests in the case of any succession struggle. It was left to Frederick's son, Philip of Swabia, to assume nominal command of the Germans for the time being. Although he eventually returned to his homeland without making much contribution to this Third Crusade, his interest in the region was far from satiated. The German expedition achieved little; most significantly its effects had been primarily negative in that Frederick's contretemps with Isaac demonstrated once again the fragility of relations between Byzantium and the West.

No other major force made its way across Asia Minor to join the Third Crusade, as the other leaders had chosen to make their way to Outremer by sea. However, the journey of King Richard I of England was to impact significantly on Byzantine interests in the area, albeit indirectly. On his way to the East, Richard was separated from the ships carrying his new bride, Berengaria of Navarre. She was, in fact, shipwrecked on the shores of Cyprus. The island was at that time under the rule of Isaac Comnenus. He was a usurper, and as such the island was not under the direct control of Byzantium. However, it was most certainly in its traditional sphere of influence as it had been under the control of Byzantium for centuries prior to the usurpation of Isaac Comnenus.

Isaac attempted to hold Berengaria for ransom. Although she managed to avoid falling into his clutches, the treatment accorded to both her and to Richard's favourite sister, Joanna, who was with her, enraged the King. When he himself arrived on the island, he was furious at Isaac's actions, and determined to conquer the island. With the help of some of the Franks from mainland Outremer, who wished to ingratiate themselves with him, Richard was successful. Thus the island fell into the hands of the West. It was to remain there for several hundred years. It was historically a part of the Byzantine Empire, and was in an important strategic location being so close to the shores of Asia Minor and the coast of Syria. Within a few years, events were to take place on the island that would add to the interest of the Germans in the East.[5] As the Germans had been opposed to the Byzantines for some time, and as their view of the Byzantines continued to deteriorate, this was a most unwelcome development as far as Byzantium was concerned.

Despite the fact that the three major rulers of Western Europe all sent armies to the East, the Third Crusade was a source of bitter disappointment. For a huge outlay of men and materials, the Crusaders had only won back a thin coastal strip of land, a poor return for such a large investment. Jerusalem, the main objective for many of those who took part, remained in enemy hands. Some successes had been achieved, but they were minor and barely sufficient to avoid the conclusion that the expedition had been futile. However, the shock of the loss of Jerusalem was keenly felt in the West, where for decades many of the leading nobles were losing interest in the crusading movement until the Muslim triumph. It was therefore very probable that a new expedition would be called before long, in order to complete the painful process of reconquest that the Third Crusade had only begun.

Apart from the problems with the German army and the conquest of Cyprus, the Byzantine world had escaped largely unscathed from the Third Crusade. However, the peripheral involvement of the Empire seems only to have encouraged its people to resume once more their journey along the road to self-destruction. Isaac's rule, it transpired, would be disastrous for the Empire. Although widely detested for his cruelty, Andronicus had at least made stringent efforts to curb the abuses so characteristic of much of Byzantine society. However, Isaac was known to be corrupt, and was resented by many of his people for it. Local lords, spurred on by the contempt that the people held for Isaac and encouraged also by his relative weakness, began increasingly to assert more autonomy. Away from Constantinople, many of the larger cities became more independent of the capital. It was a marked sign of weakness, a strong indicator of an Empire in a dangerous free-fall.

Because of Isaac's weak government, it was inevitable that there would be powerful elements in the capital scheming to overthrow the Emperor. Given his poor leadership of men, it was always probable that these schemes would ultimately succeed. Allowing for all of this, Isaac lasted a surprisingly long time. It was not until 1195 that a full-blown coup was launched, inspired, of all people, by Isaac's own brother, Alexius. Support for Isaac was desultory and doomed to failure. The plot was completely successful. Isaac was dethroned and thrown into prison. Here, shortly after his internment, he suffered the traditional penalty suffered by failed Emperors in Byzantium when his eyes were gouged out. Also made captive, although fortunately for him unharmed, was Isaac's son, yet another Alexius.

This was a particularly cruel act by the usurper Alexius, as he had been ransomed by Isaac from the Saracens, who had caught him when he tried to flee from the clutches of Andronicus Comnenus a decade or so previously. There was obviously little room for family loyalty in his plans. Nevertheless, it seems similar to any other coup, and far from an isolated example in the history of Byzantium; such violent upheavals were by no means unique. In the past, after an initial outbreak of violence, Byzantium had usually managed to stumble back onto a pathway of relative stability. Sometimes the coups occurred with disturbing regularity, and the people exchanged Emperors every few years. Even in such extreme times, however, the Empire had managed to survive.

But this time would be different. A few years before these events took place, Isaac's daughter, Irene Angelina, the widow of a prince of Sicily, had been captured by the Western Emperor, Henry VI. Henry gave her as a bride to Philip of Swabia. Despite the unusual nature of the courtship, the marriage proved to be a happy match. Both parties seem to have felt genuine affection for each other. As daughter of the deposed Emperor, Irene would have been understandably enraged at events in Constantinople. Alexius was particularly slow to identify the danger that this posed to his regime, and Isaac managed to correspond with his daughter with surprising regularity and frankness.

At the time, it may have seemed that, enraged as she was, there was little that Irene could do to express her outrage more practically. However, events were about to lend far more significance to the relationship between the German Imperial family and the Byzantine Empire than any might have imagined. A savage reaction was about to be unleashed by the failure of the Third Crusade and the ruthless overthrow of Isaac. In conjunction with the decades and centuries of distrust between East and West that had gone before, events at the end of the twelfth century would send Byzantium hurtling headlong down a road that led to catastrophe and ruin.

CHAPTER FOUR

The Adventure Begins

As the twelfth century drew to its close, tension was building between Constantinople and the West. The Venetians particularly had suffered from the change in climate between the two, but there was antipathy elsewhere in Europe too, especially from Germany. The misguided adventure of the Fourth Crusade cannot be understood without considering the context in which it took place. It would be launched at a time when the often-uncertain temper of the state of affairs between East and West had seen a marked decline. Without consideration of what had gone before – in terms of the deterioration in the understanding of the two cultures – what was about to happen makes little sense. Few things in history happen without warning and there were plenty of signs that a confrontation between the two factions was far from unlikely.

Europe itself had plenty of its own problems to distract it from the Orient. As the century neared its close, King Richard of England and King Philip Augustus of France, at one time joint leaders of the Third Crusade threw their forces at each other with a hatred born of greed and envy. The situation was even worse within the German Empire. The Emperor Henry had died before his time, and his demise acted as a catalyst for a bitter and violent succession dispute. The late Emperor's brother, Philip of Swabia, laid claim to the Imperial throne, as did Otto of Brunswick. The Western Empire turned on itself in a frenzy of infighting.

It was in the environment created by this turmoil that the Papal throne also fell vacant. Celestine III, a man of immense age (rumoured to be ninety-seven years old), expired after a long and acrimonious period of dispute with the late German Emperor. His place was taken by a young Italian aristocrat of the Lotario family. He took the Papal title of Innocent III. In some respects he appears to modern eyes to be an unlikely choice. He was only thirty-seven years of age, and was not yet even a priest (he would not in fact be ordained until over a year after his election). Yet his election was perhaps not so surprising as he was in fact the nephew of a previous pontiff, Clement III. He was also, according to his (undoubtedly prejudiced) biographer, blessed from the outset with divine approbation:

while his election was being celebrated the following sign appeared. Apparently three doves were flying around in the room in which the cardinals had taken their seats and when Innocent was elected and had been taken apart from the rest, the whitest of the doves flew to him and settled next to his right hand.[1]

If men doubted his credentials due to his relative inexperience and youth, then they misjudged Innocent badly. He would prove to be a great Pope, although, in the religious sense of the word, not always a good one. He was possessed of unbounded energy and great vision. He was firm in his ideas, and in many ways an innovator; later in his pontificate he would be instrumental in advancing the development of the infant movements of friars, the Dominicans and the Franciscans. Above all else, though, he was a man convinced of the pre-eminence of the Papacy in the world. He continued a tradition that was by now 150 years old; one that sought to establish and confirm the supremacy of the Pope over the secular rulers of the world. He was among the greatest believers in the concept of the 'Papal Monarchy', a doctrine by which the Pope was deemed to hold sway over all other men, including kings and emperors, as the ultimate ruler of Christendom. During his reign, Innocent III would not hesitate to excommunicate anyone, including the greatest secular rulers, if they did not accept his authority. He was allied to Otto of Brunswick in his battle for the German Empire but he did not hesitate to disbar him from the communion of the Church when, against Innocent's wishes, Otto attacked the island of Sicily. Much later still, he would excommunicate King John of England, the successor to the Lionheart, and force him to become his feudal vassal.

Early in his reign the new Pope set out his policy. He would firstly seek to expand the power of the Papacy. In fact, during his reign he would reinforce the secular power of the institution by confirming its control over the then substantial Papal States in Italy. His ambitions in this respect were given an early boost when the Empress Constance, widow of the late Emperor Henry, put both her kingdom of Sicily and her young son, Frederick, under the protection of the Pope.[2] He was also keen to heal the rift between the Eastern and Western Churches. For his part, the Emperor in Byzantium, Alexius III, was insecure and unsure of his throne and sought to reach some form of understanding with Innocent. Discussions between Rome and Constantinople were commenced, and a series of letters travelled east from the Papal court to the Imperial court of Byzantium and back again. Yet Alexius could not possibly deliver on an agenda of reunification of Eastern and Western Churches – his people would not tolerate it and, given the violent intrigues by which he had come to power, Alexius could not antagonise them – and he made conciliatory overtures towards Innocent without, in reality, ever offering anything tangible to the pontiff.

Despite his intense belief in the supremacy of the Church over the secular world, Innocent was presiding over the institution in changing times. This was never better illustrated than in the state of the crusading movement. The First Crusade, launched in 1095, had come about as a result of a tidal wave of religious emotion. The appeal of the armed pilgrimage touched something deep in the human psyche at that precise moment in time. And it had, of course, been crowned by success. The Holy City was taken from the heathen; surely God himself approved of the enterprise.

From that point on, however, the success of the crusaders began to evaporate. Within two years of the capture of Jerusalem in 1099, three large expeditions bringing new recruits to the East were cut to ribbons by the Turks in Asia Minor. This was only the beginning of the demise. First, the city of Edessa fell. As a result, the Second Crusade was launched. Despite the presence of the King of France and the German Emperor, the crusade achieved virtually nothing. This had been followed by the disastrous loss of Jerusalem itself and the disappointing results of the Third Crusade. Divine approbation did not accompany pilgrims from the West with the same certainty as had once been the case. Religious motivation was still important and could still inspire many to set out on crusade, but there were other factors too that would influence recruitment to any new crusade that might be launched.

In the West, one such motivation was apparent. The twelfth century saw important cultural changes in the region. It was the age of Chretien de Troyes and the early Arthurian romances. The beginnings of a new era began to manifest themselves, an era known, rather romantically to the modern world, as the Age of Chivalry. As with so many concepts in the Medieval period, chivalry was an ideal fraught with inconsistencies and apparent double standards. Chivalry meant little in the context of the sack of a Medieval city, where the men captured were often put to death summarily while their wives and daughters were ravaged in the aftermath. Yet for all that, the idea of glory, fought for and won on the field of battle, served as a spur to men of the knightly class. Such sentiments played a part in the response to the call for a new crusade that was about to be made.

Innocent decided very early on in his primacy that he would devote much of his energy towards launching a new expedition to the East. There were a number of reasons for this. Firstly, we should not doubt that he had genuine religious reasons for doing so. He was a man of the

Church and a man of his time. The fall of Jerusalem in 1187 had created much deeply felt anguish in the West and its continued occupation by the Muslim enemy could not fail to be regarded as a mark of shame. However, a complex cocktail of motives lay behind the crusading urge. It was a way of asserting the authority of the Church, part of the ongoing battle between Church and state concerning the validity of the doctrine of Papal supremacy. By summoning the crusade the Papacy gave a very visible demonstration of its authority. Yet the idea of Papal control over the crusade was illusory. Once the expedition had left and was en route to the East, it would be difficult indeed for Innocent to ensure that it acted as he wished. In reality, the Pope had always struggled to keep any semblance of control over a crusading army. The nearest that any Pope had been to retaining such control was through the Papal legate, Bishop Adhemar of le Puy, who had accompanied the First Crusade. Even Adhemar's influence had been limited, however, and Urban's direction of the crusade had virtually disintegrated when Adhemar met an untimely death. The experience of this Fourth Crusade was to demonstrate conclusively that the problems of retaining control were now worse than ever.

To a large extent, this reflected the equilibrium in the balance of power between the secular and spiritual arms of Christendom. Men were not prepared to accept blindly the supremacy of the Pope. Endowed with increased confidence because of the vitality of Western Europe, secular lords increasingly had minds of their own. They would support a Papal policy if it was in their interests to do so, they would respect the wishes of the pontiff when they did not conflict with their own aims, but unquestioning obedience was not on their agenda. The development of the Fourth Crusade was to demonstrate this all too clearly.

Innocent set about the organisation of this Fourth Crusade with great enthusiasm. He wrote to his archbishops in 1198, telling them of his plans. He commented angrily on the supposed taunts of the Muslims, who asked derisively 'where is your God?' Then he attempted to play the role of peacemaker amidst the troubles of Europe. He publicly called on the Kings of England and France, and the rival claimants for the German throne, to put an end to their petty squabbles and devote their energies instead to the reconquest of the Christian East for Christ:

> Jerusalem has been unhappily wasted and its Christian population woefully slaughtered [in fact, when the city was taken by Saladin in 1187 his treatment of the Christians had by the standards of the day been amazingly humane, in marked contrast to the bloodbath that followed the capture of the city by the First Crusade] . . . wherefore

we are stricken with anguish and weeping over so great a disaster. . . . Let us collectively and individually prepare ourselves by next March 1199 to defend the land where our Lord was born. . . . For if rescue is too late in coming, the locust's caterpillar will devour what remains and new disasters will be worse than earlier ones.[3]

Innocent then reinforced his efforts by despatching two legates to advance his desires. One of them, Peter of Capuano, was to present himself to the Kings of England and France and arrange a five-year truce between them. His efforts would, in fact, be worthless. Richard of England and Philip of France were far too resentful of each other to contemplate such an idea. Further, they had already taken part in one major expedition to the East and may have felt that they had already fulfilled their crusading obligations more than adequately. There would be no help from them. The other legate, Soffredo of Pisa, was tasked with obtaining the assistance of the Venetians – a strange choice, as Pisa and Venice were arch-rivals in the Mediterranean.

Innocent had to cope with very real problems of organisation, but he was helped by the relative sophistication of the Church, which had made great strides in its administration since the days of the First Crusade. Innocent used to the full the opportunities for communication that this offered. Bishops were enjoined to disseminate information about the crusade right down to a parish level. Detailed guidance was also provided on a range of issues, from the length of time that men were to serve on the crusade to the protection that their goods and property would receive while they were absent.[4]

The Pope involved his bishops far more in the preaching of the crusade that had been the case with previous expeditions. Previous crusades had often involved the Pope, or his leading representative, taking a leading role in recruiting men for the Cross, usually by undertaking a great, high-profile progress to the monarchs or leading lords of Europe, as was the case with Urban II and the First Crusade or St Bernard of Clairvaux in the preaching of the second Crusade. The involvement of a greater number of bishops in the preaching of the crusade had several results. From a positive perspective, it helped to take advantage of the bishops' knowledge of local relationships, and to build on their friendships at a local level to encourage men to take the Cross. It also meant that a much wider audience could be addressed than could be the case when the preaching of the Cross was in the hands of a small group of individuals. Against this, it would be difficult to maintain continuity in the messages about the Cross that individual bishops conveyed to their congregations, and as such there was a danger that inconsistencies might develop that gave a confused view of Papal objectives.[5]

Innocent also had to consider the financing of the expedition. The cost of crusading was massive. Despite the supposed lure of plunder, few men ever made money from fulfilling their crusading vows. Indeed, many placed themselves deeply in debt as a result of going on crusade. There was a huge cost involved in transportation, for which each man was usually held personally responsible. Such mundane issues lay at the heart of the problems that were about to manifest themselves during the course of the crusade.

In order to encourage men to join the crusade, Innocent meant to provide as much financial assistance to it as possible. He took decisive and unusual measures to help to increase Papal finances. The Papacy itself was to donate a tenth of all its annual revenues to the forthcoming crusade. Churches were to contribute a fortieth of their incomes to it, an innovative approach and one that did not meet with universal approval.[6] There was particular opposition to the crusade from the Cistercian order, despite the fact that they received some exemptions from the overall funding formula, and had to contribute only one fiftieth of their incomes. A chest was placed in every parish church in which the laity could place contributions that would be used to help poorer knights make their way to the East.[7] It had also become increasingly common for those who could not, for whatever reason, make the crusade in person to make a financial contribution instead and Innocent encouraged the use of this approach. It was indeed a sensible one; the large numbers of non-combatants who had accompanied previous crusades made little positive contribution to the military effort and only served to consume much more quickly the limited supplies available.[8]

Offering as much financial assistance as possible was an innovative approach towards encouraging men to take the Cross, but this was often a secondary issue to the greatest incentive offered as a reward in return for their participation in a crusade – the promise of spiritual benefits for doing so. It might appear to be a statement of the obvious to claim that the crusades were primarily a manifestation of religious beliefs in action, but this perception has become somewhat blurred by a combination of the difficulty of the modern mind in understanding the spiritual mentality of the Medieval world and the plethora of other objectives that have been offered as possible motivations for participation in a crusade. To assert, as some historians have done, that material motives were a strong incentive for men to take the Cross is a difficult hypothesis to support; there is a long history of men being driven into a state of penury by their participation in the crusade.[9]

Involvement in a crusade meant immense hardship. Crusaders put themselves in great physical peril by their involvement; not only was there the danger of being killed, or, perhaps worse, badly injured and maimed in battle, there was an even greater threat from disease and the journey to the East itself. (The relative security of sea transport should not make us blasé about the voyage; most crusaders were, by nature and experience, 'landlubbers' for whom the thought of a journey at sea in the small craft of the time was a daunting prospect indeed.) Added to the financial hardship involved, and the threat to their property while they were absent (experience from earlier crusades had demonstrated on many occasions that unscrupulous local lords had been quick to profit from the extended absence of their neighbours), it can be seen that enormous sacrifice was required if a man were to enlist for a crusade.

Given this sobering list of reasons why taking the Cross had so many disadvantages, it therefore follows that there must have been overwhelming compensation offered in return if anyone were to be encouraged to enlist. That compensation came in the form of rich spiritual benefits. This was a deeply religious age, where most men accepted that they were living in a world where the presence of God was an undoubted reality and where, fundamentally, most men were living in a state of sin. Because of this, man was threatened with suffering and punishment in the world that was to come. Only by penitential acts would he alleviate this threat of suffering in the Hereafter.

The crusade was the greatest of all penitential acts. The immense sacrifices involved added to the rewards offered in compensation. By their participation in the crusade, men were taking part in an armed pilgrimage by means of which God's kingdom on earth might be restored. In return for their involvement, the men were offered great benefits, making the crusade not only an expedition that would further the interests of Christendom but also an act of immense importance to the participant as an individual. The benefits offered were in the form of a Papal Indulgence, a statement of spiritual rewards offered by Innocent, as God's appointed representative on earth. The terms of Innocent III's Indulgence were the most generous yet offered by a Pope to those setting out on crusade, promising to the crusader nothing less than a share of the riches of Paradise for his efforts:

We grant to all those submitting to the labour of this journey personally and at their expense full forgiveness of their sins, of which they have been moved to penitence in voice and heart, and as the reward of the just we promise them a greater share of eternal salvation.[10]

Innocent made very clear that the rewards offered emanated from his own personal directive as the mouthpiece of the Almighty, and in so doing emphasised the supremacy of the Papacy over all earthly institutions as well as his own authority over all secular monarchs. The formula involved was prescriptive, requiring not only that a man should set out on crusade but that he should do so at his own expense if he were to benefit fully from the Indulgence. Partial Indulgences were offered to those who set out at the expense of another, and even to those who only contributed financially so that others might set out. This latter extension to the vicarious crusader was an important development on the benefits offered by previous Popes, as it gave the Papacy the opportunity to raise more money for the crusades.

Despite all Innocent's intense activity, the response to his appeal was initially slow and disappointing. Indeed, that of the kings of Western Europe was desultory. The region was in a state of political ferment. Philip Augustus, King of France, and Richard I of England had been involved in a vicious territorial dispute in France. Philip wished to increase his possessions in the country, much of which was still held by the Plantagenet dynasty of Richard, which had its roots in Anjou but still held vast tracts of land elsewhere in France, such as Normandy. Richard was a man of immense energy and fighting spirit. The inevitable conflict that resulted was long-standing and bitter. However, Richard and Philip Augustus did agree to put a halt to the war between them for the time being, although they would go no further than that. Whether this cessation would, in fact, have been permanent (an unlikely scenario given the past history between the two men) must remain a matter for idle speculation as Richard was to die shortly after. Following his death, Philip Augustus and Richard's successor, the much-maligned John, quickly set about each other with all the enthusiasm and alacrity of old. The monarchs of the West would contribute nothing.

Neither was much support forthcoming from other directions initially. It fell to an itinerant preacher, Fulk of Neuilly, to generate some enthusiasm for the crusade. He was continuing a tradition going back to the very birth of the crusading movement when a number of such men, of whom the most renowned was Peter the Hermit, went around the countryside whipping up religious fervour for the Cross. It must be accepted at once that even Fulk achieved nothing like the results of these early preachers, yet his role was still extremely important in the context of the Fourth Crusade. Fulk certainly bore some of the hallmarks of the men of old. On one occasion he had berated Richard of England for his excessive pride, avarice and lust, an act requiring more than a little moral backbone on his part. He was one of those most fanatical of religious men, a man who had undergone a deep Damascene religious conversion experience. Once a man who had lived an inappropriately immoral life for a priest, Fulk now threw himself into his mission with sincere passion and energy. His followers attributed miraculous powers to him, an interesting throwback to the days of Peter the Hermit, whose grubby cloak had been believed to possess healing properties. His sincerity and passion moved many ordinary men to enlist, although crucially there is little evidence to suggest that greater men were more receptive to him.

Fulk attended a Chapter of the Cistercians at the abbey of Citeaux. Innocent had sent word to the convention to pray for the forthcoming venture. So moved was Fulk by the experience that he immediately took the Cross and began to preach to others to do so. He moved around the Ile de France, proselytising with energy and enthusiasm. News of his zeal reached Innocent himself and he wrote to Fulk, authorising him to carry on with his mission. Large numbers of ordinary people were won over to the cause of the Cross by Fulk's efforts.

However, it was imperative that a response should also be forthcoming from men of substance, who could provide an army for the crusade. It was from the Champagne region of France that the critical initiative came. A tournament was held at the castle of Ecri in Champagne. This was the fortress of Tibald, Count of Champagne. Tibald had a proud chivalric heritage. It was in the court of his mother, Mary, that Chretien de Troyes had written many of his great works of chivalry. The court was renowned as being in the vanguard of the chivalric impulse that was then spreading across Western Europe, a trait that inevitably impressed itself upon Tibald. The Count was also extremely well connected, being a nephew of both Richard of England and Philip Augustus of France. Even more pertinent was the fact that his elder brother, Henry of Champagne, had been, in practice if not name, King of Jerusalem a few years previously until he met his death tragically when he fell out of a window. Tibald therefore had a family history which was connected with the crusading movement. Such familial connections were a recurring theme throughout the history of the crusades; men often took the Cross because their relations and ancestors had done so, and such family ties were a common source of recruitment.

Many leading nobles were at the tournament that took place on 28 November 1199, significantly some six months after the date that Innocent had planned that the crusade would set out. During the activities, Tibald decided that he would take the Cross. His close relative, Louis of Blois, also decided that he would commit himself to the crusade. Romantics aver that Fulk himself was present at the tournament and harangued the men to take the Cross until they succumbed to his oratory.

Sad to say, there is no evidence that this was the case. Whatever their motivations, take the Cross these great men did. It was an important breakthrough. They were the first leading lords to commit themselves fully to the cause. They were prominent members of the French nobility and, following their lead, other nobles followed suit.

The marshal of Champagne was one of them, a man named Geoffrey de Villehardouin. He would play a vital part in the expedition in two ways. Firstly, he would be one of those given responsibility for arranging transportation for the crusade, the negotiations of which would be fundamental to the way in which the adventure evolved. Secondly, he would also write of his involvement in the crusade in a chronicle that now forms one of the major sources for the background to the expedition. Although he was not one of its leaders, he was very close to the leadership and he knew intimately of what went on. His part in the affair is crucial. In his role as marshal, Villehardouin was tasked with assembling armies in preparation for warfare; he was an experienced administrator, a fact that should be noted in light of the events that followed. Although care must, of course, be taken in analysing the narrative of a man who had a strong vested interest in the events that he was describing, by his proximity to great events and great men Villehardouin provided the basis of much that is known about the Fourth Crusade.

Other leading men in Champagne, as well as throughout northern France, were led to join the expedition by this significant response. There was also notable interest from Flanders. The most prominent man to respond was Baldwin, Count of Flanders, who took the Cross in Bruges on 23 February 1200. Significantly, he was closely linked to Tibald of Champagne, being married to his sister, another example of the importance of family connection as a motivation for crusading. Baldwin was joined by his younger brothers and many of the leading lords of Flanders. He was much respected, a trusted and capable ruler whose administrative skills and experience would prove useful to the crusaders at a later date. He was also an old adversary of Philip Augustus, and he had in fact bested him in battle in the past. As such, he was not likely to be welcomed by the King of France.

There were other, much smaller contingents raised from further afield. The response from Germany was generally disappointing, which is unsurprising given the turmoil created by the war over the succession to the Imperial throne. Germany had been ruled by the Emperor Henry VI, the son of Frederick Barbarossa, from 1190. However, his premature death in 1197 had led to a divisive succession dispute. The claims of the late Emperor's son, Frederick, proved for the time being to be largely irrelevant – he was far too young to succeed. The two rivals for the throne were Philip, Duke of Swabia, the brother of the late Emperor, and Otto of Brunswick. Given their rivalry, no widespread interest in the crusade could be expected from Germany. However, there were isolated areas in the region where men were recruited. Martin, Abbot of Pairis in Alsace, had expended much energy in drumming up support for the expedition in Germany, although with far less success than Fulk. However, some men from the Rhineland were prompted to join up and there was a significant contingent from further east in Germany led by the Bishop of Halberstadt (a man whose cathedral treasury would incidentally be much enriched by his participation).

All told a fair-sized army was raised. Exactly how large this force was is speculative but, although it would have been smaller than the armies of earlier crusades, it would be of high quality. There would, of course, have been many non-combatants in the army, and also men with limited military experience, but a good proportion would have had some knowledge of warfare (a happy contrast with, particularly, the armies of the First Crusade). It therefore presented a significant military threat to any potential adversary.

However, the raising of an army was only the first of the problems that had to be solved. Equally as difficult was the question of transportation. Early crusades had taken the land route across Asia Minor to the Holy Land. As the Turks became ever more successful in their attempts to conquer large portions of Asia Minor, this became a decreasingly less viable and attractive option. The armies of the First and Second Crusade, and Frederick Barbarossa's force in the Third Crusade, had all suffered badly as a result of marching their men across hostile territory. In marked contrast, the most successful troops in the Third Crusade were the French and English armies who had made their way to Jerusalem by sea, across the Mediterranean. There were obvious tangible benefits from the sea route. It was clearly safer, despite the threat of inclement weather to the fragile ships of the day (which meant, incidentally, that there was virtually no maritime activity during the winter months). It also meant that the men would arrive fresher. But it had one major disadvantage to counterbalance these virtues; it was expensive.

The provision of a fleet to ship an army of this magnitude was a major logistical operation. Baldwin of Flanders had some ships but far too few to be adequate for the task of transporting such a large force. There were few other alternatives available. Only a select group of states in the Medieval world had an infrastructure capable of building enough ships to carry the crusade. Most of them were in Italy, particularly Genoa, Pisa and, of course, Venice (the Genoese had provided the transportation for the Third Crusade and there had many complaints about the service they provided). Several conferences were held in the spring and early summer of 1200. At the second of them, at Compiegne, a plan of action was agreed. It was decided that Venice should be approached with a view to providing a fleet.

The negotiation of the deal would be an immensely responsible task. The Venetians were renowned for their commercial acumen and, although they were people of their time and many of them would undoubtedly be spiritually inspired by the expedition, they were also a practical people who would ensure that they made a healthy return from their investment. It was decided that a party of six men would be sent to the city of Venice to negotiate. Tibald of Champagne nominated two of them, Baldwin of Flanders two and Louis of Blois, who had taken the Cross with Tibald at Ecri, selected the final two. One of Tibald's appointees was Geoffrey de Villehardouin, which was fortunate for future historians as his chronicle thus provides first-hand evidence of the negotiations that were to take place.

Charters were given to the party, confirming that they were acting with the full authority of the leaders of the expedition and that they had complete discretion to negotiate whatever deal they thought appropriate. Much has been inferred about the subsequent use, or misuse, of such discretion. Villehardouin states that the envoys were given *carte blanche* to negotiate terms on behalf of the crusade leaders, although it is difficult to believe that they were given no guidelines to work within; after all, the terms that they were to agree would be crucial to the development of the crusade.

The negotiators made their way through the Mount Cenis pass into Italy in the depths of winter. They passed through Piacenza, and on to Venice. They arrived at the city in February 1201 and sought an audience with the Doge of Venice, one Henry Dandolo. Dandolo was one of the most amazing figures of his day. Firstly, he was of immense age. The chroniclers are not consistent in the age that they ascribe to him (the date, or even year of birth is a much less common point of reference in Medieval chronicles than it is in modern times), but all sources agree that he must by this time have been at least in his mid-eighties. Some place him at an even older age. He was also extremely short-sighted; some of those who wrote about him aver that he was completely blind, although we must assume that this is somewhat exaggerated if some of the epic feats ascribed to him at a later stage of the crusade are to be believed. His appalling eyesight was commonly attributed to a wound he had received in a brawl in, of all places, Constantinople many years previously; he hardly had pleasant memories of the city. He was also possessed of an extremely strong personality. If the accounts of Villehardouin and the other leading Western chronicler of the crusade, Robert of Clari,[11] are to be credited he bestrode some of the later events in the crusade like a colossus.

The envoys presented their credentials to the Doge, giving him letters from their leaders that declared that 'the bearers were to be accredited as if they were the counts in person'. They asked that the Venetian Council should be assembled.[12] Dandolo responded that he would indeed do so, although not for four days (given the efforts to which the envoys had gone by making the journey in winter, and the obvious importance of their mission, the delay is surprising and perhaps suggests that Dandolo wished to avoid appearing overeager in helping them, an understandable example of commercial brinkmanship). The envoys accordingly presented their case to the Council at the appointed time, emphasising the holy nature of their request: 'therefore we pray you by God that you take pity on the land overseas, and the shame of Christ, and use diligence that our lords have ships for transport and battle'.[13]

Although Villehardouin at this point is vague in his narrative, the envoys would have stated the number of men that they anticipated would need transportation. It was, as Dandolo noted, 'a great thing that your lords require of us'. Even to Venice, providing ships for an army of thousands of men would require a huge building effort, and other commercial activities would be seriously effected as a result. Dandolo would not give an answer there and then, but would consult with his Council and his people generally. He asked for eight days to consider the requests of the envoys; once again, they must have been living on their nerves for what seemed like an inordinate length of time although, in fairness to Dandolo, this was an extremely significant transaction and he could not afford to proceed without being sure of support. And, of course, he could not countenance striking a bargain where the price was too low.

The envoys and the Venetians duly reassembled eight days later, and the Doge agreed that Venice would provide the transport required if their price was met. Many of the terms of the proposed contract require close examination, as they go to the heart of the future development of the crusade. The city would provide enough ships to carry 4,000 horses, and the same number of knights. There would be sufficient transportation provided for 9,000 squires and 20,000 foot soldiers. An army of some 30,000 men was therefore expected – a sizeable force by the standards of the day. It is important to recognise that Dandolo did not pluck this number out of the air. It must have been based on information given to him by the envoys who, for their part, would surely have been given an indication of the size of the force before they left for Venice. As the method for payment was to be that each man would pay 2 marks, and 4 marks would be given for each horse, it was imperative that the force that was eventually shipped should be of a similar size to that predicted; otherwise, as each man was personally responsible for paying his own way, the crusaders could be faced with a substantial deficit.

The Venetians would also provide food and provisions for men and horses for nine months. They would give the crusaders use of the fleet for a year, to start from the day that the fleet sailed from Venice. They would also provide fifty war galleys; they would not charge for this, provided that it was agreed that they could retain half of the conquests that were made during the course of the forthcoming expedition.

The total cost for all this would be 85,000 marks.[14] It was a huge sum by the standards of the time. It has been shown that the price offered, although expensive, was not hugely above that involved when the Genoese provided the fleet for the Third Crusade.[15] Nevertheless, for some of the rank and file it would be a challenge to find the fare for the voyage. That, however, was not the main problem. The fundamental flaw with this contract was that it relied on the number of men assumed in the negotiations arriving in Venice at the appointed date. In practice, it would be very difficult to predict how many men would join up, but 30,000 would be a challenging target. Further, there was no guarantee that these men would automatically join the fleet, rather than making their own way to the East.[16] And even the greater lords who had signed up to the crusade could only commit their immediate retinues to go with them. Although the lords were destined to lead the crusade, they could not bind others to go with them. Individual crusaders were perfectly at liberty to make their own way to the East. Given all this, the assumptions underlying the terms of the contract were imprudent – very imprudent indeed.

Although the Venetians had offered a high price, one should not underestimate the effort that such a major undertaking would require from the Venetians. Much commercial activity would have to be abandoned for eighteen months as the shipyards of Venice devoted all their energies to the construction of the large fleet.[17] The city itself was taking a huge gamble given the problems in organising a crusading army at the time and the lack of certainty concerning the numbers likely to arrive.

The envoys asked for some time to consider these terms, and the next day gave their answer to the Doge, accepting the treaty. The Doge then held a series of meetings, during which the deal was explained to, and ratified by, the people of Venice. He started by confirming the terms with his council of forty. He then extended his consultations discussing the terms, first 'with a hundred others, then two hundred, then a thousand, so that at last all consented and approved'.[18] The final act of ratification occurred in the great and glorious basilica of St Mark, standing proudly and ostentatiously on the shores of the lagoon of Venice itself, when according to Villehardouin 10,000 people attended a Mass to celebrate the agreement; a number which, if Villehardouin is accurate, means that the church must have been very crowded indeed!

Great emotion was exhibited at the service. It is customary among the chroniclers of the day to make much of the fact that the people and lords were moved to tears by the inspiration of such ceremonies. Villehardouin waxes lyrical about the profusion of weeping at the ceremony. We should not be too cynical about these expressions of sentimentalism. The Venetians were a Christian people, even if the profit motive was an extremely important factor in their psyche. The image of the Cross was very powerful to Medieval man, and real emotion was generated by it. At the end of the service, the treaties were duly approved and sealed. The delegation then set out on its way back to the lords of northern France and Flanders to lay before them the deal that had been struck.

One of their final acts was to borrow 5,000 marks, and to deposit it with the city as a down payment that could be used to commence production. Some of the delegation visited Pisa and Genoa first.[19] Villehardouin made his way back to France with the remainder of the delegation. He passed through the lands of Boniface, Count of Montferrat, on the way. He does not mention in his chronicle that he met with the Count, but it is highly likely that he would have done so. The Count was a major figure in Western Europe. He had many links with the East, and his brother, Conrad, had for a short time been King of Jerusalem.[20] He was experienced in politics and warfare. It was vital for the viability of the crusade that as many men as possible joined the expedition, and it is inconceivable that a man of Boniface's stature would not be visited when the envoys were passing so close to him, and he could offer potentially so many men. The point is of more than passing interest; Boniface was to play a pivotal role in the events of the future.

The envoys arrived back in France without incident. They explained the terms of the treaty to the lords who were, according to Villehardouin, delighted.[21] However, his lord, Tibald of Champagne, was not present. Grave news awaited Villehardouin. Tibald, who was regarded by the expedition as the leader, was seriously ill. Villehardouin made his way to Troyes. So pleased was Tibald with the news of the successful negotiation that he took to his horse, something which he had not had the strength to do for some time. It was a fatal mistake. He was obviously in no fit state to ride. Shortly after, he suffered a relapse. His health deteriorated rapidly until it became clear that he was at death's door.

Before he died, Tibald managed to make out a will. He had raised funds to make the pilgrimage to the East and he left them to be divided among his followers so that they could vicariously fulfil his crusading vows for him. According to Villehardouin, he made them swear to make their way to Venice, an oath that many of them were to break subsequently. Having thus made his peace with God, the Count, a man in the prime of his life (he was not even thirty years old) expired, leaving a small son and a heavily pregnant wife.[22]

The expedition was now faced with a major problem – a new leader had to be found. Baldwin of Flanders might have seemed an obvious candidate but the position was not offered to him. Instead, the crusaders looked elsewhere for a replacement. They first approached Eudes, Count of Burgundy. This was in itself not without logic. He had many followers and was not yet committed to the crusade. More recruits would therefore accrue to the expedition if he were to join. However, Eudes refused, as did the next candidate, Count Tibald of Bar-le-Duc, a cousin of Tibald of Champagne.

Why did the crusaders approach these men rather than Baldwin of Flanders? It is a plausible argument that they were perhaps already concerned at what they perceived to be a shortfall in the numbers expected at Venice, and they therefore desperately needed to attract others to the expedition. Alternatively, perhaps Baldwin's past difficulties with King Philip of France made the leaders cautious; they did not want to antagonise Philip. Whether this was indeed the case or not, their next move dramatically shifted the direction of the crusade. The leaders of the expedition decided to approach Boniface of Montferrat and offer him overall leadership.

Boniface was not without his attractions as a leader. He was much respected for his worldly experience. He also had many followers and would bring a sizeable number of recruits to the crusade. Against this, however, were several major problems. Firstly, he was closely allied to Philip of Swabia in the succession dispute, and as such he would be most unlikely to endear himself to the Pope, Innocent III. It was also an unusual move in that it potentially introduced tensions into the crusade because Boniface was a northern Italian rather than French or Flemish as most of the prominent men in the force were. Developments later on in the crusade would demonstrate that there was indeed much disunity between the French and Flemish elements and Boniface. In this respect, it was an unfortunate development.

There was, however, another factor, which was to have implications of the most sinister kind for the evolution of the crusade. Boniface knew the

East well. His father had fought in the Holy Land, and had indeed been captured by Saladin after the Battle of Hattin. His brothers, Conrad and Renier, had been associated with Byzantium closely, but their experiences had been far from happy. Renier had indeed married Maria, daughter of the Emperor Manuel Comnenus. The association benefited him little. In the aftermath of the turbulent triumph of Andronicus Comnenus Renier had been murdered. Similarly, Conrad had helped Isaac II of Constantinople to fight off a rebellion but had been betrayed in the process, if Villehardouin is to be believed.[23] Such feelings that Boniface had towards the regime in Constantinople were unlikely to be positive.

It proved to be a decision that would fundamentally change the course of the crusade. There are some accounts that describe how Innocent was uncomfortable with the idea that the Venetians were providing logistical support to the crusade, although historians are divided as to their accuracy. If, however, Innocent did feel that the reputation for adventurism possessed by the Venetians threatened his ability to control the course of the crusade, then he must have been doubly concerned by the involvement of Boniface. Whether Villehardouin had himself laid any sort of foundation by any meetings he may have had with Boniface we shall, of course, never know. There is no solid evidence that Villehardouin even saw him. Yet something must have put the idea of Boniface in the minds of the lords of the West as a potential leader, and perhaps it is not too whimsical to suggest that Villehardouin himself might have sown the seed.

As a result of these deliberations, word was sent to Boniface offering him the leadership of the expedition. He received the offer with appreciation – it was after all quite an honour. He agreed to make his way to the city of Soissons in the Champagne region of France to meet with the other leaders. On his way there, he visited the court of Philip Augustus, probably to plead for support for Philip of Swabia. Then he made his way on to Soissons.

Here, the Bishop of Soissons, who was named Nivelon, solemnly fastened the Cross to the shoulders of the Marquis, assisted by two Cistercian bishops and Fulk of Neuilly himself. However, there was little time to discuss the future direction of the crusade as Boniface set off homewards the next day, to 'settle his affairs' according to Villehardouin. But his route homewards would not be a direct one. He would visit firstly Citeaux, headquarters of the Cistercians. This was an understandable move. The Cistercians, an order of immense significance, had been lukewarm in their support of the crusade to say the least. But Burgundy itself, the region in which Citeaux was situated, was a potential source of large numbers of men, and Boniface might have hoped to see some very practical rewards for his efforts in terms of new recruits. From here, Boniface made his way to the court of Philip of Swabia, at Hagenau in Germany. As Philip was his lord, whom Boniface supported unequivocally, there were all kinds of positive reasons why the Count might want to gain his blessing before setting off to the East.

However, other more ominous motives for his visit have been suggested by historians over the course of the centuries. Philip was married, as we have seen, to the daughter of the deposed and blinded Emperor Isaac, who was even now under confinement in Constantinople. Some, at least, identify Boniface's journey to the court of Philip of Swabia as the definitive moment when a sinister change took place to the objectives of the expedition, already endangered by the over-optimistic treaty with Venice, and the point at which the management of the crusade slipped once and for all out of the hands of Pope Innocent III.

CHAPTER FIVE

The Diversion Begins

The usurper Emperor Alexius III of Byzantium was, it appears, not an excessively intelligent man. He had plotted and intrigued his way to power, in the process blinding his own brother and imprisoning his nephew. Such draconian actions should prompt a man to be on his guard. Alexius was obviously not aware of this. Failing to profit from the lessons so evident from his own disloyal example, he allowed considerable liberty to both the deposed ex-Emperor of Byzantium and to his son. Admittedly, Isaac had been deprived of his eyes and this would conventionally deprive him of any claim to the throne, as a blind man was deemed incapable of governing such a large Empire (one that prided itself on its dignity and outward expression of power, both of which qualities would, by the standards of the day, be severely impeded by a man handicapped in such a way). Nevertheless, relatively easy access was allowed to Isaac and it appears that many of his old subjects regularly came to him with their complaints about the new regime. Byzantium at this stage desperately needed a ruler that the people could look up to and worship as they had the great Emperors of old. Such men were unlikely to be seen again by Byzantium: firstly, men such as Constantine the Great were exceptional individuals, of a stature that is usually seen only once in many generations, and secondly, the Byzantium that those great Emperors had ruled was very different to the one that now existed, an Empire that was in a state of irrevocable and ultimately mortal decline.

It quickly became apparent that Alexius III was a man of few talents, an insipid imitation of the emperors of old. His subjects could not accuse him of the cruelty of Andronicus or the excessive corruption of some of the other Byzantine Emperors, but his unpopularity and insecurity was caused simply by his very ordinariness. The late German Emperor, Henry VI, had demanded a huge tribute from Alexius that the terrified Emperor meekly handed over. His subjects had been heavily taxed as a result, a move hardly calculated to endear the usurper to them. No great leadership could be expected from this man.

Isaac sent letters across Europe to his daughter, Irene, the wife of Philip of Swabia. From these, Irene appears to have possessed a level of intelligence far above that of either her father or her brother, and kept herself informed about the state of affairs in Byzantium. She would also surely have passed on news of developments in the Orient. The Germans had a long – and it must be admitted largely inglorious – involvement in the affairs of the Christian kingdoms of the East. Further, they had on several occasions come to the verge of exchanging blows with Byzantium, most notably – and ironically in the light of the current situation – when Frederick Barbarossa had been on the verge of calling down the wrath of his armies on the same Emperor Isaac who now wrote so despairingly to his daughter. The wifely complaints of Irene can hardly have done anything to improve a view of Byzantium that was, in the German court, already a jaundiced one.

The latitude given to Isaac also extended to his son, Alexius. As he remained a potential threat to the throne in the future it is perhaps surprising, given the violent mores of the time, that the usurper even allowed him to survive. It appears, however, that the young man was not only allowed to retain his life and his eyes, but he was even given considerable opportunity to escape should the chance present itself. As a focal point of opposition to a man who was a weak and unpopular ruler, such an event could have the gravest repercussions for Alexius III. He should therefore have been extremely cautious, even going out of his way to prevent this from happening. Such was not the case. In 1201 a rebellion broke out in the Balkans, and Alexius III led out an army to suppress the revolt. He evidently decided that the young Alexius could not be left behind in Constantinople. This was ostensibly a sensible move; these were dangerous times and the young man could possibly be the focus for a rebellion within the capital itself.

Evidently Alexius was not kept under close watch as he somehow managed to enter into discussions with a group of Pisans concerning an escape. It was agreed that he would make a bid for freedom on board a Pisan merchant ship. The ship anchored off the coast in the Sea of Marmora, giving the excuse that it needed to take on sand for ballast. While it was there, the young Alexius evaded the grasp of his captors and made his way out to the ship on a small boat. Naturally, pandemonium ensued when his departure was discovered. Guards were sent post-haste to the surrounding area to recapture the youth, some of whom boarded the Pisan ship. From here, we enter the realm of romance. Some chroniclers say that Alexius had cut off his long hair and dressed himself in the costume of a Pisan.[1] Another version says that he hid himself in an ingeniously designed barrel, which was half full of water but had a secret compartment contained inside it.[2] It is debatable whether any of these delightful tales are true, but the hard reality of the situation was that the young man managed to make good his escape.

Alexius made his way to the West. Unfortunately for historians, the route he took or the chronology of his journey is confused to say the least. Villehardouin places his arrival in mainland Italy in the spring or early summer of 1202, as he relates how Alexius met some of the pilgrims making their way to Venice to join the expedition. However, this version is directly contradicted by the writings of Robert of Clari. Robert was a member of the expedition like Villehardouin, but unlike the marshal of Champagne he was not an important leader, only a relatively minor knight. Long after the expedition had set out, he has Boniface of Montferrat describing Alexius to the crusader army, in the following terms: 'Lords, last year at Christmas I was in Germany at the court of my lord the emperor. There I saw a youth who was brother to the wife of the emperor Isaac of Constantinople.'[3]

Robert's account therefore explicitly puts Alexius at the court of Philip of Swabia at the same time as Boniface was there, shortly after the latter had spent so little time acquainting himself with the leading men of the crusade at Soissons. Boniface spent a considerable time at Philip's court, time that could perhaps have been better spent on organising the crusade of which he had so recently become leader. Admittedly, it was no season for travel but this had not stopped the envoys travelling to Venice during the previous winter. To those with a mind for a conspiracy theory, it was very easy to impute motives of deceit and treachery to the situation. It is not difficult to read into these stories a scenario whereby Boniface, the newly appointed leader of the crusade and long-time ally of Philip, spends a great deal of time plotting with Philip's brother-in-law, devising ways in which the crusade can be hijacked and used to restore Alexius to his rightful throne. Even at the time, there were those who said so. The anonymous writer of the *Life of Innocent* was quick to pick up on such rumours: 'Boniface made his way to have treated with Philip, duke of Swabia, who claims to be king, to the end that he should have Alexius . . . led again to Constantinople by the Christian army to obtain the empire of Roumania [Byzantium].'[4]

Such evidence would appear to be highly suggestive. Against it, however, needs to be considered the fact that the *Life of Innocent* was written by someone who, as a supporter of the Pope, wished to present Innocent in the best possible light, and who would go far to exonerate the pontiff from any blame for what went on during the Fourth Crusade. There is also the account of Villehardouin, which implicitly contradicts the story. For the moment, it is important to note that a succession of historians has chosen to side with one version or the other, and that considerable doubt exists as to which version is true.

One thing is certain. Boniface was extremely active diplomatically at about this time. As a result of his meetings with Philip Augustus of France in the previous year, he had agreed to represent French interests to the Pope. Consequently, before he left on crusade he visited Innocent to discuss affairs with him. The pontiff would have seen his appointment as leader of the expedition as a move of the most profoundly disturbing nature. One of his priorities at this time would be the settlement of the warring factions in a very disunited Europe. It is unlikely that he believed that this laudable aim would be advanced by the appointment of the avowed enemy of Otto of Brunswick, Innocent's preferred candidate in the struggle for the German throne, to the leadership of a crusade that the Pope had done so much to bring about.

At some point, Innocent also held an interview with Alexius, the escapee from the East and pretender to the Byzantine throne. It appears that he was not impressed. Apparently, the young Alexius was not well endowed with the ability or intellect to win men to his side, certainly if his subsequent career is any guide. He asked for the support of Innocent as the rightful claimant to the throne of Constantinople (although of course his father was still alive, even if blinded, and had far more right to the claim as a crowned head of state). But Innocent had been involved in correspondence with the usurper Alexius III for some time and believed, mistakenly, that he was making some progress, however small, towards the reunification of the Roman and Greek Churches. He refused to offer his youthful supplicant any comfort at all.

Boniface does not seem to have been in any great hurry to join the army that was due to arrive at Venice in the early summer of 1202. From his meetings with Innocent he proceeded to the town of Lerica, where he attempted to mediate in an ongoing dispute between Pisa and Genoa. It was not in fact until the middle of August 1202 that Boniface arrived in Venice. The fleet had been due to sail on 29 June 1202. Crusaders started to arrive from the beginning of June. Some of the more important leaders, such as Baldwin of Flanders, arrived quite early on. In the context of a supposed conspiracy this is of some significance. Boniface needed to influence primarily the Venetians, who were providing the transport, and also the French and Flemish leaders, who were providing much of the manpower, if he wished to divert the crusade towards Constantinople. Yet he chose to spend much of his time talking to men who, although undoubtedly important, would not even be with the crusade, individuals such as Philip of Swabia and Pope Innocent. If he genuinely wished to redirect the crusade's efforts then it seems highly probable that he would be best placed negotiating direct with men like Dandolo and Baldwin of Flanders. Yet he was far away from the centre of the action when the leaders began to assemble in Venice.

By the time Boniface did arrive it was clear that the crusade was already in serious trouble. Many of those responsible for organising the transportation went out of their way to emphasise to all potential crusaders that they should assemble at Venice rather than make their own way to the East. This, in many ways, of course made sense. Not only did it mean that the crusaders had more chance of meeting the demanding financial challenges presented by the contract with the Venetians, it also meant that the leadership could better coordinate the movements of the crusade to give it the maximum strategic direction. However, the Venetian terms were not cheap and it may be that many men thought that they could find a less expensive passage to the East. There may also have been some who resented the fact that Boniface had been appointed leader of the expedition, and yet others who did not particularly trust the Venetians.

For whatever reason, it soon became apparent that there was an alarming shortfall in the numbers arriving, which could only result in a huge financial deficit against the amount agreed with the Venetians. There were several worrying examples of large numbers of men making their own way to the East. Some private ships actually sailed from Venice itself. Worst of all, a large force under Jean de Nesles of Flanders, which had arranged to join Count Baldwin at Venice, omitted to keep the rendezvous and instead sailed on to Palestine alone.

Initially, it may have seemed that the lack of numbers was only symptomatic of the notoriously desultory efforts made by men to join the crusades on time. It was impossible for men of note to leave their homes without making adequate provision for their governance in their absence. This, of course, required much energetic organisation. Even allowing for the organisational difficulties, however, from the time of the First Crusade onwards men had been extremely tardy in their efforts to meet the agreed time-scales of the crusades. But it soon became clear that this was not just another delayed start; it was something much more fundamental. As time passed, it became obvious that there were just not enough new recruits arriving to make good the crusaders' bargain with the Venetians.

Those crusaders who had arrived were encamped on the island of Saint Nicholas, away from the main city. Concerned at the small numbers, the Doge made his away across to the camp to demand the payment due. His request was indeed not an unreasonable one. The people of Venice had gone to enormous expense to assemble the fleet that the Western leaders had asked of them, and it was now time for the reckoning. Something like 500 ships now lay idly at anchor, waiting only for passengers before the expedition could set out. Of these passengers, however, there were simply too few. When the contributions of all those present were added together, there was still an enormous disparity against the price charged by the Venetians. According to Villehardouin, less than half the money needed was raised.

The leaders of the crusaders were duly alarmed. They agreed that the Venetians had more than fulfilled their part of the bargain. They could not, however, begin to fulfil theirs. Much blame was attached by Villehardouin to those who had sailed from other ports, although as the deal made was partly his responsibility due caution should perhaps be exercised in taking his words at face value. We do know that many men did sail from other ports, and their contributions would, of course, have helped to bridge the gap, although whether there would ever have been enough men to use all of the transport must remain a matter for speculation. And it has to be said that individual crusaders were not obligated to sail from Venice, but could make their own decision as to how they made their way to the East.

In an attempt to bridge the gap, the leaders of the crusade sought to increase the contributions of those who had already paid, a move that, understandably, caused a great deal of complaint. Those present had already given their share of the cost; why should they pay more? To make matters worse, other discordant voices were also heard and, even at this stage, there were disturbing signs that the fragile unity of the expedition would not last long:

> Great then was the dissension among the main part of the barons and the other folk, and they said, 'We have paid for our passages and if they will take us we shall go willingly; but if not we shall inquire and look for other means of passage.' And they spoke thus because they wished that the host should fall to pieces and each return to his own land. But the other party said, 'Much rather would we give all that we have and go penniless with the host, than that the host should fall to pieces and fail; for God will doubtless repay us when it so pleases him.'[5]

Villehardouin's account does not entirely ring true. It is unclear why men should march half way across Europe and then wish to return home at the earliest opportunity. One suspects that the true reason behind the protestations was indeed that many of the men did resent being asked to pay more, and were understandably reluctant to comply with the request.

Villehardouin's concerns that everything should be done to keep the expedition together set the pattern for what was to come. Before the crusade was ended, expediency would become the dominant factor in the politics of the expedition. In an attempt to pay off the Venetians, the leading men of the crusade, Count Baldwin of Flanders, Count Louis of Blois and the Count of St-Pol,[6] scraped together as much as they could but the sum was nowhere near enough. The absence of kings was felt particularly at this stage. Crusading was an extremely expensive undertaking and few outside of royalty could afford to pay amounts of the size required to fulfil the crusaders' bargain with the Venetians. Many valuable goods were taken to the palace of the Doge as contributions towards the deficit. However, when everything was totted up there was still a deficit of some 34,000 marks – over a third of the amount originally agreed.[7]

The anger of the Venetians and the embarrassment of the crusade leaders can easily be imagined. Yet with the benefit of hindsight, it is clear that the assumptions on which the contract had been made were wildly optimistic. There were undoubtedly logistical problems in coordinating the movement of crusading armies. Communications were not very good, and to ensure that so many men would arrive at the same time in Venice was always a daunting challenge. In addition, crusading was frequently a personal affair (although family ties and feudal relationships were also important in deciding whether or not a man would go on crusade) and, when individuals decided to respond to the call, they often made their own arrangements. Only the direct vassals of men such as Baldwin of Flanders or Boniface of Montferrat would feel bound to them; others joining the crusade would owe little loyalty towards them, and would feel completely justified in making their own way to the East.

Estimates of the size of armies at this time are notoriously unreliable, but it seems that the forces of the Third Crusade were very sizeable, as were the armies of the Second Crusade. However, both of these provide a very marked contrast to the Fourth Crusade. They were armies led by kings whose royal power and influence made it easier to raise armies and, equally importantly, coordinate the movement of forces.[8] In contrast, the armies of the First Crusade, which was similar to the Fourth in that it was made up of a loose coalition of men who owed loyalty to different leaders, often worked in an uncoordinated and disjointed manner.

The state of Western Europe at this time also affected the potential size of any army. As we have seen, Philip Augustus of France was at war with King Richard of England, a struggle that if anything intensified when Richard's brother, John, succeeded to the throne. The situation within the German Empire was also parlous, with two rival claimants for the throne waging a bitter conflict. This had two effects. Firstly, of course, it meant that numbers of men who would have otherwise been available for the crusade were occupied elsewhere. And secondly, even those who were not directly involved would be keen to ensure that their interests were not compromised by their absence. It is significant in this respect that recruitment in Germany was patchy, apart from one or two isolated exceptions such as the region around the city of Halberstadt, and that England, so much involved in the Third Crusade, hardly provided any men at all as far as we can make out.

There was also another important factor to consider, and that was the mode of transportation. While the most popular option was to travel by land, geography largely dictated that any army must move through Constantinople. Now that these routes were no longer viable, and a sea voyage had become the norm, there were many more options available to would-be pilgrims. With the Christian kingdom of Outremer, and the well-developed trade routes between the West and Egypt, there was a sizeable traffic sailing across the Mediterranean from ports such as Genoa, Pisa, Amalfi and Marseilles as well as Venice. Given the fact that the price of passage offered by the Venetians was fairly expensive, it is perhaps little wonder that many men chose to plot their own course to the East. Villehardouin's accusations of treachery, understandable in the context of a man whose contract is found to be based on overly-optimistic assumptions, ignore the commercial and logistical realities of the age in which he lived.

There was much bad feeling between the Venetians and the crusaders over the money. Robert of Clari tells us that the Doge berated the Western leaders, stating that commercial activity in Venice had virtually stopped while the fleet was being built and their Treasury was under great strain as a result. In an attempt to pressurise the crusaders, they were deprived of provisions, a very real hardship in an era when armies carried very few supplies of their own. It was this action, in Robert's account, that was responsible for raising some money, which closed the gap to just over 30,000 marks.

It became obvious to the Doge that a stalemate had been reached. There was clearly little more money to be extracted from the Westerners. A vast fleet had been assembled and was now in need of a destination. Further, it should not be overlooked that the Venetians themselves had committed themselves to a military as well as a commercial interest in the venture. Fifty war galleys had been built. A large number of Venetians had been enrolled to accompany the fleet with the aim of furthering Venetian territorial ambitions.[9] These ambitions would obviously not be furthered if the fleet did not leave the shores of the Adriatic. It was time for a change of tack.

On the opposite shore of the Adriatic stood the port of Zara. Astride the Adriatic sea routes, it was in a strategically vital situation. It had for many years been Venetian territory. It was the port from which, traditionally, much of the timber was shipped for the construction of the Venetian fleet.

It was also a stopping-off point at which Venetian ships could re-victual (in those days, seafaring was a hazardous enterprise and, as much as possible, ships hugged the shoreline during their voyages, making ports like Zara invaluable). However, Zara had thrown off Venetian rule some twenty years previously and had placed itself under the protection of the King of Hungary. The citizens of Zara had also sought an alliance with the Pisans, the avowed enemies of the Venetians. Several Venetian attempts to retake the city had failed. Now the Doge sought the help of the crusaders to regain Zara. The fact that it was a Christian city, and under the protection of the King of Hungary (a fellow crusader, and the only European monarch to commit himself to the crusade) counted for little when set alongside the territorial ambitions of Venice.

It appears that Dandolo approached the problem subtly. Aware that no more funds were available, he sought to convince his people of the merits of an accommodation with the crusaders. He firstly pointed out that the Venetians would be castigated if they left the crusading army abandoned where they were. Whether this argument outweighed the commercial one that he then advanced is perhaps debatable. It would be better, suggested Dandolo, that the Venetians should cut their losses by taking the money that had been already paid to them and allowing the crusaders to pay off the remainder from any future gains that they might make. It is difficult to see what other option was available. Dandolo could not retain his credibility (and perhaps, given the example of Vitale Michiel a few decades earlier even his position and his life) unless he came up with a scheme to compensate the Venetians adequately for the enormous effort that they had exerted in assembling the fleet. The promise of future reward was enough to secure his position for the time being.

Having successfully convinced the Venetians that they should continue to support the crusade, the Doge then turned his attentions to the Western leaders. It was too late in the year, he said, for the journey to the East to be continued. He was right. The window of opportunity for long sea voyages in those days lasted for just a few summer months when the Mediterranean could generally be relied upon to be at its most tranquil. The expedition had intended to leave from Venice on 29 June, but this date was several months past. There was no prospect of completing the journey before the onset of winter, when storms whipped up the Aegean into a state that would overwhelm Medieval shipping.

There was one other complication, unknown to all but the leaders of the expedition, and that revolved around the final destination of the crusade. This had, up until now, been kept a secret from the rank and file. The three major crusades launched to date had all made their target the Holy Land and Syria (the Second Crusade ventured to launch an attack on Damascus, as at the time most of Palestine was already in crusader hands). However, this was not the case on this occasion. Perhaps it was because a large crusade would not be welcomed by the rulers of Outremer itself. The kingdom was currently in the middle of a truce with the surrounding Muslim states. It had the opportunity of a breathing space to rebuild itself after its decimation following the Battle of Hattin and the partial recovery effected as a result of the Third Crusade. It is far from probable that a new army from the West, intent on stirring up trouble in the region, would be universally welcomed by the rulers of the kingdom.

Rather than Palestine, the destination this time – eventually, after the diversion to Zara – was to be Egypt. It was not just the attitude of the ruling caste in Outremer that made this a desirable option. There were also strong strategic reasons why it might be considered appropriate. Egypt was a Shi-ite Muslim state that had only been taken over by the Sunni Muslims a few decades earlier. There was much ill feeling between these two strands of Islam (a situation still reflected in the modern world). As such, Egypt was far from integrated within the Islamic Empire. These tensions were exacerbated after the death of Saladin. The unified Islamic state that he had governed did not outlive him for long, and different rulers now governed in Syria and Egypt, adding to the attraction of the latter as a target for the crusade.

The country was also very rich and very fertile, and there was therefore much wealth to attract a would-be invader. It was also perceived to be exposed by its geographical position. It was set apart to some extent from the Eastern Islamic world, only a narrow strip of land linking it to Asia. Further, the Christian Kingdom of Outremer threatened its lines of communication. There were even large numbers of troublesome Bedouins in the region of Sinai who could pose problems by their aggressive and opportunistic tendencies (Saladin himself had suffered badly at their hands some twenty years earlier). And then there was the topography of the country. Egypt was the Nile.[10] An expedition that could take one of the major ports on the Mediterranean coast, such as Damietta, and then advance down the Nile to Cairo, could take the country.[11]

For all these reasons Egypt was perceived as something of an Achilles heel for the Islamic Empire. There was seen to be a weakness in the country that presented great opportunities for a Christian army to exploit. It was believed that no less an authority than Richard the Lionheart himself had expounded such a theory. Egypt therefore made an attractive target to the leaders of the crusade.

This being so, it might seem curious that they chose to keep their men in the dark as to the eventual destination. There was, however, a very powerful reason for this policy, which made eminently good sense. That reason was the status of Jerusalem in the eyes of the crusader. This has been made much of in many analyses of the crusading movement, but such repeated attention to its place in the Christian psyche should not make the historian blasé to the exulted place the city held.

The mystic reverence and awe that the Christian held for Jerusalem was summed up by St Bernard of Clairvaux, writing some half a century before the Fourth Crusade; his view would have been echoed, though far less eloquently, by many a crusader over the centuries:

> Hail then holy city, sanctified by the Highest as his own temple so that this generation might be saved in and through you! Hail, city of the great King, source of so many blest and indescribable marvels! Hail, mistress of the nations and queen of provinces, heritage of patriarchs, mother of apostles and prophets, source of the faith and glory of Christendom! . . . Indeed, glorious things of thee are spoken, city of God![12]

It is significant that many crusading vows were centred around an oath to complete a pilgrimage to the Church of the Holy Sepulchre in Jerusalem. It must be understood that the crusades were not warfare in any sense that modern man would understand them. They were not fought primarily for political or personal gain, although undoubtedly these motives figured partially in the development of the movement. Those who took part were rather armed pilgrims, men who wished to complete a pilgrimage to a place that they held especially sacred. In the course of this journey, they undertook to fight to free the land of God from the heathen. The unique status of the crusading movement was that the feats of arms in which the crusader was involved formed part of a penitential act for his sins. This lay at the heart of the call of the crusades to Medieval man.

Deep spiritual conviction therefore was the foundation for the motivation of many of the crusaders. The terms of the Pope's Indulgence was for many decisive. As Villehardouin himself stated: 'because this indulgence was so great, the hearts of men were much moved, and many took the Cross for the greatness of the pardon.' At the very centre of this conviction for many of the rank and file lay the elevated status of Jerusalem. Many believed that the Holy City was the ultimate destination of the crusade, and any idea that this was not, in fact, the case could have the gravest repercussions for the success of the enterprise.[13]

At any rate, the crusade's leaders considered Dandolo's offer. They discussed among themselves their best course of action and finally

1a. The city walls of Constantinople presented a formidable obstacle for the Western warriors of the Fourth Crusade to overcome.

1b. The near divinity of the Byzantine Emperor is illustrated in this mosaic of John Comnenus and his Empress next to the Virgin Mary and the Christ Child.

2. The Venetian
Doge Henry
Dandolo crowns
Baldwin of Flanders
Emperor of
Byzantium, 1204.

3. *A depiction of the city of Venice, with the four horses ransacked from Constantinople during the Fourth Crusade clearly visible (top left).*

4. A view of the attack on Constantinople (a painting by Tintoretto).

5. *The famous statues of the four horses, looted from the city and taken back to Venice after the Fourth Crusade.*

6a. A medieval siege in progress.

6b. Fulk of Neuilly,
preacher of the Fourth
Crusade.

7. *The beauty of Byzantine art is shown in this leaf from a late twelfth-century version of St Mark's Gospel.*

8. The entry of the Crusaders into Constantinople (a painting by Delacroix).

accepted that they would fall in with the Doge's plans. In reality, they had little option. If they refused, they would be marooned on the shores of the Adriatic, their wealth spent and their honour gone. If anything was to be salvaged from the great exertions they had made so far, there was little choice but to acquiesce. They could not, though, tell the bulk of their army about the diversion to Zara. It was after all a Christian city and they appreciated that the scruples of their men might be seriously compromised. They therefore kept the plans to themselves.

A great service was held in the Cathedral of St Mark, where Dandolo himself addressed the assembled congregation. He begged to be allowed to sail with the crusade, while his son assumed his role in Venice in his absence. Moved by the sight of this amazing octogenarian pleading his case, the Venetians assented. Weeping, Dandolo descended from the pulpit and had a cross sewn to his cap, inspiring many among the other Venetians present to follow suit.

Accordingly, the army at last prepared to sail. Understandably, after the months of uncertainty, and the hardship that had ensued from the crisis, the crusaders were euphoric that at last a resolution had been reached and that their journey could now begin for real (although, of course, most of them were in the dark as to where they were going). Great was the rejoicing and the exultation that prevailed among the fleet when it finally left Venice, with a sense of occasion admirably portrayed by Robert of Clari:

> And all of the high men, and the clerks and the laymen, and great and small, displayed so much joy at the departure that never yet was there such rejoicing, nor was ever such a fleet seen or heard of. And the pilgrims had all the priests and clerks mount on the high poops of the ships to chant the *Veni Creator Spiritus*. And everyone, great and small, wept with emotion and for the great joy they had.[14]

The spectacle was overwhelming. The Doge sailed with the expedition, his galley bedecked in vermilion. The sea reverberated with the fanfares of a hundred pairs of silver and brass trumpets, while drums and tabors beat out a triumphant rhythm. The brightly coloured pennons of the lords of France and Flanders waved briskly in the wind as sails billowed in the gusts that sped the fleet eastward. The sea was a blaze of colour as the ships crested the waves, their bulwarks decorated by the shields of the knights on board. Spurred on by euphoria and anticipation, the joyous crusaders made their way out of Venice and towards the Holy Land. Little did the exultant masses know that their exuberance was sadly misplaced. This fleet would never see Acre, or any other port of the Palestinian seaboard. Unknown to them, their leaders had just committed them to an enterprise that was to drive the expedition dramatically off course. Once the Western leaders had agreed to fall in with the diversion suggested by the Venetians, it would prove impossible to regain control of an expedition that was now heading towards a cataclysmic confrontation with the oldest Empire in Christendom.

CHAPTER SIX

An Attack on Christians

When Boniface of Montferrat visited Pope Innocent in Rome in March 1202 the pontiff was already concerned that the crusade might launch an attack on Christian territory. At that time, Boniface had been warned by him that the crusade should refrain from such undisciplined activity, unless the action was 'just and necessary'. While this caveat left some room for interpretation, Boniface may well have paid some heed to the injunction. When the Venetians left for Zara, Boniface was not with them. He said that he had to put his affairs in order before he could do so. Admittedly, he had been heavily involved in diplomatic activity for some time, and he had been late to join the crusade. He had much to do, and this might offer some excuse for his tardiness. Yet this seems altogether too convenient. He had been in Venice during August 1202. It is possible that he, the leader of the crusade, did not sail with the first group because he wished to avoid the embarrassment of being involved in an attack on the Christian city of Zara.

The Pope's legate had been ineffective in his attempts to stop the diversion. Innocent appointed Peter Capuano to go with the expedition, and he had been present in Venice during the negotiations. He was fully aware of the plan to attack Zara and was much disturbed by it. When he expressed his reservations to Dandolo, however, he was left in no doubt as to his role in the expedition. The Doge explained that Peter was most welcome in a pastoral capacity, but he would have no part to play in a leadership role as far as the crusade was concerned. It was at once made clear then that, although Innocent was the prime instigator of the crusade, he would play little part in the direction of the expedition. If he could not retain influence over the crusade when it was positioned only a few hundred miles away across the Italian mainland, it was inconceivable that he would retain any significant say over its evolution as it moved further away from Venice. Peter was alarmed and hurried back to Rome to report to his master.

Pope Innocent despatched a letter to the army while it was still at Venice, emphasising that attacks on Christian cities were to be avoided. Nothing must distract the expedition from its sacred mission, which was to fight the enemies of Christ. Peter of Capuano himself returned to the army after discussing the matter with the Pope, reiterating the injunction against attacking Zara or any other Christian town. Indeed, it appears that some of the army were already so alarmed by news of the proposed action that they deserted even before they left Venice. Nevertheless, as the leaders of the crusade and the Venetians insisted that they would move on Zara, inexplicably Peter of Capuano changed his mind. He accepted that the attack might be 'just and necessary' if the crusade were not to fall apart, and was therefore allowable under the terms of Innocent's instructions.

This was indeed a significant departure from Peter's previous position. It was, of course, a move based purely on pragmatism, rather than any moral consideration. Given a choice between the complete disintegration of the crusade and an attack on Zara, the legate opted for the latter as the lesser of two evils. There is no direct evidence that Innocent was involved in this change of heart. It is nonetheless curious that the legate changed his opinions so markedly, and so soon after his return, when, only a few months previously, he had been so opposed to the diversion of the crusade that he had felt compelled to journey in person to the Pope to discuss it. Was Innocent already so concerned about the future of the crusade that he had briefed his legate to change his stance if he felt that this was the only way of preserving the expedition? Conjectural as this might appear, Innocent was blessed with the gift of adaptability. Even if he disapproved of events, he was not slow to profit from the opportunities that they presented – a trait that would be witnessed later on in the course of the Fourth Crusade.

Once it had left Venice, the fleet made the short crossing to the town of Pola, where more supplies were taken on board. Then they sailed down the eastern coast of the Adriatic until they came to Zara itself. They arrived here on the 11 November 1202, St Martin's Day. Villehardouin notes that the fortifications made a great impression on the crusaders as the city was 'enclosed by high walls and high towers'. Robert of Clari adds that the people of Zara obviously anticipated the arrival of the crusade: 'The people of Zara knew right well that the Venetians hated them, so they had secured a letter from Rome, saying that anyone who should make war on them or do them any harm would be excommunicated.'[1] According to Robert's account, this letter was sent to the camp of the besieging forces to dissuade them from attacking. But Dandolo refused to be swayed, even if it meant that the army would be excommunicated en masse. This caused heated debate. The army was becoming ever more divided.

Villehardouin recounts that the people of Zara initially offered to capitulate, but were urged to resist by recalcitrant elements within the crusader army. Once again, this appears rather fanciful on the part of Villehardouin, who at times seems to be obsessed at what he regards as a conspiracy among some of the crusaders to destroy the expedition. Whatever the truth of the situation, it became apparent that the crusaders would have to take Zara by force.

They accordingly laid siege to the city. The army was well equipped with petraries and mangonels,[2] the siege engines of the Medieval world. Huge boulders were propelled from these against the sturdy walls of the city, while ladders were raised against the walls directly from the ships, so that men might attempt to cross over the parapets. The defenders suspended crosses from the walls, to remind the attackers that they were laying siege to a city populated by fellow Christians. The city at first resisted stoutly (taking a city with a direct assault was a difficult task, as the crusaders would find out at Constantinople). However, the besieging army then brought up sappers to undermine the city walls.[3] Not only did this threaten to bring down the walls, it also undermined the morale of the defenders. As a result, after a siege lasting five days, the city sought surrender terms.

The rules of Medieval warfare were harsh on a city taken by siege. If a city surrendered without a fight, it was by convention supposed to be spared the worst excesses of a sack, although this rule was not always scrupulously complied with. However, if it resisted then it was at the mercy of its captors. What happened after the attack on Zara is not totally clear. Robert of Clari and Villehardouin are both silent on the issue, as they might well be if they were embarrassed by it. Martin of Pairis,[4] the preacher of the crusade who had accompanied the expedition, says that the crusaders went about their mission with heavy hearts, and the monk Gunther, a confidante of his, said that there was little bloodshed. However, Pope Innocent, when he wrote to the crusaders after the event, castigated them for the great bloodshed involved. Certainly, Dandolo had some of the leading citizens beheaded – Zara was after all, in his eyes, a rebel city.

The city was divided in two, in accordance with the terms of the Treaty of Venice, which stipulated an equal division of any spoils. The Venetians predictably enough took possession of the port, leaving the remainder of the city to the pilgrims. However, any satisfaction that might have been felt by the conquest of Zara was quickly tempered. Apparently, menacing undercurrents were gnawing away at the fragile unity between the Venetians and the pilgrims. These swelled into open violence one night when hostilities broke out between the two parties and lasted well into the next day. This was obviously a major confrontation. Villehardouin describes the fighting that ensued as 'exceeding fell and fierce', and goes on to state that 'many people were killed and wounded'. Only with difficulty was order restored.

One of the predicaments facing the expedition was that its timing was now badly out of kilter. Crossing over to Zara had allowed the crusade to winter in a slightly more clement climate than would have been the case if they had stayed in Italy. However, they could go no further until the onset of spring. Further, the Venetians had undertaken to provide the fleet for only a year, which theoretically would date from 29 June, the day that the fleet was supposed to have sailed. By the time that the crusade set out again, the fleet would remain under contract for only a few months, and that would challenge the army with severe time constraints. We may also surmise that the army was restless. The first battle against Zara had been won but it was in fairness not against the enemy that most of the crusaders had set out to fight. Presumably, after the first scent of glory and plunder, the army was eager for more. However, they would be deprived of the opportunity for some months to come. The army was left kicking its heels – not a healthy situation for an army in any era.

There were also other issues. Supplies were being consumed at a rate that could not be sustained (the Venetians had only undertaken to provide food for six months). The crusaders were heavily in debt to the Venetians, as a result of which there was little money to replenish stocks. Indeed, despite the reconquest of Zara, the pilgrims were as much at the mercy of the Venetians as they had ever been. Ironically, the move to Zara merely meant that the army was inactive for a long period of time, and as they were now further away from home, they were more open to Venetian pressure than they had ever been.

There was also much concern at the attitude of Pope Innocent to the attack on Zara. Boniface of Montferrat had at last arrived a fortnight after the fall of Zara. With him he carried a Bull of Excommunication, directed particularly against the Venetians. However, he did not publish it, choosing to keep it from the crusade as he feared its effect on the long-term viability of the expedition. The pontiff had warned the crusade against attacking Zara, and it was always likely that he would punish the expedition for its misadventure. Given the fact that this was a crusade that had been formed ostensibly in response to a Papal clarion call, it discomfited many with the expedition that they had incurred the opprobrium of the Pope. Therefore, it was decided that a delegation should be despatched to Rome to seek his pardon for the diversion. Two knights and two clerics were chosen for the mission. The knights were Robert of Boves (one of those who had allegedly encouraged the people of Zara to resist) and John of Fraize, while the clerics were Bishop Nivelon of Soissons and John of Noyon. A ceremony was held, during which the ambassadors swore on holy relics to represent faithfully the interests of the crusaders, and to return once their mission was completed.

The mission duly made its way to Rome. Robert of Boves incurred the wrath of Villehardouin for subsequently failing to return to the army. He made his way to Syria instead, perhaps another hint of the deep divisions that lay beneath the surface within the Christian army. However, the other members of the party sought earnestly the pardon of the Holy Father. Innocent granted it, as 'he knew full well that it was through the default of others that the host had been impelled to do great mischief'.[5] Indeed, it was all too true. Innocent was nothing if not a pragmatist. He quickly reasoned that the pilgrims had little choice but to fall in with the schemes of the Venetians if his expedition was to stay together. Hurling down his wrath on the crusaders would do nothing to retain the impetus of the crusade, and accordingly Innocent granted his pardon. Nevertheless, he was surely dismayed. The army had not long set out, and already he was only exercising his influence reactively, granting his blessing to events that he had expressly forbidden, forced by circumstances to accept unpalatable diversions. Papal control was nothing more than a mirage.

Not long after the arrival of Boniface, ambassadors arrived at Zara from the court of Philip of Swabia. Their coming presaged developments of a most sinister nature. The Doge gave them audience in a palace that he had occupied. With him were the leaders of the crusade itself. They took the opportunity of delivering a proposition, made jointly by Philip of Swabia and Alexius, son of the deposed Emperor Isaac of Constantinople. They proposed that the crusaders should join forces with the young Alexius to restore him to the throne of Byzantium, made vacant by the usurpation of Alexius III.

They appealed to the crusaders on two grounds. Firstly, they argued that Alexius' cause was just. His father had been dethroned in a violent coup, by an uncle whose unprovoked treachery made him morally unworthy of occupying the Imperial throne. They then went on to state that the young pretender would restore Byzantium to the Roman Church if he were placed on the throne (a promise that it was impossible to deliver given anti-Western sentiment in Byzantium). They followed this up with an appeal to the more material instincts of the crusaders. In return for the crusaders' help in taking the throne, Alexius would give them 200,000 marks – a huge amount of money. He would also provide them with food. Finally, he would accompany the crusade on to its ultimate destination or – it were considered preferable – would provide 10,000 men for a year. He would offer the crusaders 500 Byzantine troops to stay in Outremer for the duration of his life.

It was a magnificent offer, but its very generosity should have cautioned the crusaders. It was easy for the pretender to offer these conditions when he was in no position to know whether he could fulfil these terms. If he did not recover the throne, then he would be no worse off. If he did, it would still be impossible to comply with these conditions – the Byzantine treasury would not be able to cope with demands of this size, and it would be necessary to tax the people heavily, further increasing the already deep resentment of the Latins in the Christian East. But he could worry about paying off his debt to the crusaders when the time came. Until then, he had nothing to lose.

The crusade had now reached a defining moment. From what can be ascertained from the chroniclers of the time, the offer from Alexius provoked a deeply divisive debate. To many, the plan struck to the core of what the crusade was about. Many of the crusaders were outraged. They had set out on their crusade with the aim of striking a blow for Christ against his Muslim enemies. They had not given up so much in order to become embroiled in an expansionist enterprise against the Byzantines. Prominent among these protesters was the Cistercian Abbot of Vaux-de-Cernay. He insisted that the crusaders should fulfil their vows by pushing on to Outremer, showing that even now many were unaware that they were supposedly heading for Egypt.

His opponents countered with an argument based on pragmatism. They asserted that the crusade would achieve nothing if it pushed on to Outremer. Rather, they argued, any successful attempt on the Holy Land could only be made if 'Greece' (Byzantium) or 'Babylon' (Egypt) were to be captured first. Even the Cistercians were divided on the issue, with the Abbot of Loos declaring that any attempt to push straight on to Outremer must be doomed to failure. Villehardouin noticeably implies that he did this 'to keep the host together'. There appear to have been deep philosophical divisions between those driven by strict moral considerations, who wished to push on to Outremer, and those with a less idealistic, more practical approach, who believed that the survival of the crusade as an intact fighting unit was the paramount consideration.

At the end of this debate, some of the leaders of the crusade agreed to accept the terms that the young Alexius offered. They went to the palace of the Doge, where the requisite oaths were taken. Villehardouin, a staunch supporter of the move on Constantinople candidly admits that 'only twelve persons of note took the oaths on the side of the Franks, for more (of sufficient note) could not be found' – a significant admission of the level of dissent that existed. The most important of these were Boniface of Montferrat, Count Baldwin of Flanders, Count Louis of Blois and the Count of St Pol. The contracts were duly made, stipulating that the young Alexius would arrive fifteen days after Easter.

The situation did not improve. Over the winter months, as the army endured its enforced respite at Zara, there was incessant bickering between the two factions. Those who wished to push on to the Holy Land tried to convince those who wished to support Alexius of the error of their ways, but with little success. Large numbers of the army began to desert, many trying to make their own way to Outremer. One ship carrying such pilgrims foundered, taking with it 500 souls. Others tried to cross overland but were massacred by peasants on the way. Several important men were sent on to Outremer, to explain the actions of the host to the people there. According to Villehardouin, they swore to return when their mission was completed but they failed to do so. The chronicler bitterly noted that only God could have kept the army together, as so many people wished it ill; he was obviously convinced that there were no moral weaknesses in the decision to divert the crusade to Constantinople.

Winter past, and spring arrived. The day on which Alexius was supposed to arrive also came and went. The army had been living on its nerves over the winter months, and divisions between the two different factions within it continued to rankle. The leaders of the army decided that their men could no longer wait idly for Alexius. There was ongoing and bitter debate concerning the future of the crusade. Money was very short, as were provisions. The year was moving on, and with each day that passed there was a realisation that the Venetians were one day closer to the end of their contract with the pilgrims. Given all the problems, the worst thing that the army could do was stay where it was, where inactivity could cause brooding resentment to erupt into something far more sinister.

Accordingly, the day after Easter, 7 April 1203, the army embarked on the Venetian transports. Several dramas were played out before Zara was left behind. The first concerned the city itself. It had rebelled against Venetian rule and from its port pirates had launched frequent raids against Venetian shipping. This could not be allowed to recur in the future. The city walls were levelled to the ground, with most of the buildings inside the perimeter sharing the same fate. Zara would no longer pose a threat to the hegemony of Venice. Shortly after the fleet left, Dandolo's son, Renier, would bring a fleet to the port and build a castle on an island just offshore. From this fortification he could prevent the dispossessed inhabitants of Zara from returning to their homes and rebuilding the city.

The other great drama concerned several of the leading men of the army. Simon de Montfort and his brother Guy, two of the leading crusaders, decided that they would no longer throw in their lot with the army. Simon was devoutly orthodox in his Catholicism and was increasingly concerned at the course the crusade was taking. Aware of the concerns of the Pope, and his injunction against the crusaders discouraging them from attacking other Christians, Simon could no longer countenance a course of action that he believed must incur the wrath of Rome, as well as compromising his principles. He decided that he would accompany the crusade no longer and took his men away from the army and back towards Italy. With him went the Abbot of Vaux-de-Cernay – perhaps a welcome relief to his opponents among the leadership of the crusade. From Italy, Simon took ship to Syria.[6] Shortly after, Hugh and Enguerrand of Boves, two more leading notables in the army, also left to join the King of Hungary. These were very significant departures, which did nothing to enhance the fighting capabilities of the crusade.

It was decided that the army would regroup on Corfu. The crusade made an untroubled progress to the island. In the meantime, Villehardouin reports that Dandolo and Boniface of Montferrat stayed in Zara to await the arrival of the pretender to the Byzantine throne. He was not long in reaching Zara, where he was received with great honour. The Doge fitted him out with all the galleys that he required, and the ships remaining in Zara then sailed out of port and southwards down the Adriatic. They landed at the port of Dyracchium, a strategically vital town that had played a prominent part in the journey to the East during the First Crusade. Here, the pretender was apparently received with much warmth by the inhabitants.

It is perhaps easy to be cynical, and to assume that the crusaders merely supported Alexius because of the potential for material gain that he offered. However, the chronicles of the time convey a strong sense that the crusaders felt that Isaac, his father, had been betrayed and that Alexius' claim was therefore just. The positive reception accorded by the people of Dyracchium perhaps helped to encourage a belief that many of the Byzantine people shared this opinion, and that when the army arrived before Constantinople Alexius would be accepted without demur by the people. What the pilgrims failed to understand was that the people of Byzantium would never countenance supporting a man who so obviously relied for his future on the West. The festering disagreements between East and West, and the resentment that the Byzantine people felt for the Latins, meant that Alexius could never hope to aspire to the throne without a fight.

From Dyracchium, the ships carrying Alexius, Boniface and Dandolo made their way to Corfu, where the rest of the fleet had regrouped and was waiting for their arrival. The army had set up camp on the island, and the horses had been brought ashore from their transports so that they could exercise and escape the close confinement of the ships. News of the arrival of Alexius caused great excitement and many of the knights and sergeants in the army hurried to meet him. He was welcomed into the camp of the crusaders, and his pavilion was pitched close to that of Boniface of Montferrat (who had been made his guardian by Philip of Swabia).

However, the arrival of Alexius, although much anticipated, did not solve the problems of the army; in fact, it brought them to a head. Although the views of the rank and file do not figure prominently in the accounts of the chroniclers, it seems likely that the masses knew little, if anything, of the high level discussions that had been taking place about the future of the crusade. Further, only a select few of the leaders had been involved in those discussions to date. Obviously, this situation could no longer continue. While the fleet was heading south down the Adriatic it could be going virtually anywhere. However, as soon as it turned east and hugged the land, it would quickly become clear that the army was probably not going to Syria, and definitely not to Egypt. The discussions therefore now had to be made public.

Significantly, it was Dandolo who presented the young pretender to the leaders of the army. The Doge called the leaders of the Venetians and the pilgrims together, and attempted to persuade them to support Alexius in his quest for the throne. He addressed them in the following manner: 'Lords, now we have a good excuse for going to Constantinople, if you approve of it, for we have the rightful heir.'[7] However, support for the proposal was anything but unanimous. Interestingly, Robert of Clari says that many of those who disapproved of going to Constantinople objected that it interfered with the plan to go to Egypt, rather than Outremer itself. However, to this objection the supporters of the alliance with Alexius responded that there was little to be gained from travelling to Egypt when the army had neither money nor provisions to do any good when they arrived. These men argued that it made more sense to support Alexius in his quest, to take advantage of the material opportunities that their assistance would offer, and then to go on to Egypt.

Such expedient arguments did not win over large numbers of the army. Some important men refused point-blank to go on with the crusade.[8] They would stay on Corfu until the army left, then make their way to Italy where Walter of Brienne was waiting with a substantial force to set out for the East. In terms of the distance lost, there would be little difficulty in this (Italy was not much further away from Outremer or Egypt than Corfu was), although it would perhaps be difficult to find adequate transportation or supplies to move these men without the support of the Venetians. The number of men involved was great. Villehardouin, who as a supporter of the move on Constantinople was hardly likely to overstate the extent of opposition to the plan, said that over half of the host meant not to go on with the army.

It is no exaggeration to say that the whole enterprise was on the point of collapse. Perhaps 11,000 men had been in the pilgrim army that left Venice (as well as, of course, the Venetians who accompanied the expedition). This figure must have suffered from desertion and natural attrition, as well as some losses at Zara. Several leading men, such as Simon de Montfort and Enguerrand of Boves, had already left with their retinues. Now if over half of the remainder refused to go on, only a few thousand would be left to attack Constantinople; hardly enough to assault a city that had remained unconquered behind the most massive walls in Christendom for over a thousand years.

The divided nature of the host was exemplified when those who had no desire to be diverted from the original purpose of the expedition took themselves out of the camp, and set up their tents some distance away in a valley. The import of this threatened mass desertion was not lost on the leaders of those who wished to push on to Constantinople. Boniface of Montferrat met with Count Baldwin of Flanders, Count Louis of Blois, Hugh of St-Pol and all those who sided with them. According to Villehardouin, they well understood that should so many men leave, then the crusade was finished: 'Lords, we are in evil case. If these people depart from us, after so many have departed from us aforetime,[9] our host is doomed, and we shall make no conquests.'[10] They decided to take themselves to the camp of those that did not wish to go on with them. Accordingly, they set out with their retinues and made their way towards the camp of the dissentients. The scene must have been a dramatic one, as those in the camp espied the retinues of Boniface, Baldwin, Louis and the others making their way towards them, perhaps fully armed. They well knew the difficulties that their actions had caused for the plans of these magnates, and they could not be sure that their approach was entirely, if at all, peaceful. The air was pregnant with threat and menace as those in the camp lived on their nerves, waiting for the barons to arrive.

However, as the barons approached, tensions relaxed slightly as it became clear that their actions were not aggressive. Then the drama increased again. The barons threw themselves on the ground in front of the deserting masses, weeping profusely and begging their audience not to leave the crusade. They refused to pick themselves up off the ground until they were assured of the support of the army. Of the ordinary men in the army, we have little first-hand information – even Robert of Clari provides little detail as to what their thoughts were. In fact, he does not report the confrontation in the camp at all (the details belong to Villehardouin's account) but he merely describes how the barons sought the sanction of the bishops with the army before agreeing to the move on

Constantinople. However, we can perhaps speculate. For many of those in the army, their presence on the crusade was the physical manifestation of a quest for spiritual benefits. Many were too poor to finance the journey from their own resources, and had been forced to seek the help of the Church in funding their voyage. This money would be repayable to the Church unless they returned home with a signed statement from one of the leading notables in Outremer (such as the King or the Patriarch of Jerusalem) that they had indeed arrived in the Holy Land. There were therefore strong practical and material reasons why they would be extremely reluctant to be diverted from their mission.

In every sense, this was the defining moment of the crusade. If those who had threatened to abandon the cause followed through their declarations with actions, then the crusade would to all practical purposes be at an end. If, however, they resolved to support the plan to aid the young Alexius, then another Rubicon had been crossed. Innocent had already greatly criticised the crusade for the attack on Zara. There could hardly have been much confidence that he would forgive the crusaders for an attack on one of the oldest cities in Christendom.

Perhaps the clue to the decision finally taken lies in the account of Robert of Clari, and his description of the attitude of the Churchmen:

> Then the bishops were asked if it would be a sin to go there [Constantinople], and the bishops answered that it would not be a sin but rather a righteous deed; for since they had the rightful heir who had been disinherited, they could help him to win his rights and avenge himself on his enemies.[11]

This was a Christian expedition, indeed one called by no other authority than the Pope himself. It is significant that the attitude recorded by Robert of Clari is not even ambivalent; according to his account, the bishops stated that the deed was not only not a sin, it was positively righteous. One wonders whether this would have been the case if the outspoken Abbot of Vaux-de-Cernay were still with the army, but he, of course, had long gone. He had acted as a focal point for ecclesiastical opposition, and in his absence the bishops encouraged the waiverers to throw in their lot with those who wished to go to Constantinople. This may well have been decisive.

Whether through the efforts of the bishops, or the tearful pleas of the barons and their entreaties to the army not to abandon them, the decision was finally taken that the army would go on to Constantinople. Even then, there was obviously still a great deal of uncertainty about the justice of this course of action. The dissenters within the army insisted on a clause in the agreement that they would only stay with the force until Michaelmas (29 September) and that they might effectively give the expedition fifteen days' notice of their intention to depart at any time in the future. The barons were very eager that this clause should be kept secret, but the dissenters insisted that it should be made public. Significantly, so weak was the barons' position that they were forced to concede to the requests that the clause should not be hidden.

This final obstacle being thus overcome, the crusade made ready to depart. The people of Corfu had not been welcoming to the army, and at one stage had even bombarded them with stones propelled from their petraries. The local clerics had been no more accommodating. When one of the Latin priests argued with a Greek cleric that the Byzantine Church should accept the hegemony of the Pope, the latter replied ironically that as far as he could see the only argument supporting the primacy of Rome was that a Roman soldier had held the cloak of Christ at the Crucifixion. The incident spelled out once again the huge gulf that existed between the world-views of East and West.

The horses were loaded back on to the ships. On 24 May 1203 the Venetian fleet set sail from Corfu, hugging the coast of Greece as it made its way towards Constantinople. On board was a Christian army that had been intended to best a Muslim foe. Despite the intentions of many on board, most of this army would never see a Muslim other than as a merchant in Constantinople. Not one drop of Infidel blood would be shed by this crusader army (at least not in the Holy Land), nor would Jerusalem be won back from the heathen by it. Instead, this crusade was now on a collision course with an Empire that had acted as the outward bastion of Christendom for a millennium. It would set in motion a chain of events that would strike a hammer blow at the foundations of that Empire, a blow so heavy that it would help to topple it. By its actions, it would help to open up the whole of Christian Eastern and Central Europe to the threat of Muslim domination for centuries to come.

CHAPTER SEVEN

Into Battle

The fleet sailed with the help of favourable weather conditions. The shipping of the time was not robust by modern standards, and the men on board no doubt gave thanks to God for the mostly uneventful voyage. There were nevertheless a few incidents of note that took place before Constantinople was approached. As the fleet rounded Cape Malea, at the southernmost extremity of Greece, two ships were spotted heading west. Although the craft were Western ships, they did not seem eager to hail the great flotilla heading eastwards. Count Baldwin of Flanders sent a boat over to investigate. It transpired that those on board were in fact men who had set out on their own for Syria through Marseilles. They had arrived in Acre, the major port of Outremer, to find the city in the grip of plague. Further, the kingdom was at that time in the middle of a long-standing truce, and the rulers of the country were eager that this peaceful interlude should last as long as possible. Therefore, the presence of these pilgrims achieved little. They soon became disillusioned at the lack of action, and resolved to return home. According to Villehardouin, they were too ashamed to show themselves to the crusaders heading east.

Villehardouin was enraged at what he saw as the treachery of those who chose not to join the crusade at Venice; indeed, condemnation of those who did so is a constant theme throughout his chronicle. Therefore, he takes delight in describing how one of those returning home, his vows unfulfilled, could bear the shame no longer. A sergeant on board one of the ships climbed down into the boat that Baldwin had sent over, declaring that he had resolved to join the great fleet as he perceived that the expedition would conquer much territory. As a parting present, he declared that those on board the ship that he was quitting could divide his possessions (which we should assume were meagre) among themselves. A great fuss was made of the new recruit to the expedition, Villehardouin noting that 'much did we make of the sergeant, and gladly was he received by the host. For well may it be said, that even after following a thousand crooked ways a man may find his way right in the end'.[1]

The fleet made landfall on the island of Nigra (Euboea), an island just off the coast of mainland Greece itself.[2] Here the leaders discussed the next move of the expedition. It was decided that the fleet would divide into two. One half would make for Asia Minor, while the other, which included Boniface of Montferrat, Baldwin of Flanders and the young pretender Alexius in its number, would make a diversion to the island of Andros. Apart from the fact that the island was only some 7 nautical miles away from Euboea, there is little obvious reason why this move was made, unless perhaps it was to find more provisions (the island was amply blessed with fresh water). The people of Andros were overawed by the Western armies, who 'over-rode the country'.[3] They quickly sued for peace, handing over many of their goods to the young Alexius as a token of their subservience.[4]

The group then took to its ships again, sailing towards Asia Minor and the other half of the fleet. On the way, Guy, the castellan of Coucy in Champagne, died and was buried with as much ceremony as could be mustered at sea.[5] They eventually reached Abydos, a city astride the Dardanelles. Here they found the other portion of the fleet, which had arrived eight days previously. The people of the city, which Villehardouin described as 'very fair, and well situate', had no wish to resist the claims of Alexius and his Western supporters being, as Villehardouin describes them, 'men without stomach to defend themselves'.[6] However cowardly Villehardouin feels that the people of Abydos might have been, they were certainly not without wisdom. The reputation of Western warriors as men of ferocious appetite and awesome military power had proceeded them, and no help could be expected from Constantinople in time to resist any attack that the Franks might make. As a result of their timid actions, the population at least saved itself from the horrors of a sack, as Villehardouin himself states.

The area was very fertile, and the crusaders had arrived at harvest-time. They therefore helped themselves to the ample provisions available. All in all, the pleasant climate on the shores of the Dardanelles and the abundant harvests must have provided a very welcome tonic to the crusade. Having stocked up well, the reunited fleet pushed eastwards up the Sea of Marmora towards Constantinople. On 23 June they reached the Abbey of St Stephen, which lay three leagues from Constantinople itself. Here the fleet beheld Constantinople, the object of their mission, for the first time.

Villehardouin is not a chronicler prone to hyperbole. His descriptions are mostly factual and to the point. This makes the awe with which he describes the city even more noteworthy:

Now you may know that those who had never before seen the city looked upon it very earnestly, for they never thought that there could be in all the world so rich a city; and they marked the high walls and strong towers that enclosed it round about, and the rich palaces and the mighty churches – of which there were so many that no one would have believed their eyes – and the height and the length of that city which above all others was sovereign.

The first reaction then was one of wonderment. Only those who had visited Constantinople previously would have seen anything like it before, for there was no other city in the Christian world that could match it for size, grandeur or richness. Yet the admiration that the crusaders felt for it soon transformed itself into another emotion: 'No man there was of such hardihood but his flesh trembled; and it was no wonder, for never was so great an enterprise undertaken by any other people in the world.'[7]

It is perhaps easy to imagine the reactions of the crusaders when they saw the city for the first time. Never can they have even dreamed that so vast a city existed. The walls of the city towered above the sea, which lapped at their very base. They were immense. They had been built some six centuries before but had been well maintained and retained all of their original grandeur. They stood atop a steep counter-scarp, and were liberally interspersed with huge towers, dominating any would-be attacker. Behind these walls, far greater in scale than any West European could previously have imagined, rose a veritable forest of churches and palaces. The sight was at once both exhilarating and indescribably intimidating to the Franks. It was a city of a frightening heritage to any that dared consider attacking it. For a thousand years, right back to the time of the great barbarian invasions that presaged the fall of the Roman Empire in the West, the city had been assailed by a variety of attackers, many of whom had swept all before them in other parts of the world. Yet even when defeat had seemed imminent, this great city, to its people the 'eye of the world', had stubbornly refused to submit, secure behind those very same walls which glowered menacingly over the waters that now separated it from the fleet of the Franks. No wonder the Franks were terrified.

Now that they were on the threshold of the great city, the crusaders needed to plot their course of action. The leaders assembled to discuss this in the Church of St Stephen. The conversation lasted for some time, and many different views were expressed. According to Villehardouin, it was Dandolo who, once again, had the final word. He reasoned wisely. He argued that the crusaders were so short of food that, if they were to land on the mainland, they would quickly be tempted to start foraging for themselves. The discipline of the army would be lost, which, so close to the city of Constantinople, could be a dangerous situation indeed. Rather, the Doge argued, the fleet should sail to some nearby islands that were bounteously supplied with provisions (a very fortunate by-product of the Venetians long-standing links with the region was that the crusaders had access to a vast store of local knowledge). Sagaciously, the veteran campaigner explained that the army should resupply itself before moving on the mainland, for 'he that has supplies wages war with more certainty than he that has none'.

All of the leaders assented to the Doge's sound advice and they took to their ships again. They stayed where they were overnight and in the morning set sail. The fleet, several hundred ships strong, made a magnificent sight. It went out of its way to present a wonderful spectacle, with banners unfurled to the breeze and colourful shields festooned around the decks. Their onward passage necessitated sailing right next to the walls of Constantinople.[8] Perhaps the crusaders wished to impress the people of the city, who would undoubtedly rush on to the city walls as they passed. It is also possible that they wished to intimidate the Byzantine fleet, which was widely regarded in the West as being large and powerful.[9] In any event, it appears that the crusaders were under no illusions that they would come under attack when they came into range of the city; even if the citizens were believed to be favourably inclined towards the young Alexius, the current incumbent of the throne was hardly likely to welcome him with open arms. In fact, the fleet was susceptible to much damage as it sailed in the shadow of the towering city walls that hugged the shoreline. Accordingly, the crusaders made sure that they were armed and ready to fight.

The wind was kind to the fleet. The ships were carried along in the general direction of their desired destination. As they passed the city, they shot at many of the Byzantine vessels that were close at hand.[10] They passed Constantinople without major difficulty. However, at this point the wind conditions, or the local current, must have turned against them, for they did not make for the islands as they had planned.[11] Instead, they landed at the city of Chalcedon, just across the straits from Constantinople. Here they found a palace of the Emperor Alexius, which the leaders made full use of, revelling in its sybaritic delights. The palace was not, of course, available to the rank and file, who pitched their tents, as was their wont, around the city walls. The horses were once again brought ashore from their transports so that they could retain a good level of fitness. Only the sailors stayed on board the ships – everyone else took the opportunity of transferring to terra firma.

Although the fleet failed to reach the islands as planned, the site at Chalcedon was not without its compensations. The country round about was fertile and the harvest had just been reaped. In fact, the timing of the crusaders' arrival appears to have been perfect. The men already ashore helped themselves to as many provisions as they needed, and probably more besides. After three days here, the fleet removed to Scutari, where they remained protected by the narrow waters of the Bosphorus. The men ashore made their way to Scutari by land. The Emperor Alexius, knowing full well the intentions of the Crusaders, despatched a force to take up position opposite them with the instruction to watch out for any attempt to force a landing close to Constantinople.

From Scutari, foragers were sent out to search the surrounding countryside for provisions. Supplies were a constant headache for the Medieval commander, and even if the army was well provided for at Scutari, a sizeable force such as this could soon clear out even a large city. The detachment detailed to search the area consisted of some eighty knights. About 10 miles out from Scutari, the party spied a contingent of Byzantine troops camped in some foothills. The Franks instantly decided to attack, although they were heavily outnumbered as they were faced by five hundred troops.

The numerical disparity might have appeared an alarming one, but it was not just weight of numbers that was important in warfare at this time. The Byzantine army, although by no means a rabble, had declined significantly since its heyday several centuries earlier. Many of the army were mercenaries. This in itself created difficulties. Mercenaries were notoriously unreliable, and they also lacked the passion possessed by warriors who are fighting to protect their homeland. The morale of the Byzantine army, which had thirty years before suffered a shattering defeat at Myriocephalum, had never recovered.

In contrast, the Western knights were the finest fighting men of their day. They were superbly armed, their armour giving them substantial protection against most of the blows of their enemy.[12] The shock of a cavalry charge from these men on their powerful steeds was widely regarded as one of the most terrifying aspects of Medieval warfare. If coordinated properly against an immobile enemy, the cavalry charge would crash over opposition like an unstoppable tidal wave. Many times during the course of the crusades the man-for-man superiority of the crusader knights would be wasted by the breakdown in discipline and overconfidence that often ensued from a cavalry charge. However, to untried troops or those who had never faced such a charge before the prospect could be an awful one.

The Byzantines drew themselves up in battle order in a defensive position in front of their camp. The crusader knights thundered over the plain, their momentum seemingly irresistible to those arrayed against them. They crashed against the Greek soldiers, who staggered back at the shock of the impact. The so-called battle lasted but a few moments. Appalled at the impact of the Western soldiers, the Greeks resisted halfheartedly and then, dropping all further pretence, ran from the field, pursued for several miles by the euphoric victors. The crusaders were delighted at their triumph. The camp was full of rich pickings, especially horses. These prizes were invaluable. A constant problem for cavalrymen involved in the crusades was the high rate of attrition among their steeds; we may assume that, even on a relatively uneventful crossing such as that enjoyed by this crusade, there would be some losses. Even if there were not, the addition of fresh horses to the army was an invaluable asset to a force whose greatest weapon, as this small-scale skirmish had amply demonstrated, was their cavalry.

The next day, an envoy from the Emperor Alexius reached the camp of the crusaders. Diplomacy was, in many ways, the greatest weapon of the Byzantines, an ally that had served the Empire well over the centuries and had managed to buy it out of trouble, sometimes literally, when all else had failed. In contrast to the West, where military virtue was prized over all other qualities, warfare was not gloried for its own sake by the ruling caste of Byzantium. Over the centuries, there had been some outstanding Byzantine generals who had won some great victories, yet war was treated as a scientific exercise rather than the passionate pursuit it often was in the West. A diplomatic approach from the Emperor was, therefore, only to be expected.

He sent as his ambassador a man called Nicholas Roux. He was a fellow countryman of Boniface of Montferrat, a Lombard by birth. He found the barons holding council at Scutari, and obtained an audience with them. He presented his letters of accreditation to them, which they perused and acknowledged. He was given the floor, and asked to state his mission to the assembly. He did so in words that offer an object lesson in the art of diplomacy.[13]

The first words he uttered were words of fawning flattery to the Franks, describing them as 'the best people uncrowned . . . [who] come from the best land on earth'. Having dispensed with this thinly veiled attempt to massage the egos of the leaders, the next tack was to express incredulity at what the Franks could possibly be doing in the region: 'he [the Emperor Alexius] marvels much why you have come into his land and kingdom.' An appeal to the Franks morality followed. The Franks were, the Emperor knew, Christians on their way to Outremer, stated the ambassador. The implication was clear. The crusaders had made vows to deliver the Holy Land from Muslim interlopers and an attack on fellow Christians would therefore be unthinkable, amounting in fact to a great outrage against the very principles that the crusaders had espoused when they took the Cross. There then followed an appeal to the Franks' material instincts; the Emperor would, Nicholas stated, provide as much food and supplies as the expedition required provided only that they would quit the Emperor's lands as quickly as possible. Finally, came the threat; the Emperor did not want to hurt the crusaders, although as he had twenty times as many men as them he could easily do so (the performance of the small Byzantine party against the even-smaller group of Western knights on the previous day might, perhaps, have made this seem an idle boast).

In a nutshell, here was a classic demonstration of Byzantine diplomacy in action, even if it was delivered by a Westerner (another example of the subtle Byzantine mind, which reasoned that the Westerners were far more likely to listen to one of their own kind than they were a Greek). We may be sure that Villehardouin's succinct account is a concise summary of what was said, and that the ambassador's oration lasted much longer than the chronicler describes. Yet the whole rings true. It was an appeal to all kinds of emotions; to morality, to materialism, employing sycophancy, disbelief and bluster. Past experience, however, should probably have told Nicholas that he was wasting his breath in employing his considerable eloquence on the Western leaders. Clever words and pleasing platitudes were not generally successful with such men of martial prowess and great, heroic deeds.

The honour of responding was given to one Conon of Bethune. Conon was a much-respected and very experienced man, who had taken part in the Third Crusade. He was also renowned for his skill as a troubadour. That he was highly regarded by the Western knights is evidenced by the fact that he was one of the six ambassadors who had been despatched by Tibald of Champagne and the other leaders to negotiate with the Venetians for the fleet when the crusade was first being formed. In response to the arguments of the Emperor, Conon presented a challenge of his own. The crusaders had not entered into 'his' lands as they were not his to own. The Empire had been stolen from the rightful Emperor, and the current incumbent of the throne was nothing save a usurper. The throne in fact belonged to the young Alexius, who was with them (the fact that Isaac was still alive seems to have been conveniently overlooked by Conon in his arguments). If the usurper would give up his claim to the throne then, it was implied, he would be left alone to live in luxury; a claim that, given his treacherous conduct in seizing the throne from his brother, the Emperor Alexius would surely have had difficulty in believing. If, however, he would not stand down, then the time for talking was over. Nicholas took his leave of the crusaders and returned to Constantinople, in no doubt as to their aims.

The gauntlet had been well and truly thrown down. Now that the crusaders had openly declared their intentions (which must surely have been obvious to Alexius in Constantinople for some time), it was time to force the issue. They talked among themselves of their next move. It was decided that they would sail the fleet past the city walls with the young pretender on display. They would present him to the populace whom, it was correctly assumed, would flock to the city walls when they heard that the crusaders were sailing by. Accordingly, Alexius boarded a galley with Dandolo and Boniface the very next day and they set sail, accompanied by nine other ships.

When they were close to the walls, they hailed the Greeks, proclaiming 'Behold your natural lord!'. Quite clearly they assumed that the population needed no convincing that the claims of the young Alexius were unassailable, and that they would rise up as one, throwing open the city gates and ejecting the usurper from the Imperial palace. Unfortunately, this belief was based on some gravely erroneous interpretations of the situation. The crusaders had made the fatal mistake of believing their own propaganda. Whatever the merits of his claims, Alexius had never been a very prominent or popular figure in Constantinople. Even if he had been, this would count for nothing now. He had come back to claim his inheritance as a puppet of men from the West, men with whom the Byzantine Empire had been increasingly at odds for a number of years. Nothing was more guaranteed to debar Alexius from succeeding in his claims.

So the people did not, or would not, recognise Alexius as their rightful Emperor. Villehardouin claims that it was because they were afraid of the Emperor. He may be partially right of course; the current Emperor was hardly likely to surrender his throne meekly, and might well have set his feared and terrifying Varangian Guard on the people if they attempted to open the gates to the Franks. The mob had been a powerful player in Byzantine politics for centuries; indeed, they had brought down Andronicus Comnenus only two decades earlier. And the Emperor was not popular. Therefore, a popular revolt was not unthinkable if the people genuinely wished to be rid of him. The fact that they did not, and the way that they rallied round the Emperor in the following days, suggests unequivocally that any unpopularity that the people had for him was more than outweighed by their hatred and distrust of the West.

In desperation, the ships sailed backwards and forwards in front of the walls. They shouted across the waters to the assembled masses, asking them if they did not recognise the man on board the Doge's ship. The people replied in the negative. Even when the Westerners shouted back that he was none another than Alexius, son of the cruelly treated and wrongly deposed Emperor Isaac, they still refused to recognise him. The crusaders' mission was a complete failure, as indeed it was destined to be from the start. Disappointed and completely disabused of the naïve notion that the population would do their hard work for them, the crusaders made the short crossing back to Scutari.

Nothing had been achieved from this pointless exercise, although a chastening lesson had been learned by the crusaders. They had completely misjudged the temper of the Byzantine people. This was not altogether surprising – the young pretender would hardly have gone out of his way to overstate the difficulty of the plan to place him on the Imperial throne. Now there were no doubts remaining, no misconceptions left about the challenge facing them; if the crusaders wished to place their charge on the throne – which, if they wanted to be paid, they had to do – then they would have to fight for the privilege.

The ten ships returned to Scutari with these sobering tidings. The people were assembled at a parliament to discuss the next move. In reality, they met to discuss tactics and not strategy. The aim of the expedition was clear enough. They had sailed to Constantinople primarily to raise money with which to pay off the debt to the Venetians, and to finance the next stage of their mission. The distraction would profit them nothing unless they fulfilled the desires of the pretender. This they would have to do by force. The only question was how.

They held the parliament in a field. There was no debate about whether or not they should fight. The discussions centred on the division of the army into battalions. The talking lasted for some time. At the end of the debate, it was agreed that there would be seven battalions in all. The first of them would be under the command of Baldwin of Flanders, who had with him many men, including a number of archers and crossbow-men. In fact, his men formed the largest single group in the army. His brother Henry would lead the second battalion, along with Matthew of Walincourt and Baldwin of Beauvoir. The third would be led by the Count of St-Pol, with Peter of Amiens, and the fourth by Count Louis of Blois. Then came the men of Champagne, under the command of Matthew of Montmorecy; Villehardouin would be in this detachment. The sixth group consisted of the Burgundians, who included Odo of Champlitte in their number. The last detachment, which was led by Boniface of Montferrat, was 'very large'.[14] It numbered all those men that were left – the Lombards of Boniface, the Tuscans in the force, the Germans and those from the eastern marches of France.

It was agreed that the army would attack early in the morning. A short time after this council of war the men in the camp were aroused at daybreak to be told that the attack was imminent. The scene is not difficult to picture. Men roused themselves from their broken sleep, in tents if they were lucky, out in the open if they were not. They rubbed the dust from their eyes and prepared a simple breakfast to fortify themselves. It crossed the minds of some that this could be their last meal on earth, for the challenge of the day ahead was a great one, and it was certain that some in the camp would never see another sunrise.

After their bodily needs were attended to, it was time to prepare spiritually. Regardless of each individual's motives for being there at that particular time, most of the men present were, in their own very simple and uncomplicated way, religious men. Many had after all set out with the expedition because of the enchantment of the Cross. They felt deeply the need for their Lord to be with them, to protect them from the arrows and spears of the enemy throughout the battle ahead. It was also vital that a man should prepare himself to die. Death was a part of everyday life in this insecure age when men died young. It was unthinkable that a man should die unshriven, without his confession heard by a priest who could remove the burden of sin from his shoulders. Eternal suffering for those who died outside of the love of Christ, without remission of sins, was a reality for these men. Most therefore sought a priest, to make their peace with God lest they should not survive the day ahead.

The men then took up arms. The knights who could afford high quality armour, largely impervious to the arrows and sword thrusts of their opponents, dressed in the mail suits that formed a steel barrier round their frame. These weighed over twenty pounds but, if they were padded properly, they were reasonably comfortable, even in hot weather. A layer of padding would also protect them from any hammer blows that might force the chain into the body, and most of the knights would have worn such underneath the mail. Their legs were protected by more armour, helping to ward off the slashing swords of any infantrymen foolish enough to stand in their way.

Last of all, they put on their helmets. In preparation for war, knights would have cut their hair short, as this helped their helmets to fit more closely. First of all, they would put on a mail coif, then the helmet. Great helms had been developed in the twelfth century, and probably many of the richer knights, especially those from Northern Europe,[15] were in possession of these. They were very large helmets, covering virtually the whole face. More resistant armour had developed in response to the evolution of the crossbow as a weapon (it had fearsome stopping power) and the power of the lance. The crossbow was particularly feared and for a while the German Emperor had even attempted to have it banned as a weapon of war against other Christians, though without success.

For most of the troops such refined protection was out of reach. Many of the infantry sergeants would wear the brimmed helmet, known as the *chapel de fer*, which was characteristic of the period. However, thick leather quilts were the best that most could hope for as protection against the enemy. They were, after all, expendable. The success or failure of crusader armies at this particular moment in history would almost certainly revolve around the performance of the heavy cavalry, although the infantryman would become far more important in Medieval warfare in the very near future.

Having prepared themselves as best they could, the men took to their ships. The way would be led by Venetian galleys, which would be packed with archers and crossbow-men whose task was to sweep the chosen landing grounds with their arrows and drive back the resistance that would undoubtedly be waiting. The galleys towed in their wake the transports. These carried the heavy cavalry and the infantry. Some of the transports were, in fact, very crude landing craft. They had doors that could be swung open as the craft neared land, and planks serving as bridges along which the knights could guide their horses. The crossing was short but the current flowing through the Bosphorus was very difficult, and the towing ability of the galleys, which were propelled by oars, was invaluable.

Shortly after daybreak, on a fine, warm morning, the fleet moved out from Scutari. There in the near-distance, not far away, not far away at all, stood those massive walls, daring the crusader army to come on and storm them. This would have been an ideal moment for the strong Byzantine fleet that the West believed was present to move out from the harbour of Constantinople and attack the transports while they were at their most exposed. But no Byzantine ships appeared. The myth of Byzantine naval power was exactly that, a mirage that no longer reflected reality because of years of short-sighted economy drives.

The fleet made its way unchallenged towards the suburb of Galata, which was on the east side of Constantinople. As the ships moved in towards land, they were met with a ragged volley from the Greek archers who had assembled on the shore to contest the landing. From the walls of Constantinople, petraries rained down rocks on the crusader fleet, while inquisitive and frightened citizens watched from the roofs of the houses that were closest to the action.

At first, the fire was quite hot. Villehardouin, in the thick of the action, claims that 'the Greeks made a goodly show of resistance'.[16] But the sight of this approaching armada was too much for them. Unsettled by the clarion calls of the trumpets and the driving beat of the drums and tabors of the Franks, the Greeks were terrified by the approaching fleet. From the leading galleys, the crusader archers unloosed their arrows and crossbow bolts, soon beginning to exact a heavy price from those contesting their landing. The Greeks began to lose heart. Then the doors of the transports were opened, and the knights, already mounted, began to descend gingerly into the waist-deep water.

In any amphibious attack, this is the moment at which the attacking force is as its most vulnerable. The attackers are inevitably cramped together as they make their way from the transports, and their difficulties are increased because, in the water, they are out of their natural element and their movements are restricted. If the Greeks were to drive the invaders back into the sea, now was the time to do it. It was not to be. The knights lowered those piercing, heavy lances and aimed them towards the defenders. The Greeks took a last look at the crusader knights and decided that this battle was not for them. Broken and demoralised, they streamed away from the shore towards a nearby bridge, over which they fled and made their way back into the city.

The first serious confrontation then had effectively been a no-contest. The Greeks had no stomach for battle with the Frankish knights, who owned a terrifying reputation. The sight of these heavily armoured warriors of Christ heading for them had been more than enough to decide the battle before it had even begun. It was a revealing insight into the state of Byzantine arms and morale. Yet this was only the beginning. The first battle had been won, and won easily. However, the Byzantine army now sheltered behind those terrifying, menacing walls, mountains of stone towering over the crusader forces. Those vast walls, unbroken for centuries, would need to be scaled and conquered if the city were to be taken. The future was pregnant with the promise of harder battles ahead. If the crusaders were to place their man on the throne, they could only hope to do so after the effusion of much Christian blood and a great deal of sacrifice. The Greeks may have been weak but they were fighting for their homes and their lives. Many of the Franks must have reasoned that, if the crusade were to take the city, they would not be alive to see it.

CHAPTER EIGHT

Under Siege

A bridgehead had been won on the shoreline but this was only the opening skirmish of what was likely to be a prolonged assault on the city. It was imperative for the security of the fleet that it should find safe harbour as quickly as possible. The logical next step was for the ships to push further up the inlet known evocatively as the Golden Horn and find an anchorage in the port of Constantinople. This was easier said than done. Opposite the massive walls of Constantinople stood the suburb of Galata. Here there was a tower. From this tower, a large chain, as thick as a man's wrist, was stretched across the waters to the city, effectively barring the way to any Venetian ships that might attempt to force their way upstream. It was therefore impossible for the fleet to progress further without first taking this tower.

The crusaders were well satisfied with their gains so far; the Emperor Alexius had been thoughtful enough to desert his camp so hurriedly when fleeing back into Constantinople that he left behind a great deal of plunder for them to enjoy. However, another fight was now imminent and there was more work to be done. The crusaders set up camp by the Jewish quarter known as Estanor and prepared themselves for the assault on the strongly fortified tower at Galata.

There, understandably nervous that they might be counter-attacked at any moment, they spent a harrowing and disturbed night, not daring to sleep in case the Byzantines should steal up on on them without proper warning. The sentries took extra care, keeping their eyes and ears sharply focused, their nerves stretched by every stray dog that barked and their tired eyes mistaking innocent night-time shadows for a deadly enemy. Despite their fitful sleep the night passed uneventfully, and the camp awoke after what had been, perhaps surprisingly, a night of little incident.

It was a short-lived respite. At the hour of tierce,[1] the doors of the tower at Galata were swung open, and a large body of warriors charged down on the Western army, their hoarse war cries and shouts of abuse resounding across the Golden Horn. At the same time, men from Constantinople itself, able to see what was going on across the inlet, sailed over towards the crusaders in a number of barges. Faced with this two-pronged attack, the crusader camp quickly roused itself to face the challenge. The fighting developed into a hand-to-hand mêlée, swords slashing and hacking at close quarters and sparks flying as cold steel struck down onto thick armour.

At the height of the battle, one of the leading crusader knights, James of Avesnes, was hit in the face with a lance and severely injured. For a moment, it looked as if he must be captured or slain on the spot but, in the heat of the moment, a hero of the crusader host, one Nicholas of Jenlain, dug his spurs into the side of his steed and charged headlong into the thick of the fray. He managed to beat aside the sword-thrusts and spear-points of the Byzantines and, with his help, James of Avesnes was brought back to safety. Nicholas won himself honour and glory with this daring rescue of his lord; a fine example of feudal chivalry at its best, a virtue in marked contrast to some of the less savoury actions of the crusade.

The Byzantines pressed home their attack but the fighting qualities of the Western knights were again to prove decisive. Despite the ferocity of the Greek efforts, the crusaders managed to resist until their enemies began to tire. Sensing that the moment to fight back was at hand, a great war cry went up throughout the crusader host, who charged with savage force at the Greeks. Once again, the sight of these men of steel bearing down on them, their heavy swords gleaming in the morning sun, was more than they could stand. They turned and ran, desperately seeking succour from imminent defeat and oblivion. Many of them tried to make for the barges but were unable to do so. Large numbers fell into the swift-flowing waters of the Golden Horn, to be sucked down to their deaths. Others tried to regain the relative security of the tower. But they had begun their retreat too late. As they reached the doors and tried to get inside, the crusaders were very close to them. It was too late to shut the gates; the huge weight of the Western forces prevented them from being closed. Slowly but inexorably the doors were pushed open and the Greeks, powerless in the face of the weight of numbers against them, were forced to yield ground. It was soon over as a battle. Those Greeks whose life-blood was not ebbing away from mortal wounds gave themselves up to the doubtful mercy of their enemy. The tower was taken, and a significant barrier to further progress was thereby removed.

The capture of the tower presaged another event. Shortly after, a great Venetian galley, named *Aquilea*, moved swiftly up the Golden Horn. As it approached the vast chain barring the way, the rowers onboard the galley frantically worked up its momentum until it was at ramming speed. Moving at great pace, the iron-tipped point of the galley, designed precisely for such a ramming manoeuvre, crashed against the iron of the chain. With a crack, the chain broke asunder. There was nothing now to stop the Venetian fleet from moving on.

Behind the broken chain, the Venetians came across a few Byzantine ships, which were eagerly seized as prizes, but the much-vaunted Byzantine fleet was again conspicuous by its absence. Truly, it now existed only as a faded memory, a sad and pathetic echo from a time when Byzantium was a far greater power. The Byzantines were to all intents and purposes powerless to prevent the crusaders from laying siege to the city. However, the city walls still presented a formidable challenge to the crusaders. The perimeter stretched for miles, way too far indeed for the Western army to contemplate a complete investment of the city. Constantinople juts out on a peninsula, and the land walls therefore formed only a small proportion of the total length of the fortifications. Far more of the city bordered the sea than it did the land. With their large fleet and experience of maritime warfare, the Venetians argued that the whole of the force's efforts should be concentrated on a naval assault. However, the men of the army, who 'said that they did not know so well how to help themselves on the sea as on the land',[2] were strongly opposed to this plan. The land was their natural element. Of course, a siege presented little opportunity for their heavy cavalry to be used, but few of the army felt comfortable on the sea at the best of times, and the thought of a battle being fought on ships – particularly when it could be easily avoided – filled them with trepidation. Despite the best efforts of the Venetians to persuade them otherwise, the army was adamant; they insisted that their efforts be concentrated on a land assault.

Finding that they could not move the army on this issue, the Venetians reluctantly acquiesced. It was agreed that the operation would be a two-pronged one. The army would storm the walls alongside the Blachernae Palace, as this was perceived to be a weak spot.[3] The Venetians would launch a simultaneous assault by sea on the walls bordering the Golden Horn, just to the south of where the army would strike. It was perhaps not an ideal solution. The crusader forces were not large enough to be divided with impunity, and a massive onslaught launched in one area might have been a better option. On the other hand, there were some advantages. An assault in two places also split the defending force, and they would be forced to deploy their forces on several parts of the wall at the same time.

It would take time to prepare for the siege. Siege towers had to be built, and the artillery of the army made ready. The Venetians had ideas of their own for their part of the attack. They built bridges, which they planned to position up in the rigging of the ships.[4] They were built wide enough to carry three men abreast. They were intended to be as high as the ramparts of the city itself, so that men could cross over from the ships onto the walls, and hopefully gain a foothold there. Handgrips were provided for the men on the bridges to grab hold of when they crossed over to the walls. In addition, hides were placed along the sides of the bridges, with the aim of protecting the men there from the arrows of the defenders. They would also help to inhibit the effectiveness of the dreaded 'Greek Fire', which would be rained down on the ships from the city. This was a particular nasty incendiary substance that was naphtha-based. Once it took hold of any flammable areas, it proved virtually impossible to put out. The bridges were an innovative move, but it must have been a harrowing experience for any of the men using them; high above the decks, swinging precariously over the sea and the walls as the ships rose and fell with the waves, fired on by the defenders, the attackers unfortunate enough to be delegated to use them faced a traumatic and precarious ordeal. It is little wonder that the bulk of the army preferred to attack by land.

It took four days for the siege engines to be prepared, time no doubt well spent in rest for many of the crusaders after the exertions of the contested landing and the attack on the tower of Galata. On the fifth day, the camp prepared to move off. The next stage of the enterprise was more daunting than any to date. The crusaders were now going to test themselves against those massive walls. The fighting quality of the Byzantines was perhaps not as great as it had once been. There were many people in the city, but they were more noted for their effectiveness as a mob rather than an army. The mob is essentially a bully; it senses weaknesses in its prey and moves in for the kill. Whether it could be employed with much use against an efficient and well-armed force, such as that of the crusaders, was of course a moot point. However, what could not be disputed was that these people were fighting for their homes. They could not retreat, as they had nowhere else to run. They hated the Westerners passionately. If the city fell, they could expect their possessions to be ransacked, their womenfolk raped, their young men to be killed. Given all this, it was probable that the Greeks would resist spiritedly.

As the army moved towards the Palace of Blachernae, it had to cross over a bridge. The Greeks had wisely broken it down to hamper the advance of the crusader army; far less wisely, they had chosen not to defend the crossing itself. Therefore, the army was able to repair the damage to the bridge, and what should have been a major obstacle was nothing more than a minor inconvenience. The bridge was not wide, and a strong force could have made the crusaders' crossing a torrid one indeed. Yet this was not done. This demonstrated a lack of leadership from the Emperor, who seemed to be so overwhelmed by the prospect of the force facing him that he was paralysed into inactivity. Thus little hindrance was placed in the way of the crusaders. Even Villehardouin was surprised, remarking incredulously that 'no one came out from the city against them; and this was a great marvel'.[5]

The army set up camp opposite the Palace of Blachernae, in between the city walls and an abbey known as 'The Castle of Bohemond'.[6] Most sieges of the Medieval period were not decided by assault. There would often be a negotiated settlement if the attackers had a clear advantage over the defence; by so doing, the horrors of a sack might be avoided. Alternatively, if the defenders did not immediately capitulate, then a period of blockade would often ensue, whereby the attackers would hope to starve out the defence. On many occasions, they themselves would run short of provisions and be forced to quit the siege as a result. There would be sporadic outbreaks of violence when, for example, the defenders launched surprise raids on those besieging them. However, these would be interspersed with long periods of comparative inactivity.

It was likely from the outset that this siege would be different. The crusaders were certainly outnumbered by the defence, and it would be very difficult for them to starve out the city, although they could certainly interfere with supplies into the city, both with their land forces and, as a result of their naval dominance, from the sea. However, they themselves were running short of supplies. They had enough flour and bacon to last them only three weeks, and although it was possible to forage the surrounding countryside for provisions, this was not without its dangers. If a large raiding party were to be despatched, it would invite a raid on the depleted camp from the besieged city, and the crusaders were more than aware of the dangers of such an event. Within a short space of time, therefore, they were forced to eat the flesh of horses killed in battle if they wished to enjoy fresh meat.

Neither were the people of Constantinople disposed to capitulate meekly. Their detestation of the army from the West outweighed even their low regard for the Emperor Alexius. When the Franks launched their attack, scaling the walls from strategically placed ladders, resistance was fierce. Bitter hand-to-hand battles were fought on top of the walls. Fifteen men from the crusader army managed briefly to gain a small foothold but the weight of numbers against them was too great. Some were cast down over the walls and two were captured. The small group of crusaders was forced to give up its attempt. The men returned to their comrades, their pride dented and, in many cases, their bones broken.

The assault from the sea was equally fierce. A long line of galleys formed up, and sailed straight for the walls. The sky was criss-crossed with the trail of crossbow bolts and arrows, from both defenders and attackers, interspersed with huge boulders, catapulted through the air from mangonels and petraries, to land with a sickening thud as they crashed into walls and timbers, or crushed the heads and limbs of those unfortunate enough to get in the way. The tumult was deafening, the cries of the injured and dying mingling with the war cries of the attackers and the taunts of the defenders to form a Hell-like cacophony. The ships drew adjacent to the walls, and the bridges were suspended over them. The clash of steel on steel added to the nightmarish hubbub, as the Venetians determined to make some headway on the walls. However, it was not to be. The defence once again proved too resilient. The first attack failed, beaten off after much exertion and bloodshed on both sides.

The Venetians retired to lick their wounds, no doubt now painfully aware of the full extent of the challenge facing them. The rebuff was more than the proud Doge, Dandolo, could bear. Incensed at the failure of his men to carry the walls, Dandolo demanded that he be led to the prow of his galley. Here, he haughtily unfurled the flag of Venice, and cried indignantly to his men to carry him to the shoreline. He threatened them with all kinds of ill treatment if they failed to fulfil his wish. The men of Venice, tired and dispirited after their hard and unsuccessful battle on the walls, looked on astonished at this man, who was nearly ninety years of age and, according to most chroniclers, completely blind. There he stood, exposed to the missiles of the defenders, not caring whether they should strike him or not. How could they fail to respond to such amazing leadership? It was a tragedy for Byzantium that they had no leader of their own who could match this incredible old man.

Inspired, as they could not fail to be, by the Doge, the Venetians aimed their galleys for the shore again. They ran his galley aground in front of the walls and, grabbing his flag from the prow, rushed at the Greeks once more. It was not only those on Dandolo's galley who were fired up by this action. The rest of the Venetian fleet, seeing their flag flying proudly on the shore, also made for the thick of the battle. Those who were in larger ships, whose draft was too great to approach through the shallow water, loaded themselves into barges and threw themselves into the fray. Villehardouin – who was not, of course, a Venetian – speaks of the engagement that followed in terms that amount to reverential awe, calling the fight that ensued 'great and marvellous'.[7] In the thick of the press, a Venetian flag appeared atop the battlements. No one saw how it got there, but the sign gave further encouragement to the attacking Venetian forces.

The Greeks fought desperately but resistance started to crack as more Venetians came over the walls, coming across on their 'flying bridges' in the mastheads of the Venetian galleys or arriving in a somewhat more prosaic fashion after climbing a ladder. Spurred on by this weakening of the defence, the Venetians pushed home their advantage. They ran along the walls, taking tower after tower as they went. Faced shortly before with humiliating defeat, the Venetians had, by the example of one outstanding individual, won a resounding and incredible victory. The city was certainly not theirs as yet, but this was a very significant breakthrough indeed. Elated, the Doge despatched the news post haste to the army attacking the walls by the Blachernae Palace, who could scarcely credit it.

The Venetians had little time to rest on their laurels. News that a large number of towers, some twenty-five to thirty in all, had been taken spread like wild-fire through the city. Reinforcements in the form of none other than the famed Varangian Guard were sent to eject the invaders. This was an elite warrior group, formed of mercenaries, primarily Danes and Saxons, renowned for their strength and valour in battle. Now they rushed towards the Venetians, swinging their battle-axes menacingly above their heads. The Venetians were understandably alarmed at the imminent arrival of such aggressors. Deciding that they were not numerous enough to fight off the counter-attack, they adopted desperate measures in a bid to hold on to their gains. They set fire to the buildings between them and the Varangian Guard. Quickly the blaze worked up a searing heat, devouring any building that stood in its way and passing on to the next when it had finished its work. The smoke became so thick that the Byzantines could no longer even see where their enemies stood. The Venetians for their part retired to the towers that they had gained, determined to hold on to them at all costs.

To those in the city, there was no doubt that a crisis point had now been reached. The Emperor Alexius realised that, if he were to have any chance of saving his city, his Empire and, in all probability, his life, then he had to act quickly. He shook himself from the lethargic stupor that had characterised his response to the Western invasion to date, and assembled as many of his army as he could lay hands on. Then he led them out of the city gates, some distance away from where the camp of the Franks had been set up.

Whatever the quality of the troops in the Byzantine army, they certainly outnumbered the Western army comfortably. As those in the Frankish camp became aware of the vast crowd, as yet in the distance but unmistakably heading towards them, they were assailed by a sense of deep foreboding and apprehension. Villehardouin describes the scene as looking as if 'the whole world were then assembled'. Robert of Clari, who was to be heavily involved in the battle that was to follow, wrote that the Emperor had with him 100,000 cavalry alone.[8] Even allowing for Robert's customary difficulty with figures – sadly, the chronicler is notoriously unreliable when dealing with statistics – it may safely be assumed that the army sent to deal with the Franks was, compared to the Western army, a very large force indeed.

Already the great siege engines directly outside the walls of the Blachernae were under threat. The Byzantine Emperor had arranged that there would be sallies from three of the gates of the city while he himself would strike against the Franks defending the engines in their flanks. He planned that the Franks, trapped between overwhelming numbers, would be crushed in an iron vice. It must have become quickly apparent that this was the defining moment of the campaign. The Emperor Alexius was gambling all on a massive attack on the Franks. He could, of course, regain the city if he were defeated, but his people, who had never in truth loved him, would turn on him in fury. For the Franks the choice was stark. If they were defeated in this battle, there was nowhere to run. Backed up against the sea, if they were driven back then some of their number might be rescued by the Venetians (who were, of course, busy elsewhere) but they would be a minority. Defeat here would mean a catastrophic end to the dream of taking the city.

The army of the Franks was divided into seven battalions. Four of them were to be left under the command of Boniface of Montferrat to defend the camp itself. The other three were to venture out to meet the mighty army opposing them. The honour of leading the vanguard was given to Baldwin of Flanders, while the other two battalions were led by, respectively, Count Hugh of St-Pol and Henry, brother of Baldwin. Every man available in the camp was called to arms. Even the cooks armed themselves, using their pots as makeshift helmets and their cooking utensils as weapons. On no account were those in the camp to move from their defensive position, for if they were to do so the camp would be lost, and with it the campaign.

The battalions deputed to meet the enemy moved out of the camp across the plain in front of the city walls to meet them. Robert of Clari was particularly impressed at the way the horses of the knights were dressed in splendid colours, with coats of arms liberally draped over them. Behind the cavalry walked the sergeants, the infantrymen, who were to support the knights in the battle that was expected. But the force had advanced only a few hundred yards when Baldwin of Flanders' advisors urged him to stop — it was advancing too far. It was a strange piece of advice. If the cavalry were to act in a purely defensive capacity, then it would have made more sense to stay put at the camp, and add to the numbers there. But the strength of the Frankish cavalry was in the charge (which was renowned and feared around the world for its ferocity), and to leave these men to defend the camp would not have utilised their skills. Surely they would be best employed in an aggressive manner? However, it seems that, perhaps understandably, Baldwin's advisors were unnerved by the huge force heading in their direction, and thus called off the advance.

Baldwin heeded the advice of his counsellors. He ordered his men to stop, face around and start to retreat towards the camp. His move caused consternation among the rest of the army. The Count of St-Pol, who was leading the second battalion into battle behind Baldwin, conferred with his lieutenant, Pierre of Amiens. He stopped his force where it was, refusing to return to the camp. When Baldwin saw that the Count's battalion was not retiring, he sent a messenger over to it, asking him to head back. Pierre of Amiens responded. He would not, for any reason, comply with the request. To Pierre, and no doubt to many of the other men gathered round him, including Hugh of St-Pol, to retire before the enemy without even coming into contact with them was a disgrace. The army stubbornly refused to budge an inch. The Western knights were a proud breed –and oft-times in the crusades their vanity led to disastrous situations.

In vain, Baldwin despatched another messenger, virtually begging the second battalion to comply with his orders. Baldwin was in a predicament. It would of course be disastrous for the well-being of the crusade if the army were caught in two minds. In addition, Baldwin himself was a proud man. For him to quit the field of battle while others refused to retreat would be a stain on his character; in that era, he would carry with him to his grave such a blot on his reputation. His name would be destroyed forever should he leave the second battalion to its fate. Even the knights in his own battalion felt the slur keenly. They turned on Baldwin, pleading with him to change his mind: 'Lord, you are doing us great shame not to advance, and know that if you do not now ride forward, we will no longer held ourselves bound to you.'[9]

In those few words, Baldwin was faced with the stark reality of the situation. If he were not to take up his place at the head of the army and lead it towards the enemy, then his men would no longer obey him. The oath that a feudal knight took to his lord was more than a contract, it was a solemn vow made in the presence of God himself. As such it was, in theory, irrevocable. Only in extreme circumstances, where the lord had betrayed his trust, could the vow be ignored. Now, in the opinion of Baldwin's vassals, such an occasion was imminent. It was a message that Baldwin could not possibly ignore. Like it or not, he had to lead the army into battle against the enemy.

There is no reason to doubt Baldwin's bravery, or indeed the sense of pride that he held for his position in the social hierarchy. In all probability, Baldwin led his force forward willingly. It may have been more prudent to retire on the camp, but, after all, heroes are noted not for their caution but for their martial deeds. With alacrity, Baldwin dug the spurs into the flanks of his charger and led his men on until they were again level with the Count of St-Pol. They now rode together, forming an extended front that moved towards the huge force of Alexius. In between the two armies was a small slope that partially obscured the forces from each other. The Western knights charged up to the top of the rise and stopped.

They were now extremely close to the army of Alexius. Indeed, the two forces were so near each other that their archers and crossbow-men exchanged fire. However, they did not attempt to close. Robert of Clari asserts that the army of Alexius was so alarmed by the sight of the enemy that they were too afraid to come nearer. Given the reputation of the Western knights, this is perhaps understandable. Equally, however, the Franks did not move on the Emperor.

Robert offers the opinion that this was because a canal lay between the two forces. He states that the leaders of the crusader battalions knew that they would suffer great losses if they attempted to cross it. He does not, however, state that it was impossible to do so, merely that it would be expensive in terms of the casualties that would accrue as a result. Villehardouin, for his part, gives sound tactical reasons for the decision. The army would be too far away from the camp if it were to charge on Alexius. Indeed, there was a great danger of an encircling movement as Byzantine troops made their way out of the city to attack the Franks from the rear and as others attempted to outflank the army. The battalions led by Baldwin of Flanders could therefore find themselves cut off.

There is indeed every indication from the available evidence that the crusaders now believed that they were in a truly perilous position. The actions of Baldwin and the other leaders at this time suggest that there was clearly a great numerical difference between the two armies. Crusader knights were not renowned for their caution in battle. Minutes before, Peter of Amiens had been all for charging headlong at the Byzantines. Now his colleagues refused to budge from where they were. What else can have changed the minds of the crusaders but the fact that they could now see the extent of the enemy who previously had been obscured?

The Venetians had also got wind of the crisis. So perturbed were they by the messages they had received from the Franks that they abandoned all the gains they had made on the walls of Constantinople. Those gains had been hard won, and much Venetian blood had been spilled in the process. The danger to the crusade that was posed by this counter-attack of the Emperor is best evidenced by this act alone.

The armies stood where they were, within sight and bowshot of each other. But nothing happened. The two forces stood on the edge of all-out conflict but neither side attempted to move on the other. Bemused, the ladies of Constantinople, who had gathered on the city walls to watch the battle, waited for something to happen, assuming that this stand-off was merely some tactical device employed by their menfolk, who knew far more about warfare than they did. Then, to their surprise and evident dissatisfaction, the Emperor ordered his army to turn about and make its way back into Constantinople. He may have heard that the Venetians had abandoned their conquests in the city. Some commentators, wishing perhaps not to think too harshly of this man who was so plainly out-of-his-depth in his current position, gently hint that this might even have been his plan all along. Sadly, such tactical subtleties do not accord with the rest of Alexius' career as a warrior. Knowing the man and his actions, it is far more probable that he had just been stared out by the enemy, and that, in the process, his courage had completely failed him. As he moved his army back through the gates out of which they had so proudly marched a few hours before, Alexius was a marked man. By his failure to bring the enemy to battle despite great numerical advantage, he had signed his death warrant as Emperor.

The events of the next few hours are speculative, although their end is clear enough. The Emperor was not a man possessed of great courage or the ability to inspire men to fight to their last drop of blood on his behalf. He had been a nonentity as an Emperor. His very ordinariness marked him out as a man completely unsuitable to be on the throne of the world's oldest Empire at this, its moment of greatest danger. In the small hours of the morning, those who were still awake would have heard a sizeable retinue heading out of the gates of Constantinople. If they could have inspected the wagons accompanying the party, they would have seen that they were loaded with treasure. Alexius, like Balshazzar, had seen the writing on the wall. Unlike the Babylonian of old, he was not placidly and meekly going to stay put and await his fate. He saw his end writ large, and fled the city.

Like a thief in the night, the usurper hurried out of Constantinople in the shadows of darkness. He had won the Empire with dishonour, and now he lost it in the same manner. He abandoned everything – his city, his people, even his wife and several of his daughters – to the mercy of the Franks.[10] It was a disgraceful end to a reign that had promised little and delivered less. As the rays of the morning sun rose over the city a few hours later, it looked down upon a people without a leader and without hope, with nothing to expect in the near future save a violent retribution from the forces of the West.

CHAPTER NINE

A Brief Respite

The flight of the Emperor caused great difficulties for the citizens of Constantinople, welcome as it was, in some ways, to many who despised him for his weakness. The walls of the city were surrounded by a strong and implacable army, whose avowed aim it was to restore the young pretender to the throne. Within the past day, that same enemy had taken a significant part of the city's outer defences (even if it had subsequently abandoned them for strategic reasons), and had forced a large Byzantine army to leave the field of battle by the strength of its reputation rather than armed conflict. There was little doubt that, unless the demands of the Western army were complied with, then the walls would be stormed again. Given the state of morale in the city at this moment in time, there can have been little confidence that another attack would be repulsed.

It was in the hours following the rapid and cowardly departure of the Emperor that the Byzantine genius for self-preservation reasserted itself. It was not by chance alone that the imperial city of Byzantium had outlived the imperial city of Rome by a thousand years. The Byzantines realised early on that martial prowess alone was no guarantee of survival. Guile and cunning, ruse and counter-ruse were just as important, if not more so, than the armaments relied upon by the warriors of the West. Thus it was that in the consternation created by the flight of Alexius a plan was developed which, if not totally undermining the scheming of the Western leaders, was at least guaranteed to introduce an element of confusion into their thinking.

It was the imperial treasurer, a eunuch named Constantine, who was the initiator of the plan. The crusaders case had revolved around the legitimacy of the recently departed Emperor, who had usurped the throne from his properly anointed predecessor. They argued that he had no right to govern Byzantium, and that his crown was forfeit to the legal heir, the young Alexius. The crusaders were, of course, correct. The throne had been usurped, in a most brutal and perfidious manner. Yet they had made a fatal flaw in their analysis. In their assumption that the blinded ex-Emperor Isaac would no longer be considered a worthy ruler in Byzantium because of his physical debilities, they had completely overlooked the fact that he was still alive. He had been crowned and, in the eyes of God, was the rightful ruler of the Empire. True, convention dictated that his blindness would debar him from the throne but, to Byzantine minds, rules were made to be broken. As always in the Greek world, expediency would triumph over custom.

Thus in the early hours of the morning Isaac was brought back to the Blachernae Palace. One can only conjecture at his feelings. At first, the sound of footsteps coming towards his door at an out of the ordinary time may have led the feeble invalid to believe that his end was imminent. As it opened, he may have expected that at any moment the bowstring would be placed around his neck and tightened until his face went scarlet and the breath was squeezed out of him. Perhaps he was aware that his treacherous brother was rapidly losing any popularity he may have had in the city, and reasoned that he had determined to eliminate Isaac so that he would not become a focus for opposition. Fear then became bewilderment as he was led out of his rooms. Where were they taking him? Why not kill him where he was? On the way to the palace there was perhaps a muttered explanation, words of reassurance and protestations of loyalty. When he arrived at the palace, he was bedecked in imperial splendour and led once again towards his throne. They seated him there, and then, to the astonishment of Isaac who, if he could have seen, would scarcely have believed his eyes, they knelt before him, and 'did to him obeisance as their lord'.[1]

It was a masterstroke. It at once countered the crusaders' claims that the now deposed Alexius had been illegitimate. They could not take the moral high ground and argue further that Isaac had no right to reign; indeed, the claims of their young pretender were primarily relevant because he was Isaac's son. Even the old man's blindness caused little difficulty; after all, Dandolo himself was blind. The necessary courtesies having been paid to the now restored Emperor, the Greeks got together a delegation to break the news to the crusaders.

Messengers were sent to the camp of the Western army, seeking an audience with the young Alexius. They were ushered in to his pavilion, where they told him the news that his father had been released and restored to the throne. His reaction is not recorded but it must surely have been a blow to him. There is little evidence that he had any great love for his father, and only the day before he presumably felt that a great prize was within his grasp. Now, in the space of a few hours, the situation had been transformed. He was no longer on the brink of glory, he was restored to the position of being merely heir apparent.

Alexius summoned Boniface of Montferrat and the other barons to his tent. There the news was given to them; the rightful ruler had been restored. Villehardouin says that 'when they heard it, their joy was such as cannot be uttered, for never was their greater joy in all this world'. For once, the chronicler's words fail to convince. Isaac had been no friend of the West when he had been Emperor. Frederick Barbarossa had been on the verge of pulverising Constantinople during the Third Crusade and Isaac had sent words of congratulation to Saladin when he reconquered Jerusalem for Islam. Further, he was no party to the deal made between Alexius and the crusaders at Zara, and there was no guarantee that he would agree to abide by the extravagant terms of the treaty. The clue to the true temper of the crusaders appears shortly after, in Villehardouin's account: 'Then the day began to dawn, and the host to put on their armour; and all took hold of their arms throughout the host, because they did not trust the Greeks.' Mutual distrust and antipathy had existed between East and West for centuries. For weeks they had been fighting each other. Neither side had any intention whatsoever of trusting the other.

As the day progressed more envoys made their way from the city to the camp of the crusaders. They all told the same tale. It became clear that the unlikely story was indeed true and that the usurper had abandoned the city. The Western leaders conferred among themselves and decided that they themselves should send a delegation into Constantinople. They were particularly anxious to gauge the intentions of the restored Emperor, especially with regard to the covenants that they had entered into with his son.

The delegation was to consist of four men: Matthew of Montmorency and Villehardouin himself, along with two Venetian representatives.[2] When they were ready, they rode out of the camp and stopped outside one of the great gates of the city. Here they dismounted. Slowly, the gates were swung open to receive them – a state of affairs that would have been quite inconceivable only twenty-four hours earlier. The procession to the Palace of Blachernae was conducted in an atmosphere of some threat. The gates, and the streets from them to the palace, were flanked by contingents of the Varangian Guard, veteran warriors all, who had on the previous day been only too keen to trade blows with the same army whose representatives were now parading before them. No doubt the people of the city were also there to watch, their emotions a strange mixture of curiosity and loathing as they watched the men from the West making their way to negotiate with their Emperor.

The great Palace of Blachernae was one of the two major imperial palaces of Constantinople. Its huge walls towered above the surrounding streets, including the walls of the city itself, inside of which it was just situated. Indeed, the palace had been the target of some of the artillery attacks during the siege that had ended so unexpectedly, although whether the rocks and boulders directed at it had actually made much impression on its massive walls is not recorded. The palace was, as usual in Byzantium, sumptuously ornamented and filled with treasures of great value, a unique combination of imperial grandeur and unrivalled opulence. It was certainly a fitting edifice in which to house the imperial throne.

The envoys were led in to the Emperor's palace. The imperial court had turned out in force, no doubt many of them trying to ingratiate themselves with the restored Emperor. Some of them perhaps feared for their place in the new regime, though presumably those who had done most to harm Isaac's cause had fled the city with Alexius. The palace was filled to the brim with courtiers, 'of great men and women there were so many that you could not stir for the press'.[3] They were arrayed in a dazzling display of colourful and expensive finery. After the rigours of the siege, many were determined to make the most of this opportunity to show off.

At the centre of it all sat Isaac, once more on the imperial throne. Next to him was his wife, a woman of great beauty. The ambassadors of the West were led towards the Emperor to be given the chance to state their case. They must certainly have been impressed by the presentation, a very tangible manifestation of the great wealth and unrivalled heritage of this fabled city. The display was certainly not accidental. Such demonstrations were a standard part of Byzantine protocol, designed to impress and overawe ambassadors from other lands who sought audience with the Emperor. Certainly the sight must have been a spectacular one, even to hardened negotiators like Villehardouin. Yet they were men of great experience and, although they would have appreciated the show laid on for them, they would not be fooled by it.

Indeed, this public audience with the Emperor was only a formality, a prelude to the real negotiation that was to take place. Having courteously presented themselves to Isaac and properly honoured him, the delegation asked for a private session. This was duly granted, and the Emperor, his wife, his chancellor, an interpreter and the delegation were led out of the main audience chamber into more private rooms where more intimate discussions could take place.

It was, according to his account, Villehardouin himself who spoke on behalf of the delegates. They had come, he explained, on behalf of Isaac's son, Alexius. The young man was very anxious to take his place alongside his father in the city but he could not do so until he had certain assurances from the Emperor. Primarily, he needed to know that Isaac would ratify the treaty made with the crusaders. They had gone to great trouble and expense to restore Isaac to his throne, and it was only right that the agreed recompense should be given to the Franks, even if the father had been handed the throne rather than the son.

Isaac asked for details of the covenants made. Deliberately and precisely, Villehardouin recited the formidable list to him; 200,000 marks of silver, food for the expedition for one year, the despatch of 10,000 cavalry and infantry to Outremer for one year, the maintenance of 500 knights in that land for perpetuity. Isaac listened to the list and, as he listened to it, he must have become increasingly appalled and incredulous. The cost of the covenants was enormous. It was, of course, some years since Isaac had been on the throne, and it is unlikely that he would have had any detailed briefing of the state of the treasury since his dramatic resurrection. Yet he would have heard enough surely to have established that there had been no miraculous revival in Byzantine economic fortunes. Although not possessed of intellect or talent, he was totally aware that there was not the remotest possibility that the price demanded could be met.

He prevaricated with the ambassadors, saying that 'this covenant is very onerous and I do not see how effect can be given to it'.[4] Yet, like his son, he was entrapped. If he wished to remain as Emperor he knew that he had little option but to go along with the demands of the Franks, however unrealistic they were. He had, after all, spent some time away from the throne, and his restoration to imperial privileges would be something that he would certainly not give up lightly. The arguments went on for some time but, as far as Isaac was concerned, they were all in vain. After his initial well-founded protestations concerning the impossibility of the impositions placed upon him, he was forced by circumstances to accept the terms that his son had agreed to. He swore a solemn oath to abide by the covenants and witnessed the same by appending his gold seal to a charter that had been drawn up listing the terms.

The ambassadors returned to their comrades outside of the city walls, ecstatic that they had achieved all that they had set out for. The news was received with great joy in the crusader camp. Shortly afterwards, Isaac's son, Alexius, was dressed in his finest regalia and led back in through the gates of the city that he had escaped from in such dramatic fashion a year or two before. He was received enthusiastically by the population (or so we are told) as they lined the streets to cheer his progress towards the imperial palace. Once there, father and son were re-united in a scene of touching emotion, inspired by both affection and disbelief at their change in circumstances. Great were the scenes of celebration that followed, both inside the great city and in the camp of the crusaders.

But even this air of jubilation could not disguise the great distrust that existed between the people of the city and the Franks. Not long after the restoration of the Emperor and his son had taken place, it was suggested to the Franks that their presence inside of, or adjacent to, the city was likely to cause trouble among the populace. It was therefore mooted that they should withdraw their forces to the shoreline opposite the city, across the Golden Horn, between Galata and Estanor. They went along with this suggestion, ostensibly because they had no wish to argue with their erstwhile patron, Alexius, but in reality they were pragmatists. Even across the water, they were close enough to provide an intimidating reminder that there was still a debt to be paid to them. They also had completely open access to enter the city when and where they wished, so that they could easily see for themselves if the mood in Constantinople were changing at all. In addition, they intended to take no chances. Soon after, a stretch of the walls was torn down. The implication was clear for all to see; the crusaders believed that they might have to enforce their claims by force at some time in the future, and they wanted to make it as easy as possible for them to do this. Absolutely no one in the city was fooled by the open displays of friendship between the Franks and their patrons at the court of Constantinople; neither side trusted the other one jot.[5]

This mutual mistrust was quickly reinforced. As a condition of their support for Isaac, the Franks insisted that Alexius, son of Isaac, should be declared co-Emperor. This was by no means unique in the annals of Byzantium but one can detect the hands of the Western leaders at work here. They had not come this far to give up the chance of retaining their influence in the Byzantine court through the pawn they had helped to recover his heritage. It was likely that this was a condition of their support for Isaac.[6] This condition was agreed to. Shortly afterwards, on 1 August 1203, the son of Isaac was crowned in the most holy church of St Sophia as the Emperor Alexius IV. The ceremony was conducted with all the dignity and solemnity characteristic of this most sacred of Byzantine rites. Such affairs were a visible manifestation of statecraft in the Empire, the ceremony being an event that had, over a period of a thousand years and more, acquired a mystique all of its own. Beneath the hallowed and ancient domes of this most marvellous of churches, Alexius was reverently handed the imperial diadem. The coronation was a magnificent occasion; it was sadly a completely inappropriate portent for the reign that was to follow.

Shortly thereafter, a letter was despatched to Innocent in Rome, appraising him of events and reassuring him that the army would resume its journey in the spring. They also asked for more help to be sent from the West. Innocent replied in February 1204, asking that more should be done to reconcile the churches of Rome and Byzantium. He even asked that the Patriarch of Constantinople should journey to Rome to recognise the authority of the Papacy offcially. Such ambitions, however, were totally unrealistic.

At least the Franks were shortly to recover some of the money promised them, although it would profit them little. The co-Emperors managed to raise a sum of 100,000 marks to pay off part of their debt to the Western army. Half of this was given to the Venetians, in line with the terms of the contract between Venice and the army. From the remaining 50,000, the Franks gave a further 34,000 to the Venetians, to pay off the remaining part of the down payment owing to Venice since the non-appearance of so many crusaders at the start of the expedition. The army did not even benefit much from what was left; many of them had borrowed money in Venice to help them finance their journey, and the money from the Byzantines was used in many cases to pay off these individual debts. For most of the soldiers in the expedition, these payments from the co-Emperors did little save whet their appetite. They amounted to a tantalising glimpse of the wealth that might be theirs in the future, and only served to make them more determined to wait until the remainder of the debt was paid. Only the Venetians really benefited from this money; if nothing else, it was a suitable indication of who had always been most likely to profit from this particular crusade.

Over the next few weeks, men from the army regularly made their way into Constantinople, either making the short crossing over the Golden Horn by barge or travelling over the bridge. Some renewed old acquaintances. The sister of the King of France, Agnes, lived in the city, having married a Greek noble named Vernas.[7] She was no friend of the new regime, and refused angrily even to speak with those from the West who came to see her. The only visitor who had any success with her was Count Louis of Blois, who was in fact her nephew.

The sights and sounds of the city inevitably fascinated the crusaders. Robert of Clari particularly was amazed at some of the things that he saw. On one occasion, the crusaders met a pilgrim whom they found especially notable, 'whose skin was all black'. He was none other than a royal from Nubia. He bore a cross on his forehead, branded deep into his skin. He had set off from his hot desert country long ago, with a view to making a pilgrimage to Jerusalem, 'a hundred days' journey' away. He was accompanied at the start by a retinue of sixty. Only ten survived the journey. From the Holy City, they had made their way to Constantinople; seven of those remaining perished on this leg of the expedition. He wished to complete his pilgrimage by visiting first Rome and then St James of Compostella in the north of Spain. His people were Christians, he told the Franks through the medium of an interpreter, who were all marked with the brand of a cross in the same way as he was. Unsurprisingly, the Franks gazed at him in awe and amazement.

As time went on, there was little sign that the co-Emperors were in much of a position to repay the crusaders the remaining part of the debt. The position of Isaac and Alexius was, in reality, extremely uncertain. The old Emperor, the deposed Alexius III, had set up a rival dynasty, with its headquarters in Adrianople. Further afield, a Bulgarian king, Ioanittsa, had conquered much of the northern part of the Empire. The young co-Emperor, Alexius IV, was a regular visitor to the camp of the Franks. On one visit he came to them with a specific proposal. He assembled the leaders in the pavilion of Baldwin of Flanders. He began by explaining that his position was still far from secure. He was widely despised by his people because they knew that he owed his position to the Western army. Soon, it would be time for the crusaders to depart. The time was fast approaching when the contract between Venice and the army was due to expire. If they were then to leave, Alexius had little doubt that the people of Constantinople would rise up against him at the earliest opportunity. He would be dethroned and killed.

It was a good enough analysis of the situation. The mob knew perfectly well who was responsible for the fact that Alexius was their Emperor, and they had no love for the Westerners. Undoubtedly, given recent history his life expectancy would be short if he were to be left by the crusaders to his fate. The implication for the Franks themselves was also clear enough. Alexius had no money to pay them off as yet, and if he were to die then they would never receive what was owed to them. Expediency therefore demanded that Alexius' plea for an extension to the agreement between the crusaders and the Emperor should be complied with.

There were, as usual, sound strategic reasons why the extension made sense. Apart from material considerations, winter was approaching once again and the season for crossing the seas was almost at an end. However, the leaders would not commit themselves to the deal without obtaining the agreement of the mass of the army. They therefore assembled the lesser leaders of the host and presented the plan to them. The response was an outpouring of furious indignation. Many of the army demanded that the barons comply with the bargain they had struck earlier in the campaign, when they had promised to supply ships to those who wished to leave the expedition.

It is easy to sympathise with the rank and file. The fine strategic arguments presented by the leaders were lost on them. They were simple folk, and their presence on the crusade had little, if anything, to do with material considerations. The politics of the Fourth Crusade can easily obscure the fact that this expedition, like all other crusades, was motivated primarily by spiritual factors. Many of the men had vowed to complete the pilgrimage to the Holy Sepulchre in Jerusalem. Here they were, still no nearer fulfilling that vow. Until the pilgrimage was completed, they could not return home without losing the spiritual benefits for which they had risked so much. The barons had put pressure on them to agree to the diversion of the crusade on several previous occasions. The last time they had done so, they had promised that they would release all those who wished to leave with only a couple of weeks' notice. Now the leaders were arguing for yet another delay. What would be the excuse next time? It is little wonder that they were so angry.

The debate was long and heated. Villehardouin states that those who wished to destroy the crusade tried their utmost to do so, but once again he protests too much. Many of those opposed to remaining surely had well-motivated personal reasons for leaving. At the end of the debate, the army agreed to extend the contract with Alexius. There was ample excuse to abandon the Emperor in the present circumstances. There was also a firm commitment for the leaders to provide assistance to those who wished to leave. Yet the decision made was that the army should stay in Constantinople. There is little evidence of any conspiracy to destroy the crusade here, rather perhaps an attempt to justify the actions of the leaders of the crusade from a man who was one of them.

It was vital that Alexius should show himself to his subjects as soon as possible. At the moment, his power base did not extend far beyond the walls of Constantinople itself. He therefore decided to travel around his Empire and display himself to his new subjects. This was partly at the instigation of his Greek advisors and partly at the advice of the Franks. Just before he set out, the camp of the crusaders was much affected by the death from sickness of Matthew of Montmorency. He was a much-respected man, who had only a short time before been sent into Constantinople as one of the Franks' two negotiators when Isaac had been restored to his throne. His loss was immense, described as 'one of the greatest that had befallen the host by any man's death'.[8]

After burying the great lord with all due honour and ceremony, Alexius and many of the leaders of the army set out on their journey around the Byzantine hinterlands, although some important Franks did stay in Constantinople. It was an impressive company that accompanied him. Boniface of Montferrat, Hugh of St-Pol and Henry, the brother of Baldwin of Flanders, were among their number, along with James of Avesnes and William of Champlitte. This was a high-powered embassy indeed – and it needed to be. Villehardouin does not describe the journey in much detail, although he admits that Ioanittsa, who owned nearly a half of the Empire in its European guise, would not submit himself to him. Robert of Clari is more specific, describing how the army (according to Robert half the Western host accompanied the Emperor on his progress) conquered twenty cities and forty castles. In all, the army was away for three months and although there were a large number of subjects who swore allegiance to their new liege lord, Alexius did not succeed in bringing his immediate predecessor, the deposed Alexius III, to book.

The Emperor's progress was an unavoidable act on his part if he were to cement his position more securely. However, he could not be in two places at once. While he was away from his capital, he could obviously not keep a close watch on events in Constantinople. Unfortunately, what happened in his absence only served as a crystal clear reminder to him that, worried as he understandably was about increasing his profile with his subjects around the Empire, he could not even be sure of their behaviour on his own doorstep.

While Alexius was away from Constantinople, two events in particular took place which would turn the relationship between East and West on its head. The friendship between the two was never more than cosmetic to begin with; after these events, even the pretence was dropped. With the Emperor and many of the leaders of the Crusade far away from the city, the populace began to get restive. Although only half of the debt had been paid off, Alexius had had a considerable job raising even this amount. The people of the city had watched as much of their wealth made the short crossing over the Golden Horn to the camp of the crusaders. Many of the leading families had seen their treasures confiscated as Alexius attempted to pay off the crusade. After a short while, he had been forced to turn his attention elsewhere. There was one institution prominent above most others in the Empire in terms of its wealth; the Orthodox Church. Some of the silverware used in church services was melted down to help to pay the Franks, and even icons were not safe from being used for this purpose.

To the people of Constantinople this was a profane act. They looked at their new Emperor and they remembered him, when he was still in the city, spending his days drinking with the Franks. They remembered the terms of the treaty with the West, which stipulated that the Eastern and Western Churches should be reunited. And their anger increased still more.[9] They then saw the Franks, arrogantly strolling or riding around their city as if it belonged to them; perhaps some of the Byzantines, seeing how much their Emperor appeared to be in the pockets of the Western leaders, believed that in reality it did. It was all too much.

One evening, for reasons that are not recorded, a fracas broke out in the city. What started as a small localised skirmish intensified rapidly as news spread that the Greeks were fighting the Franks. Weeks of pent-up anger erupted. The Greeks rushed out on to the streets, striking down every Westerner they came across. There were old, established Western communities in the city, many of whose members had proved staunch friends to Byzantium, particularly the Pisans who had been trustworthy allies for years. This counted for nothing. No one was immune; everyone with Western affiliations was fair game for the soulless, cruel mob. Those who could fled to the harbour and grabbed whatever transport was available, making their way across the water to the camp of the crusaders. Thousands of men, women and children made the journey. Villehardouin estimated that over 15,000 people escaped in this manner.[10]

The riot, which took place on 19 August 1203, was a disaster for Constantinople. It is dangerous to make moralistic judgements about events that happened 800 years ago – paradigms were so different then – but it was an indefensible act on the part of the Byzantines. It mirrored previous massacres by the people of the city (the slaughter of the Venetians in 1171 being the most notable precedent), and was the result of a deep-rooted xenophobia in the Byzantine psyche. Probably such outpourings were also the consequence of a deepening sense of inferiority as the Greeks desperately sought to hang on to a sense of imperial pride and grandeur that had been ebbing away through a series of military disasters (Manzikert and Myriocephalum, for example) and second-rate Emperors. Whatever the reasons, by its collective stupidity the mob had alienated friends who might have helped them, and enflamed their enemies. Their action sealed the death warrant of the city.

If this rioting was a blow to the city, the event that followed was a catastrophe. Shortly after this outbreak, a group of Franks made their way into the Muslim quarter of the city. The Muslims had traded without obstruction with the Byzantines for many years and had a vibrant trading community in Constantinople. The Franks could not understand how the enemies of Christ were allowed to do business so openly with a Christian people.[11] The party of Franks apparently contained its fair share of zealots. Incensed at the presence of a mosque in the quarter, the small group of Franks started to lay about any Muslim they came across. Quickly, the Greek neighbours of the Muslims came to their aid. As the fight intensified, more Franks made their way across the Golden Horn to join the skirmish.

In the mêlée that followed, a fire broke out. Apart from the royal and noble palaces, the houses of the city were closely packed. There was a large amount of timber in these buildings, mostly bone dry. There was little or no organisation in place to cope with outbreaks of fire. This cocktail of factors was a recipe for disaster. The fire spread before it could be put out. The wind fanned the sparks across the city, causing numerous smaller fires to break out. Soon it had taken hold of whole streets, and leapt easily across from one timbered building to the next.

Nothing could stop it. People of all ages died in their hundreds, unable to out-run the flames so quickly did they spread.

In a tragedy of immense proportions, buildings that dated from the heyday of the Roman Empire were consumed. Part of the Hippodrome – the ancient setting for the chariot races – was damaged. The Forum of Constantine was completely destroyed. Even parts of St Sophia suffered, though thankfully the bulk of the fabric survived intact. It was only when the fire had exhausted itself, and devoured the combustible materials in its path, that it burnt itself out. The conflagration had lasted for nearly two days. Many people had died and the material loss was immense. It was shortly after this disaster – one of the greatest fires in recorded history – that the Emperor Alexius came back from his imperial progress to find that his city was, both literally and metaphorically, smouldering.

According to Robert of Clari, the Franks left behind at Constantinople had sent word to the leaders accompanying Alexius, requesting them to return because they were not being paid any of the outstanding debt by Isaac. Ironically, the progress of the young Alexius had only made his financial problems worse as he had been forced to pay large sums to the leaders to accompany him in the first place, leaving even less to pay off the remaining debt. On his return, the Franks demanded that the Emperor prevaricate no longer and pay them what they were owed. For a time, the Emperor paid small, insignificant amounts to the Franks; then even this trickle dried up.

Boniface of Montferrat pleaded with the Emperor to pay more, perhaps seeing his plan to have a friend of the German Emperor on the imperial throne under threat. According to Villehardouin, Alexius, buoyed up by the triumphs of his recent progress around his domains, 'was filled with arrogance towards the barons'. It seemed he had forgotten how much he owed to them. This may, of course, be true. His courage might also have been boosted by the fact that his people had decided to rebuild the stretch of walls that the Franks had destroyed after the recent fracas in the city. Yet it was also true that Alexius was in an impossible quandary. He could not hold the city without the support of the Franks, yet if he stayed on friendly terms with them he would be loathed by his people. The Franks would not stay in Constantinople forever, and when they eventually left he would find himself toppled in another of the interminable Byzantine palace coups. There were intensely practical considerations as well. However much he wanted to pay off the debt, he simply did not have the resources to do it. Therefore, no further payments were forthcoming.

Eventually, the Franks decided to send a delegation to the Emperor and present him with an ultimatum. The eloquent Conon of Bethune was in the party, along with Miles of Provins. The third representative of the army was again Villehardouin himself. There were also three Venetian envoys in the embassy. The description that follows in Villehardouin's account is among the most convincing in the entire chronicle.[12] He describes how the party 'went in great peril, and on hard adventure'. This time they went mounted through the city, the pommels of their swords close to hand. One can imagine the glares of the Greeks as they passed, full of hatred and enmity, hands on daggers, waiting for the least provocation to strike. It must have been a terrible ordeal for the small delegation, surrounded by those who wished to see them gone, or even dead. One false move could have precipitated their lynching.

Dismounting at the gate of the Palace of Blachernae, they strode once more through its great portals into an audience chamber packed with the good and great of the city. They made their way towards the imperial throne, where the Emperor Isaac and his wife stood, along with his co-Emperor and son, Alexius. Conon of Bethune was nominated as the spokesman for the group.[13] He launched into his appeal with enthusiasm, reminding the Emperors that they owed their status to the Franks. He quickly cut to the point of his oration. He had come to ask the Emperors to recognise their covenants with the Franks and pay the money owed them. If they did this, all well and good. Peace would be restored and everything would be forgiven.

However, if the money was not paid the result was unequivocal: 'be it known to you that [the Franks] will not hold you as lord or friend, but will endeavour to obtain their due by all means in their power.' There was little room for misinterpretation in this threat. If the money were not paid, then they deemed that the regime had lost their right to claim the support of the Franks. The crusaders had already acted as kingmaker once; they could do so again.

The result was uproar. The Western ambassadors had not sought a private audience with the Emperors on this occasion, and everyone present at court had heard what was said. There was an explosion of rage in the palace and its precincts. No one had dared to insult the Byzantine court in such a fashion before, according to Villehardouin. To an Empire that prided itself on its place in the world, this public humiliation from upstart Westerners, one stage removed from barbarians, was an unbearable disgrace. Angry looks were cast at the envoys, who decided that they should beat a hasty retreat. They made their way as quickly as possible to their horses, waiting patiently outside the palace gates. Then they rode as rapidly as they could through the streets of the city and back to the camp, deeply relieved that they had not lost their lives at the hands of the Greeks.

The tirade launched against the Emperors, in such a public manner and in their own audience chamber, was either an incredibly foolish piece of misjudgement on the part of the ambassadors or part of a very brave and premeditated act. On the one hand, it is possible that the envoys calculated that if they were to bully the Emperors publicly then their people, terrified of an imminent attack from the Franks, would help them raise the funds required to pay off the outstanding debt. If this was their ploy, it was sadly misguided. Such an action took little account of the Byzantine sense of pride, an inner emotion that would never forgive such a public insult.

However, the crusaders may have reasoned that they needed to make the break with the Emperors as public as possible. By so doing, they could demonstrate that they had given every possible chance for them to pay their debts. In short, the ambassadors may have been playing to a wider audience. Such a move was an important factor in convincing a whole host of people of the good intentions of the leaders of the Franks; from the body of the crusade itself to dignitaries such as Philip of Swabia and Pope Innocent hundreds of miles away. This latter interpretation suggests great courage on the part of the ambassadors as they risked their lives to fulfil their mission. But then, lack of courage is not often found in the list of faults that historians have attributed to the crusaders of this and every other crusade. The ambassadors were all experienced negotiators, who had been quick enough to seek a private audience when it suited them. The fact that they chose a public audience to berate the Emperors, and that they chose one of their more inflammatory orators to deliver the tirade, suggests that the manoeuvre was a quite deliberate act.

The camp of the crusaders was alive with anticipation as the ambassadors relayed their report to the leaders. The tension was no less tangible in Constantinople. A very public ultimatum had been delivered, and few believed that its terms would be met. Only a small inlet of water separated the two parties, yet the gulf that existed between the Franks and the Greeks formed a massive barrier. No one believed that this gap could be bridged by any method other than force. The city had already survived one siege, though then only barely. Now, conflict loomed once more. This time, the battle would be a fight to the death, with nothing less than the soul of the world's oldest Empire as the victor's prize.

CHAPTER TEN

Palace Coup

When Isaac was released from his extended period of captivity, various other notables were also freed. One of them was a man named Alexius Ducas Murzuphlus.[1] He was an interesting character. Strong-willed and capable of great ruthlessness, he had an impressive pedigree, being directly descended from none other than the mighty Alexius Comnenus himself. He had been imprisoned during the reign of Alexius III. His release would not have been welcomed by the Franks as he was known to have strong anti-Latin tendencies. Possibly, this was the very reason that he was set free in the immediate aftermath of Isaac's restoration – he was potentially a source of opposition to the crusaders. Whether or not Isaac had anything to do with his freedom is unclear, but it seems unlikely. Certainly, however, in the days to come, Isaac and his son, Alexius IV, would have much cause to regret that Murzuphlus had ever re-entered the public arena.

Murzuphlus was a decisive and determined man. He was possessed of much energy and no little bluster. He was never happier than when he was at the heart of affairs, whether in the world of political intrigue or in the heat of battle. Such qualities, when combined to his imperial heritage through the royal blood line and his anti-Latin pedigree, were guaranteed to endear him to many of the people of Constantinople, who longed for the Frankish threat to be eliminated. However, they also marked him out as a source of great danger to the co-Emperors.

Or, at least, they should have done. Murzuphlus quickly ingratiated himself into the circle of the co-Emperors. Isaac soon proved to be an irrelevance. This might have been expected all along. The leading families in Constantinople were, in all probability, delighted to have a man on the throne who served merely as a token figurehead and, perhaps more importantly, as a stumbling block to the ambitions of the crusaders and their perceived client, Alexius IV. Isaac soon demonstrated that he had little interest in assuming anything other than the trappings of state. He had always been a lover of luxury, renowned for his sumptuous feasting and his exaggerated pride in his personal appearance.[2] Now, apart from his cronies who constantly talked up his importance, he was an anachronism. Increasingly, he was excluded from power. To have co-Emperors in any environment creates difficulties.

Given the weakness of Isaac, both physically and mentally, it was inevitable that his position should suffer in the current circumstances.

Additionally, Isaac probably suffered lasting effects from his period in captivity. As we have seen, his confinement was not particularly onerous in that he still had regular access to many of his supporters even when he was imprisoned. However, the constant threat of imminent death while his brother, the usurper Alexius III, was in power proved too much for a weak constitution, particularly when allied to the physical effects of his mutilation. More and more of his subjects began to note that now he was Emperor once more, Isaac appeared to be constantly distracted and his mind regularly wandered. His effectiveness as a co-Emperor, never marked from the beginning, reduced to nothing. As this happened, a vicious circle ensued. Even those who, at the outset, had supported him noted which way the wind was blowing and, fearing the effect of being associated with a failure, slipped away from Isaac. In his periods of coherence (which were becoming increasingly rare), the father bemoaned the increasing dominance of his son. Most of his time was spent in consultation with his soothsayers and in the search for an elixir, which, he had been promised, would miraculously restore his sight.

Neither was the position of Alexius IV secure. Events had forced his hand. Unable to pay off the crusaders, and obliged by anti-Latin sentiment to distance himself from them, his stock presumably increased with his citizens after the showdown at the Palace of Blachernae. However, such feelings were unlikely to be any more than short-term. The effect of any increase in popularity was illusory. If Alexius was to retain the support of his people, he had to deliver results. But his Empire was in a more parlous state than ever. Bitterly divided, with a rival Emperor still in existence and the terrible Ioanittsa carving up a huge kingdom for himself from the Byzantine territories in Bulgaria,[3] a fearsome enemy still threatened the city in the form of the crusader army, separated from it by just a few hundred yards of water. The Franks were not simply going to accept the change in circumstances as a fait accompli and up camp and leave. They had invested much, in terms of money, men and lives, in the investiture of Alexius, who had freely entered into a contract with them to pay the sums agreed, large though they were. They would insist on what was due to them, and enforce their demand if necessary. In their opinion, right was on their side. The crusaders had a simple perspective on morality, and one that they believed in implicitly. In their view, Alexius IV was morally obligated to pay over the remainder of the outstanding debt. The Emperor had acted perfidiously and dishonourably (no doubt many of the more extreme members of the army believed that this was typical of the behaviour of the Greeks throughout recent history), and the crusaders had every right to stay and claim what was theirs.

There were of course selfish, personal reasons as well. Many of the leaders, men such as Baldwin of Flanders, Boniface of Montferrat and especially Henry Dandolo, had invested huge capital, both material and personal, in the plan to place Alexius on the throne. They had, on many occasions, been forced to beg, cajole, persuade or bully the host to follow them to Constantinople. Large numbers of the troops had never wanted to divert the expedition to the city in the first place. They had ultimately only been persuaded partly because of the lucrative payback offered to them to do so. If the prize were feebly abandoned now that the crusaders had delivered on their part of the bargain, the effect on the leaders personally would be unthinkable. There was never any doubt that the crusade would stay where it was and fight for what was owed them.

Alexius was not an unduly bright Emperor, but he must have seen the threat posed by the crusader army and, of course, the ever-present Venetian fleet, which could move around virtually at will given the complete non-existence of a Byzantine navy. In such circumstances, he did what the weak man often does in a moment of danger. He looked about him for strong allies, men who were popular in the eyes of his people and from whose reflected prestige he could benefit. Men, indeed, such as Alexius Murzuphlus. Sadly, he failed to realise the inherent risk in his patronage of such individuals. Murzuphlus quickly became Alexius' most trusted advisor. In his advancement of the hirsute lord, Alexius identified only the benefits to be gleaned from the arrangement. Through his own feebleness, or perhaps through a simple desire to not see what he did not want to see, he did not spot the dangers. And men such as Murzuphlus sense weakness; like a wild animal, they stalk their prey silently, lulling their victim into a sense of false security. Then, when they sense that their target is at its weakest, they strike and destroy it.

Robert of Clari detects the hand of Murzuphlus in the refusal of Alexius to pay over any money.[4] Allowing for the fact that the Emperor could not pay the debt even if he wanted to, and that Robert cannot possibly have been in a position to know this firsthand, the accusation nevertheless rings true with what we can detect of the personality of Murzuphlus. Certainly, his influence on Alexius was marked, and became more so as time went on.

Alexius' refusal to pay the debt placed the crusaders in a quandary. The city still presented a formidable obstacle to their ambitions, and it would be much better if they could even now reach a negotiated settlement. Against the evidence of their own eyes, they attempted one last time to persuade Alexius to fulfil his obligations. According to Robert of Clari, Dandolo himself offered to make one final attempt to persuade Alexius to change his stance. He sent word to the Emperor that he would make his way over to the city in his galley, suggesting that Alexius should come to meet him. Accordingly it was done. The Doge was rowed across the Golden Horn to the harbour of the city itself. Alexius came to meet him on horseback. The two men faced each other; the grizzled elder statesman who had seen it all after so many years in the corridors of power in Venice, and the young, upstart Emperor who had so quickly forgotten the great debt he owed to the Western armies.

No doubt Dandolo thought Alexius an ungrateful whelp; he certainly did not mince his words. He bluntly asked the Emperor what he thought he was doing, reminding him that he only sat on the throne of his Empire because of the aid of the crusaders, and asking him even now to repay what was owed to the West. Alexius was equally blunt, responding that he had done all that he was going to do as far as repayments to his former patrons were concerned. Dandolo's final words were forthright and unequivocal, leaving no doubt that the Emperor had been given, and had failed to take, the final opportunity to redeem himself: 'Wretched boy, we dragged you out of the filth, and into the filth we will throw you again. I defy you, and from this moment on I will do everything in my power to harm you.'[5]

It was tantamount to a declaration of war, a chilling warning that from henceforward this would be a fight to the finish, with the Emperor forced either to pay over the vast sums owing or to forfeit his throne. Dandolo's galley, along with the three that had accompanied him on his seemingly futile mission, made its way back towards the crusaders' camp, where the Doge broke the news that the army must now prepare for certain conflict. In truth, the other leaders knew this already. If Alexius was influenced by anyone, it was by Boniface of Montferrat. But, despite his attempts to convince the Emperor that he ruled only by the say-so of the crusaders, Boniface had singularly failed to move him. There was never any real possibility that Dandolo should fare any differently. Nevertheless, this final rejection must still have come as a blow to the army. Constantinople would not be taken without much hardship and great effusion of blood.

The next few weeks were to see something of a phoney war taking place. There were many small skirmishes but no major battles. The chroniclers differ as to the outcome of these minor fights, splitting approximately along party lines, with Villehardouin saying that the Franks were nearly always the victors while the Byzantine chronicler, Nicetas Choniates, says that the result was more equal, with the Greeks coming out on top as often as not. These small-scale confrontations however, were just a prelude to the much greater test that was to come.

The Franks were reluctant to risk an assault in winter, even given their proximity to the city. They had enough problems keeping themselves supplied over these harsh months, and they had to forage ever further afield to keep the camp adequately provisioned. As food became scarce, inflation took hold; prices rocketed for basics such as eggs and chickens as their availability decreased, while wine stocks also ran low. Only biscuit was widely obtainable but, although it provided a form of nutrition, it was not a very palatable one.

However, the crusaders still had one major advantage over the Byzantines, and that was control of the sea. The presence of the immensely powerful Venetian fleet served a twofold purpose. Firstly, it interfered with the free-flow of goods into Constantinople and therefore exerted economic pressure on the city. Secondly, it allowed communications to be maintained with the West, and gave some opportunity for provisions to be shipped in from further afield. Later in the winter, for example, a supply ship arrived from Brindisi; for a short time, these provisions made a significant difference to the well-being of the crusaders.

The Greeks were well aware of the importance of the fleet to the crusade and resolved to challenge the naval supremacy enjoyed by the Western forces. But conventional attacks on the fleet from the Byzantine navy were not an option – years of neglect had seen to that. The Byzantines therefore adopted more unusual methods. They gathered together a number of old hulks and packed them full of combustible materials. Dry wood, fat, pitch, anything that would burn, was thrown into the dilapidated vessels. Then the Greeks waited, until the wind was right. In the early hours of a mid-December morning, before the day had dawned and while the camp of the crusaders was still asleep and off its guard (or so the Greeks hoped), it was deemed that the wind was blowing in the right direction. Torches were thrown into the old wrecks, which quickly shot up in flames. The fires quickly took hold, flaming fiercely and unstoppably, illuminating the cold, dark sky with flashes of terrible brilliance.

The wind did its job, speeding the death traps over the Golden Horn, heading for the Venetian vessels, which were lethargically moored in front of the crusader camp. Straight as an arrow, the ships aimed for the heart of the fleet. However, the camp was more alert than the Greeks had hoped. The desperate shouts of alarmed sentries interrupted the quietness of the early hours, and both the camp and the Venetian fleet roused themselves and sprang into action. The Venetians had not idly won their reputation as great sailors, superior to most others in the world. Quickly, the master mariners in the fleet took control of their ships, skilfully manoeuvring them out of the way of the lethal fire-ships, dextrously avoiding them by controlling their vessels as capably as any knight controlled his steed. By their great technical ability, allied to more than a little courage, the threat was avoided.

The crusaders were naturally buoyed up by this success. Inspired by its escape from potential disaster, the Venetian fleet was involved in several more small confrontations during which some Byzantine vessels were taken. However, the tactic of the fire-ships was used again by the Greeks who, rightly, saw an opportunity, perhaps the only opportunity, of destroying the Venetian fleet, an action that would leave the crusader army high and dry on a strange shore, hundreds of miles from home. On the first day of the year 1204, the wind was once again right for an attempt. More hulks were requisitioned and packed with flammable materials. The Greeks had learned from their experience on the previous occasion. This time the ships would be chained together, making it much more difficult for the Venetians to move their ships out of the path of the Byzantine vessels.

The silence of that new year's morning was broken by the clarion calls of trumpets in the crusader camp, as the sentries once again beheld the terrifying spectacle of a wall of fire heading for the fleet. The camp sprang into action, fully expecting that the Greeks would be seeking to exploit the situation by launching an attack from the land at the same time as this assault from the sea. Such a tactic would indeed have been a great threat to the crusaders, divided as their attention would have been, but it was not to materialise. From the far shore, the citizens screamed their abuse at the crusaders, mocking their predicament. However, harsh words do not win wars. For all the bravado of the Greeks, no attempt was made to push home their advantage by an attack from the landward side. It epitomised only too well the essential weakness of the mob; the people were prepared to shout and hurl insults at the enemy but they could not, or would not, fight. The Greek army was demoralised and ineffective; its morale was low, while the stock of the armies of the West was high. In any pitched battle between the warriors of Eastern Christendom and those of the West, the result was considered by most to be a foregone conclusion. The Byzantine army had lost its will to fight.

While the camp stayed on its guard, waiting in vain for an attack to come, the Venetian sailors quickly manned their ships and moved out to meet the wall of fire bearing rapidly down on them. The threat posed by the Byzantine hulks was much greater this time than on the previous occasion. The fact that they were chained together meant that the Venetians could not simply take evasive action. More desperate measures were needed if the fleet were to survive.

The night was rent with the cries of the blood-crazed Greek mob on one side of the Golden Horn and, on the other, by the war-cries and shouts of alarm of the army as the Venetians moved close to the fire-ships with grappling hooks. They were attacked by some small craft making their way out from Constantinople. From these boats, Greeks fired arrows and whatever other missiles they could lay hold of, wounding some of the Venetian mariners. Showing no little skill and even greater reserves of courage, the sailors moved alongside the hulks, at every moment risking their ships and their lives for, if these fires were to take hold of their own ships, then the resultant blaze would be almost impossible to restrain. The hooks cut deep into the wood of the rotting hulks, and the Venetians began to drag them away, almost imperceptibly at first but, as confidence increased, with ever more enthusiasm. Each passing moment lessened the danger to the fleet. Eventually, the flaming ships were dragged into the main current, which quickly caught hold of them and pulled them away.

The Greeks watched on, distraught. The spectacle and the noise resembled a scene from Armageddon,[6] but the threat had been averted. Although flames still illuminated the night sky, the fire-ships were now drifting harmlessly away, out to the open sea, where they would burn themselves out. In marked contrast to the dejection of the Greek mob, the crusaders were euphoric. Only one ship was lost, and, ironically, even that was not a Venetian craft. A Pisan merchantman that, until the recent pogrom in the city was far more likely to be found supporting the Byzantines, was too slow to move out of the way of the wall of fire. In a salutary reminder of what might have been, the flames quickly took hold of the ship, which blazed up, like an inferno. In a short space, the whole ship was aflame and quickly sank. Apart from this one, almost incidental loss, the only ships that lay on the ocean floor were the Byzantine hulks, their last glorious action sadly for the Byzantines no more than a despairing and futile gesture.

As the two parties reviewed the events of the night in the cold light of the following day, there were indeed great differences in the emotions abroad. For the Greeks there was now desperation. Limpet-like, the crusaders stuck stubbornly to the shore, refusing to move until they had won what they believed was rightfully theirs. Great hopes had been based on the fire-ships, which the people of the city seem to have genuinely believed would rid them of the troublesome enemy. These hopes had been dashed. Now all that could be anticipated was a protracted siege, a battle to the death. As the threat from the fire-ships flickered out, so too was hope extinguished for the Greeks. By nature they were a pessimistic people, and the effect on morale was disastrous.

Of course, for the crusaders the feelings were somewhat different. No doubt being good Christian men, they praised God with sincerity for their escape from danger. In addition to their relief, there was an air of celebration in the camp. And there was something else too; admiration. Villehardouin was a knight and, by definition, not a man of the sea. His feelings for the Venetians stand out clear in one memorable phrase: 'never did people help themselves better at sea than the Venetians did that night.' It was a fitting accolade by a man who, although no seaman himself, recognised real bravery and valour when he saw it.

Not only did the failure of the raid signal the beginning of the end for Constantinople itself, but it performed a similar role for the short reign of Isaac and Alexius IV too. Isaac had continued to withdraw into a world of his own. It was widely believed that his mind had been affected by his captivity, and there was certainly much evidence that his health had been seriously compromised. Within a short time he died, believing to the end that he would find a miracle cure for the ailments that affected him, and that his eyesight would be marvellously restored. At the end, only his astrologers had much time for him. He was a nonentity, and his demise would not affect the affairs of Constantinople one iota.[7]

That left Alexius. His people woke every morning and stared into the near-distance over the narrow waters of the Golden Horn to the camp of the crusaders. The Western army showed no sign of moving. Their very presence was an insult to the imperial prestige of Byzantium and a constant threat to the well-being of the city. With the camp in such close proximity, it was impossible for the Greeks to ignore the crusaders. Despite all the efforts of the citizens to date, the enemy showed no intention of meekly giving up his quest. Every attempt to shift them had failed, and for that failure someone had to be held to account. There was no doubt whatsoever about where the blame would be laid.

It was, of course, thanks to Alexius that the crusade had come to the city in the first instance. For that alone, the people would never forgive him. If he had managed to drive them away, then the citizens might be disposed to offer their support to his regime. But although he had spoken strong words (no doubt egged on by the outspoken Murzuphlus who, as events would soon demonstrate, was indeed a man of strong will and brave words), Alexius' defiant talk had not been matched by actions. He was perceived for what he was, a weak man, little more than a youth, who was helpless in the face of events and personalities that were demonstrably bigger than he was. Those close to him probably recognised soon enough that the power behind the throne belonged to his increasingly influential chief advisor, Murzuphlus. The mob smelt blood. Sensing the vulnerability of the ineffectual emperor, the people grew more and more tense until they reached a point when they could be controlled no longer. Then they exploded in a blind, irrational fury. Alexius had brought the pestilence into his lands and he had failed to make it go away again. For that, he must be punished.

The irrationality of the mob had already been demonstrated earlier on in the siege. In the city was a statue by the master sculptor, Phidias. The ancient Athenian was one of the greatest figures in the history of art; his most famous creation was the statue of Zeus at Olympia, which was one of the Seven Wonders of the ancient world. Constantinople housed another of his masterpieces, a statue of Athene. She stood with her arms outstretched. One day, the mob, in a crazed and savage frenzy, decided that her posture suggested that she was beckoning the Franks to come and take possession of the city. Incensed at the arrogance of this treasure of antiquity, the mob hacked the statue to pieces. Thus a work that had lasted for nearly two thousand years, a product of the greatest age of one of the world's greatest civilisations, was lost forever. Neither was this action unique. There were two columns in the city, dating back to imperial Roman times. They were renowned for the carvings etched into them, which were believed to outline events that were to happen in the future. Early on in the siege, the mob had seen in some of these carvings what they perceived as scaling-ladders and an enemy making their way over the walls into the city. To the mob, this clearly referred to the Franks. They therefore hammered away at the carvings until they were obliterated. Cultural barbarism was obviously not the exclusive preserve of the West.

Such was the myopia of the mob, which read all kinds of interpretations into meaningless inanimate objects. The irrationality extended to their need to punish a scapegoat for their predicament, and to find a means of salvation from it. On 25 January 1204, the underlying tensions could be suppressed no longer. With little warning, and even less purpose, the mob exploded. They met at the ancient and hallowed church of St Sophia, a place where so many of the great events of Byzantine history had their beginnings. They declaimed that Alexius should no longer be their emperor. To this extent, their intention was clear. But who was to replace their ineffectual lord? They offered the throne to several leading members of the aristocracy, who were also present at the meeting, but they all declined. This prize, they all knew, was a poisoned chalice. The challenge facing the city was a great one, to many, indeed, it seemed insurmountable. Given the pessimism then current within the city, any prospective Emperor would have reasoned that within a few weeks he himself could expect the mob to be baying for his blood. To have the responsibility of Empire without the power was a reward that enticed nobody.

Some of those who were offered the throne went to great lengths to avoid it. One potential candidate, a noble named Radinos, was offered the throne in absentia. So eager was he to escape the dubious honour that he dressed himself as a monk and fled the city immediately. In vain the mob then harangued his wife to reveal his whereabouts but she refused to cooperate with them. Eventually, three days later, the mob foisted their attentions on another noble, Nicholas Canibus. He had apparently just made his way to the church of St Sophia to take part in his daily devotions. When the mob saw him, they asked him to be Emperor. At first, Canibus refused. However, he was persuaded by their persistence to change his stance. He declared that he would indeed be their Emperor. Events would quickly show that his first instinct had been the correct one. The acceptance of the throne proved to be a fatal personal mistake.

While these tumultuous events were unfolding, Alexius stayed within the confines of his palace, seemingly powerless to react to, or interfere with, events. His inactivity during this time of dramatic upheaval provided a perfect epitaph for the brief reign of the Emperor Alexius, epitomised as it was by indecisiveness, weakness and lack of leadership. In these last moments, Alexius made one last desperate attempt to retrieve the situation. He sent word to his former protector, Boniface of Montferrat, telling him to come with his troops and take possession of the Palace of Blachernae. He despatched his most trusted confidante, Murzuphlus, to the camp of the crusaders with his frantic plea for help. In so doing, he sealed the fate of his reign, his city and his Empire. His error was to cost him his life.

Alexius obviously trusted Murzuphlus implicitly – and nothing serves better to illustrate his inability to gauge the souls of men. There is a real element of tragedy in the life of this pretender to the ancient Imperial throne of Byzantium. He had sought greatness when he was plainly not ready for it. Indeed, his lack of any innate abilities meant that he was always destined to be a poor Emperor. Through a unique combination of events, a huge prize had been granted him when he had neither the talent nor the experience to take advantage of the opportunity. He was naïve, weak and immature, a pawn in the hands of greater men and stronger personalities who would use him for what he could do for them and then, when they judged the time to be right, discard him. He was at the mercy of adventurers and opportunists. Such a man was Alexius Ducas Murzuphlus.

Murzuphlus fulfilled his mission to the letter. He gave the message to Boniface and promised his support in the scheme. He then returned to Constantinople and divulged the plan to the Greek nobles in the city. By this act, he doomed the reign of Alexius to extinction, as he well knew.

He had also put himself at the head of the list of those who were likely to replace him. He was popular with the people for his anti-Latin stance and his robust and aggressive attitude towards the invaders. He had an imperial heritage and had shown himself to be capable of taking difficult decisions and acting upon them. He was the ideal candidate to be the next emperor.[8]

Later that evening, completely unaware of the treacherous behaviour of Murzuphlus, Alexius was roused by a message that he was outside, urgently seeking an audience. He was immediately admitted. Breathlessly, he advised his Emperor that events had taken a marked turn for the worst. The mob was making its way to the palace. Their intention was clear; the Emperor was to be dethroned. Alexius must escape quickly if he were to survive. Alexius thought for less than a moment. Perhaps he remembered his father and the terrible mutilation that he had suffered all those years ago or, even worse, the horrific fate of Andronicus Comnenus. Barely pausing to reflect, Alexius rushed out of the palace with Murzuphlus.

He walked into a viper's nest. Murzuphlus led him to his tent. Here, the pretence was abandoned. The bemused Emperor, realising suddenly the awfulness of his predicament and the completeness with which he had been duped, was led away to a dark and unhealthy prison cell. He was put in chains. He would never taste freedom again in the few weeks that remained of his abbreviated life. According to Villehardouin, Murzuphlus tried to poison Alexius on several occasions without success. Then, seeing that the deposed Emperor stubbornly refused to die, Murzuphlus went to his prison cell, took a bowstring and tied it around his neck, and strangled the life out of him.

Murzuphlus immediately took up the reins of power. One of his first cynical acts was to arrange a state funeral for Alexius, protesting that he had died of natural causes. It is unlikely that many of the citizens believed him, though whether they cared must also be debatable. News of the demise of their ex-client soon reached the camp of the crusaders. Sympathisers inside the city shot an arrow into their camp with a message attached. Whatever the public protestations of Murzuphlus and the show of grief that he made, Villehardouin was in no doubt about the moral position. He writes in his chronicle that 'murder cannot be hid', and in this instance he was surely right. That a young man in the prime of life could die unexpectedly of natural causes at a time so convenient to Murzuphlus was pushing credibility altogether too far.

The crusaders called a parliament to discuss their next move. Their claims to repayment revolved exclusively around their connection with Alexius, who had entered into a contract with them for the recovery of his throne. Now that he was dead, the contract no longer existed. However, after its great sacrifices so far, it was inconceivable that the army would meekly accept this situation. There was some debate about the right course of action to take. Some were unequivocal in their condemnation of the perfidy of Alexius: 'a curse on anyone who cares whether Alexius is dead or not', they said.[9] Yet these views were apparently in the minority and, in the end, they did not win the day. There were obviously sound practical reasons why the army should continue the siege after so much had been committed to it thus far. In addition, some strongly held moral opinions were also expressed. The oath that a vassal swore to his lord was, in this era, the most sacred of covenants. In the eyes of the crusaders, by his treachery Murzuphlus had committed the most heinous of sins, which made him a man devoid of honour and moral worth. He was not worthy to sit on the imperial throne.

The debate passed back and forth without clear resolution until the clerics with the expedition were asked to express their moral opinion. Throughout the crusade, the Church largely reacted to events rather than drove them, yet this should not obscure the great weight that its views carried. In times of crisis and, more pertinently, uncertainty, the views of the Church could indeed direct the actions of the crusade down one particular path or another. This was just such an occasion. The clerics weighed up the moral arguments, but stated decisively that the crusade would be fully justified in continuing the attack on Constantinople. Their line of reasoning is interesting and fundamentally important. Firstly, they stated that the war was 'lawful and just'. The choice of words was fitting. One of the greatest influences on the theological thinking of the Medieval Church was St Augustine. A millennium ago, he had laid out clearly the narrow confines within which war could legitimately be waged. He had coined specifically the phrase 'the just war'. The use of terminology was so similar that it can hardly have been coincidental. The clerics were claiming the support of one of Christianity's greatest thinkers to buttress their arguments.

They then proceeded to what was, for them, the crux of the matter. They stated that 'the Greeks had withdrawn themselves from obedience to Rome'.[10] Of course, there was nothing new in this. As we have seen, the differences between the Latin and Greek Churches had existed for centuries. On the eve of the crusade, the Pope had been in negotiation with Alexius III to reunite the Churches. Now the pretence that a peaceful resolution could be found was openly and clearly abandoned. The clerics finished their reasoning with a flourish. They stated that any man who were to die in the attack on Constantinople would, provided he was properly confessed, receive the full benefits of the Papal indulgence.

The attack on Constantinople was being linked unambiguously with the status of a crusade.

The importance of this move cannot possibly be understated. For many in the army, the crusade was primarily, perhaps even solely, a religious act on their part. The benefits of the indulgence offered at the start of the expedition were great. The fact that the attack on Constantinople now so clearly had Papal blessing was of great meaning to the crusaders. It was not the Pope himself of course who had given his approbation; but those who sanctioned the move were his appointed representatives and the army was entitled to believe that they faithfully represented his views. Thus Christian theology had gone full circle. A few centuries before, the Church had been undecided about whether violence was justified in any circumstances, against any people. Then the crusading concept had legitimised it, if it was directed against those who were not Christian. Now Christians could fight and kill other Christians with the full blessing of the Church. Neither was it the first time that such a concept had been mooted. As we have seen, Pope Paschal II had considered calling a crusade against Byzantium nearly two centuries earlier. That said, the first major expedition which was, effectively, a crusade against Christians had not actually been launched until 1199, when one had been summoned against a rebel baron, Markward of Sicily. The man who had given his Papal blessing to the move was none other than Pope Innocent III. There was therefore a clear, and very recent, precedent for the Papal delegates to follow.

Encouraged by the approval of the clerics, the army resolved to fight on until Constantinople was theirs. From this point on, there was never any mention of appointing a pliant Greek as Emperor. Henceforward the aim was clear and unequivocal; the conquest of Byzantium for the Franks themselves. The crusade had taken, almost imperceptibly, a huge lurch in a different direction. The Westerners, however, would be faced with a resilient foe. Soon after taking control, Murzuphlus sent word to the Franks, telling them to quit his lands peaceably or he would force them back into the sea. Knowing that the answer to this bluster would be negative, he had set about fortifying the defences of his capital. The walls, already formidable, were heightened and strengthened. With energy and enthusiasm, the new Emperor began improving the position of Byzantium. The people were in sympathy with his tough line. Many were exhilarated at his plain-speaking rejection of the demands of the Franks. Unfortunately for him and for them, although the presentation of the message had changed, beneath the surface little had really altered.

The realities of life were demonstrated all too clearly soon after. Over the winter months, the Franks were forced to widen their search for provisions. The war in the meantime continued, increasing in intensity although it still consisted of skirmishing rather than pitched battles or an out-and-out attack on the city. In order to ease the supply position of the Franks, it was resolved that a raid in force should be launched into the countryside surrounding Constantinople. It was to be led by Henry, brother of Baldwin, Count of Flanders. With him were many of the prominent knights of the army, including men such as James of Avesnes and Odo and William of Champlitte. They left at vespers[11] in the twilight of a January day. The force rode through the night and arrived on the Black Sea coast at a port named Phile. They stormed it and found many provisions inside the town as their prize; animals, clothing and food as well as a host of prisoners.

This was a very welcome boost for the raiding party, and they made the most of the opportunity of basking in the glory of their conquest. For two days they stayed in Phile, before starting to make their way back towards Constantinople. In the interim, word of the fall of the port had reached Murzuphlus. Determined to strike a blow against the Franks at every opportunity, he quickly assembled a large force and made his way towards the returning raiding party. He hid his force in some woods abutting a road along which he knew the Franks would have to ride. Sure enough, the party was not long in arriving at the spot.

Murzuphlus instructed his troops to stay hidden until the rearguard was before them. Then, he shouted the order to attack. The Franks were completely off their guard, and were horrified to see a large number of Byzantine troops heading for them. They were vastly outnumbered and their foe was cock-a-hoop. The Byzantines had with them an icon of the Blessed Virgin. It was one of the most sacred relics of the city, and in a metropolis that was awash with relics that was no mean attribute. The Franks in the rearguard were unsure what to do. If they fled, then much of their hard-won booty would be lost. Worse, panic might spread throughout the rest of the raiding party, which could be overwhelmed as a result.

Once again, at the moment of crisis the superior morale of the Franks re-asserted itself. They reasoned to themselves that flight was not an option: 'if we flee we are all dead men. It becomes us better to die fighting than fleeing.'[12] Thus they faced up to the threat of the Byzantines. They assembled a tiny force of crossbowmen, consisting of only eight men, as a token screen in front of their horsemen. The battle quickly degenerated into a slogging match. The Franks threw aside their lances; presumably the fighting was at such close quarters that they were of no use. Instead, they stabbed and hacked around them with their swords. They did fearsome damage, their armour protecting them from the weapons of the Greeks. Not one horseman was thrown from his mount by the Greeks, according to Robert of Clari. The seemingly impervious wall of steel demoralised the Greeks. The attacks of the Byzantine soldiers grew less fierce as time went on. Thinking that the moment was right for a counter, the Franks charged into the ranks of the Byzantines.

This was all too much for the Greeks. Faced with a full-frontal attack from cavalry of such fiercesome reputation, they broke and fled. There was no order in their retreat, which quickly degenerated into a rout. Much booty was captured by the Franks, meekly abandoned by the shattered Greek forces. For the Greeks, the reverse quickly began a tragedy. In the chaos of their hasty departure, nothing less than the imperial diadem and, worst of all, the sacred icon fell into the hands of the Franks. Elated by their success, the Franks gave up the pursuit. Certainly, the prize of the icon was a huge one to the Franks. It was magnificently fashioned, forged from solid gold and finished with precious stones. However, that was not its main relevance to either the Franks or the Byzantines. This was an age that prized relics above all other things. A mystical aura surrounded them. They were deemed to have immense power, and men would go to extraordinary lengths to gain possession of them. After the capture of the icon, every other prize available was superfluous. News of the attack had filtered back to the crusaders' camp and a force was hurriedly assembled to help the raiding party. When it arrived, their only role was to help to take the booty back with them.

For Murzuphlus, the loss of the icon was a disaster. News of its capture would be an immense blow to his prestige and, given the infancy of his reign, that might prove terminal. His people would be incensed.[13] Indeed, soon after his return the people did begin to ask where the icon was. Murzuphlus told them that it was so precious that it had already been returned to safe keeping. News of this deception reached the camp of the crusaders.[14] They saw in this an opportunity to undermine Murzuphlus. They took hold of the icon and put it aboard a galley. The ship was rowed in front of the walls of Constantinople and the icon was prominently displayed to the many citizens who had gone to watch. His duplicity uncovered, Murzuphlus blustered that the loss of the icon only made him angrier and more determined to exterminate the Franks than ever.

Thus the winter months drew to a close. Their had been some hardship in the crusaders' camp but no reports of great losses to disease or malnutrition, two of the great killers of Medieval warfare. The Greeks had tried their utmost to drive out the Franks but they had failed. With each Byzantine failure, Greek morale sank and Crusader spirits were boosted. Now spring was near, the time of year when the earth came to life again and crops began to grow, and the time of year when Medieval armies began once more to wage war after the inactivity of the winter months. The tenacity of the Franks was not in doubt. They were well armed and had acquired much experience of warfare during the siege of the city. In contrast, the Greeks were bitterly divided, and led by yet another usurper Emperor who had, so far, promised the world and delivered nothing. In the fight that was now imminent, there was only ever likely to be one winner.

CHAPTER ELEVEN

The Fall of the City

For a thousand years, the city of Constantinople had resisted every assault directed at it. The prospect of an attempt on the city was a daunting one but it does not seem to have appalled the crusaders unduly. Despite the enormity of the challenge facing them, they were confident enough to spend much time in planning how the city would be divided after it was captured. It was decided that a committee of twelve men would be set up once the city fell, consisting of six Venetian representatives and six from the leaders of the army. The remit of this group was to adjudicate on the subject of who should be Emperor after the city had been captured. It was agreed that if the man chosen were one of the leaders of the army then the new Patriarch of Constantinople should be a Venetian, or vice-versa. The Emperor should receive a quarter of all the wealth that was gained from the conquests of the crusade, with the remainder divided equally between the army and the Venetians.[1] The new ruler would also receive the two major palaces in Constantinople, the Blachernae and the Bucoleon.[2] There would also be another committee set up, this consisting of twenty-four men, who would decide on the apportionment of minor titles and fiefs when the crusaders' conquests were completed.

This arrangement was solemnly attested to by a formal swearing of oaths on holy relics. All this was a sign that, although undoubtedly well aware of the magnitude of the battle ahead, the crusaders were nevertheless in confident mood. If anything, their mood was over-confident. Much time was expended in discussing the details of the division of the Empire, but the crusaders perhaps misread the situation. They seem to have assumed that the capture of Constantinople would automatically mean that the rest of the Empire would meekly accept that it was consequently in thrall to the West. In fact, although the city was obviously of great importance, the increasing autonomy of much of the Empire in the past few centuries meant that some provinces of it were more than capable of being self-sufficient. Even after Constantinople was captured, many parts of the Empire would refuse to recognise the rule of the invaders. The crusaders would have to fight hard to gain the Empire even if they conquered its capital.

There was implicit recognition that it was highly unlikely that the majority of the crusade would now make its way on to the Holy Land once the conquest was completed. Those who wished to would be released to complete the journey to Outremer in a year's time (March 1205) but those who remained within the Empire 'would be held to the service of the emperor in such manner as might be ordained'.[3] To give legitimacy to the enterprise ahead, the clergy declaimed that those who did not adhere to the covenant would be excommunicated.[4]

The political issues having been discussed and resolved, it was also necessary for the crusade to complete its military preparations for the battle ahead. Murzuphlus had used the break given by the winter months to strengthen the defences of his capital. His fighting talk had been intended to raise the spirits of the citizens. Wooden towers had been erected to cover the gaps in the city's defences, which the attack of the Venetians the previous year had managed to exploit. Petraries and mangonels were placed liberally along the length of the walls to cause maximum discomfort to the enemy. Even psychological warfare was used to demoralise the enemy. Three Venetian prisoners were drawn on hooks and burned alive on the city walls, in full view of their comrades.[5]

The crusaders, however, were equally thorough in their planning. The Venetians protected their vessels by reinforcing them with house timbers and draping grapevines over the side; this would help to protect the timbers of the ships from projectiles fired at them from the Greek artillery. They also built more flying bridges high up in the vessels, which their men hoped to use to climb over onto the city walls. The French, who would attack by land, built 'cats' and 'sows' to protect their soldiers when they approached the walls of Constantinople; this would protect their engineers as they attempted to mine underneath the defences. These devices were rather like large mobile buildings, complete with roofs, which could be wheeled right up to the wall and offered some shelter to the miners who were tasked with tunnelling beneath the fortifications.

There was one last matter that the crusaders discussed, and that was the way that the city was to be treated once it fell into their hands. Constantinople was, to them, a fabulously wealthy city – its many treasures were a matter of fable throughout the world. Such great wealth would inevitably be an enormous temptation for the army, many of whom were very poor. In order that some control might be exercised over the flow of booty, it was agreed that the army could only help itself to minor items like tools and food. Any gold, silver or expensive cloth was to be brought straight back to the camp and handed over for safe keeping and subsequent distribution. Further, there was to be no sexual abuse of any of the women in the city. Finally, no one should lay hands on any priest or violate the sanctity of any church or monastery. Robert of Clari insists that the crusaders were forced to swear on holy relics that they would abide by these conditions; sadly, in so doing many of them perjured themselves. If they believed in the sacred nature of the oaths that they took, many of the men placed their souls in great peril because, when faced with the great prizes on offer in this city, the baser elements of human nature would take over.

The preparations finally over, the army steeled itself for the assault. It was decided that the attack on Constantinople would take place ten days before Palm Sunday, that is to say 9 April 1204. The siege engines of the army were carefully loaded onto the ships, already bristling with large numbers of petraries and mangonels with which the crusaders hoped to break down the colossal walls of the city. High above the decks, those delegated the unenviable task of fighting their way across the flying bridges onto the walls prepared themselves mentally for an ordeal that would be perilous in the extreme. No doubt, in these last moments of safety, all of the men braced themselves for what lay ahead. As soldiers have done through the ages, some probably felt euphoria at the prospect of the challenge, but, on considering their mission to attack an enemy protected by such immense fortifications, most would be filled with a fear so intense it pervaded their very being. Stomachs churned and heads spun, making some perspire, others feel physically nauseous, as their minds filled with horrific images of the dreadful, painful death that awaited many of them, their bodies transfixed with pointed spear, their limbs cut off by the heavy, hacking swords of the enemy or their skull caved in by a violently swung Varangian axe.

And then these apocalyptic images were suddenly interrupted as the loud calls of the marshals split the morning air. The order to set sail across the short stretch of the Golden Horn that lay between the camp and the city was shouted along the length of the fleet, which was so large it stretched across a front a mile long. The ships were arranged so that the men of individual divisions were in vessels next to each other, so that the cohesion of the attack might be maintained. It was not long before the ships moved into range of the defences of the city. As they did so, the nightmare of battle began. From the length of the walls, the petraries and mangonels flung their mighty projectiles at the transports arrayed before them. With a sickening thud, great boulders crashed into the side of the ships, testing to the full the improvised defensive precautions that the Venetians had prepared. Others hammered on to decks, crushing all who were unfortunate enough to be in their path, causing death or, perhaps worse, horrific injury to those in the line of fire.

Through it all the Venetian ships came on, firing their own artillery back at the city, knocking chunks of stone off the massive walls. From a prominent hill inside the city, Murzuphlus himself watched on. He had set himself up in the Church of Christ Pantepoptes.[6] From this elevated position, he could see right over the walls of the city and out to the attacking fleet. He had ensured that there were a large number of trumpets and timbrels around him; from these he demanded a fearful racket to keep up the spirits of the defenders and strike fear into the crusaders.

Through this hail of missiles, the fleet advanced. Despite the intensity of the defence, the crusaders managed to draw up adjacent to the walls. Here, the battle began in earnest. The Venetians in the flying bridges desperately struggled to gain a bridgehead on the walls. Equally determined, the defenders pushed them back. Separated by only a few feet and a length of steel, men hacked and parried, thrust and stabbed at each other. Above the cries of the defenders and the fearsome exhortations of the attackers, over the clarion calls of the trumpets, rose the screams of those who were grievously wounded in the mêlée. In a hundred different places the scene was repeated.[7] The crusaders gave their all in increasingly ferocious attempts to dislodge the defenders, while the Greeks threw themselves body and soul into the terrifying conflict atop the city walls. The fight lasted all day until the hour of none.[8] Despite the enormous efforts of the crusaders, the result was everywhere the same. In a hundred different places they had launched their assault. And in a hundred different places they had failed.

In the intensity of the battle, scores of attackers lost their lives. In contrast, few of the defenders were killed. The Greeks were overjoyed at their success, as they had every right to be. By whatever standard the outcome of the battle was judged, there could only be one winner. In contrast to the euphoria of the Greeks, the Crusaders were devastated. Seemingly so confident of success before the battle was joined, the extent of their reverse had caused the exact antithesis of optimism to spread through the ranks of the crusaders. A black cloud of grim despair and wretched dejection descended over the host as it reassembled at Estanor to lick its wounds.

Dandolo called a parliament, and great was the soul-searching that took place at the assembly. Some suggested that the Venetians should sail down the Golden Horn and attack a weaker section of walls on the other side of Constantinople. The Venetians pointed out that this could not succeed, as the strong current would carry them out to sea. So profound was the distress of the crusade that there were some of their number who thought that this would be no bad thing, provided that the ships took them away from those awful, intimidating walls that had proved impervious to the best efforts of the army during the day.[9]

In these defeatist comments of Villehardouin concerning the morale of the expedition there is an extremely strong clue that the depression spreading among the army was not simply as a result of its immediate rebuff. Signs of complacency could be read into the involved discussions about what the army would do with the city when it was captured that had taken place before the assault. After the successes of the winter, the negation of the threat from the fire-ships and the victory in the skirmish with Murzuphlus on the way back from Phile, the army perhaps overrated its own powers, believing that their dominance was so great that the assault on the city would be a mere formality. The city had after all been ruled by three different Emperors in the space of a year (four if one includes the irrelevant figure of Isaac). Such instability could hardly have given the impression of a united city whose citizens would fight to the death to protect their rights. However, Alexius had, through his connection to the Latins, been a divisive influence. Murzuphlus, for all his faults, was a robust and aggressive Emperor around whom many of the Greeks could rally.

Now that complacency had been demolished, and the seemingly unshakeable confidence of the crusaders had been shown to be something far more frail. Over a hundred of their colleagues lay dead, having paid the ultimate price for underestimating the defensive qualities of a people who had nowhere to run to, indeed whose very survival was at stake. It was a chastened force that debated in depth its next move, with the discussions going on for some time as the leaders of the army attempted to make some sense of what had happened. 'Angry, sorrowful and greatly troubled',[10] they resolved that they would rest for the next two days, that is Saturday and Sunday, to better prepare themselves spiritually, mentally and physically for another attack on Constantinople.

On the Sunday the whole camp assembled to take communion, all the men confessing their sins to the priests with the army, almost as if they were ritually purifying themselves so that, their sins made known to the Almighty, they would once more have divine approbation on their efforts. Self-evident as the fact might appear, it is worth repeating that involvement in the crusade was essentially a spiritual act. Failure was widely regarded as a sign of God's disapproval, His judgement of the unworthiness of the expedition. The outpouring of religious emotions that took place on that Sunday had been matched many times before throughout the history of the crusading movement.[11] All the leading clerics of the expedition were conscripted to preach sermons to the army. There were probably some 20,000 people in the camp, the numbers swollen by the many people who had fled from Constantinople during the recent pogrom. Logistically, therefore, it would be impossible for one cleric to be responsible for the religious devotions of such a crowd of people. The Bishop of Soissons, the Abbot of Loos and the Bishop of

Troyes all took part.[12] Having preached fervently to the congregation to repent of their sins, and extolled the crusaders to even greater efforts, the priests gave communion to everyone present.

On the previous day, the Saturday, the clerics had been called upon for a different reason. The reverse suffered by the crusaders had once more called into question the legitimacy of the attack on the city. Even at this late stage many harboured grave doubts about the morality of this action. Therefore, the bishops were again asked to offer guidance as to whether or not the assault on Constantinople was just. The clerics were for their part unequivocal in their rulings. The city had in ancient times recognised the sovereignty of the Latin Church, but it had rejected the Papacy and by so doing it had become a legitimate target for the expedition. The bishops were categorical in their assurances, saying that 'they [the crusaders] were right to attack them [the Greeks], and that it was not at all a sin, but rather a righteous deed'.[13] The role of the Church during the crusade should not be underplayed. Reactive though that role may have been, the moral fibre of the expedition was strengthened consistently by the pronouncements of the clerics at critical stages of the crusade. Although it is hard to accept that the siege would be abandoned at this late stage even if the clerics had come out against the morality of the undertaking, it would nevertheless have considerably weakened the resolve of the attackers. By its lack of a strong moral lead against the attack, and indeed by its positive acceptance that the deed was a righteous one, the Church played an important part in the events that took place.

Following the intense religious devotions of the Sunday, one final act of purification took place. All the women in the camp were put aboard ship and taken away from the menfolk. Sexual abstinence was another important penitential act on the part of the army. The men should stay well clear of all unclean thoughts and acts so that they would be better equipped to undertake God's work on the morrow. Its sins confessed and its morale reinforced by the earnest exhortations of the priests, the camp settled itself for the long night, knowing that in the morning the great undertaking would begin again. The very understandable fears of those who would be in the thick of battle were heightened by the experiences of the previous assault. There would be no overconfidence among the ranks of the crusaders this time.

The last few days had also been used to make some tactical adjustments to the plans of the crusaders. One hard lesson taken to heart was that it was no use attacking the towers of the city with a single ship. Those on board were outnumbered by the defenders and, given the difficulties experienced by the men exposed high above the ships in the flying bridges, they were easily beaten back. This time the ships would be linked two-by-two, thus the manpower available would be doubled, and the Venetians would stand a much greater chance of overpowering the defenders. It was also decided that the attackers would strike the city solely from the sea, despite the reluctance of the army to take part in such a venture. By so doing, the strength of the attackers would no longer be diluted, again increasing their chances of victory.

Meanwhile, the defenders were understandably buoyant after their successful efforts to drive back the crusaders. Now they packed the walls, confident that the Franks would enjoy no more return on this occasion. Once again, Murzuphlus took up a prominent position so that he could inspire his people to push their assailants back into the sea. Defiantly the Venetian ships came on again, launching an assault that was described by Villehardouin as 'proud and marvellous', with a noise 'so great that it seemed to rend the earth'.

Robert of Clari seems to have been in the thick of the fray. He describes in great detail what took place in his particular part of the battle, which seems to have been critical to what followed. He writes with a gusto and verve that could only come from one who was intimately involved in the conflict. According to Robert, the Venetian ships dropped anchor when they were as close to the city walls as they could possibly be. Even before they reached the shoreline, the petraries of the defenders hurled boulders incessantly at the ships, crashing into timbers and sending splinters flying. Again the defensive measures taken by the Venetians, the unusual combination of grapevines and housing planks, proved resilient enough to prevent serious damage from taking place. The ships, however, were at a disadvantage. So high were the improvised towers erected by the people of Constantinople that only four or five ships were large enough to launch a serious assault on them.

For a while each side hammered away at the other, the well-manned defence proving capable of holding its own against the frenzied attacks of the crusaders. Then two ships, the *Pilgrim* and the *Paradise*, were driven against one of the towers by the current. High up in one of the flying bridges three men tried to jump over onto the walls, one Venetian and two Western knights. Desperately leaping across the gap, the Venetian succeeded in hurling himself onto the walls, clinging on precariously with his hands until he managed to gain a more secure foothold. But one man could do nothing against the packed defence. The tower was manned by a combination of Varangians, Danes and English, and Greeks. They charged at the impudent Venetian, hacking at him with axes and swords until he was a lifeless, bloodied corpse.

The next time that the sea drove the ships forward, one of the knights, Andrew of Dureboise, threw himself across. The defenders flung themselves at him, striking him continuously. However, his armour prevented them from causing serious damage. Battered but defiant, he rose to his feet, daring his assailants to come at him again. As he moved towards them, the defenders nerve broke. They charged down the stairs to the lower storeys of the tower. Once Andrew had driven them off, other knights joined him. The ships were tied to the tower, allowing more and more crusaders to cross over onto the walls. The first breach had been made.

However, the fickle tides of the Golden Horn were not at this moment on the side of the Franks. So violently did the Venetian ships move around in the current that they threatened to pull down the tower, and reluctantly, the attackers had to untie the thick ropes that had attached the ships. Nevertheless, the defenders were disheartened by the successful incursion of the Franks, and abandoned the tower to the crusaders completely. Murzuphlus sent troops to drive back the attackers but, as they were on their way, another ship, that of Peter of Brachaux, also struck against one of the towers, which in its turn also fell quickly.

Despite these successes, stalemate ensued for a time. The defenders were too numerous for the crusaders to contemplate moving out of the towers and pushing into the city. Great numbers of Greeks and Varangians blocked their progress, forming an impressive and intimidating obstacle to any further progress. It needed a dash of courage and improvisation to overcome this impasse, and this came, initially at least, from Peter of Amiens. He descended from his ship to a narrow strip of land between the city walls and the sea. Here, he came across a false postern, a gateway that had been bricked up. He led his small force of ten knights and sixty other armed men to the postern. Frantically, they laid into it with picks, axes, their swords and even pieces of wood, desperately trying to knock a hole in it. The defenders were quick to spot them. Equally frantic, they hurled masonry down from the walls and directed the fire of their crossbows into the ranks of the crusaders. Some of those trying to gain access used their shields to protect others, who were digging and hacking at the postern. Their predicament did not improve. Pots of boiling pitch were hurled at them and then, worst of all, Greek fire was directed at them.

Five centuries earlier, Constantinople had looked doomed to fall to the Arabs until it was miraculously delivered by the use of Greek fire. It could be directed onto an enemy through primitive hoses. Once it was ablaze, it was virtually impossible to put out. Since its first, shattering use half a millennium ago, its reputation had grown so that now an enemy quaked at mere mention of it. As this dreadful weapon was aimed at the crusaders, their desperation turned to terror. Panic-stricken, they charged at the postern with energy inspired by the thought of imminent incineration. At last, the postern began to give.

At first, the gap that they made was only big enough to peer through. On the other side of the wall, the crusaders could see a vast crowd waiting to drive them back should they break through. Nevertheless, they continued to hammer away at the postern until the hole was big enough for a man to crawl through. The sight of the large number of defenders waiting for them, however, was a daunting one. The crusaders hesitated, reluctant to push on, until one of their number, a man named Aleaumes, charged into the breach. Desperately, others – including Robert of Clari – tried to hold him back, convinced that the man was on a suicide mission. Nothing daunted, Aleaumes rushed on at the enemy. The defenders threw rocks at him and struck out in an attempt to force him back. They did not succeed. Instead, Aleaumes turned to his comrades in arms and boldly declared, 'Lords, enter heartily! I see them draw back dismayed and beginning to run away'.[14] His heroic efforts inspired those who still faltered outside. They charged after Aleaumes. As they did so, Murzuphlus, who was barely a stone's throw away, moved towards them. He had been exhorting his people to greater efforts, his defiant declarations backed up once more by the clarion call of his trumpets and the rhythmic beat of his timbrels. He hoped to swing the battle against the Franks by frightening them off but, instead, the crusaders, who were never afraid of a good fight, pushed on towards him led by Peter of Amiens. When Murzuphlus saw that, rather than retreating, they were advancing towards him, he drew back.

This was now the decisive action of the battle. Nearby was a larger gate. As soon as he possibly could, Peter ordered his men to open it so that those still outside could make their way into the city. The horses were unloaded from the transports and the knights mounted them, spurring them through the open gates of Constantinople into the streets of the city itself. Murzuphlus clearly realised which way the tide of battle was flowing. He retreated quickly into the heart of his capital, abandoning his tents and great booty to the Franks. When the rest of the defenders of the outer walls saw that their Emperor had fled, they followed suit. They left their towers and escaped as quickly as they could into the streets of Constantinople itself.

The outer defences of Constantinople at last fell to the crusaders. However, this was by no means the end of the battle. The inner walls of the city still remained intact. There was much fighting to be done, and much blood to be spilt, before Constantinople was secured. It was by now late in the day. As evening approached, the crusaders decided wisely to stay where they were. Even if they should break into the inner city, behind the second line of defence lay a labyrinth of cluttered streets criss-crossing through densely packed buildings. It would be a dangerous place in the daylight for an army not familiar with the layout of the city; it was certainly no place to be during the night. The crusaders therefore sought accommodation in the areas they had taken during the first day of the battle. Count Baldwin occupied the tents so recently abandoned by Murzuphlus.[15] His brother, Henry, took the Blachernae Palace, while Boniface secured a position in another part of the city. The army then settled down for the night, no doubt well satisfied at their day's work but apprehensive of what the morrow would bring, certain that the people of Constantinople were still far from beaten.

During the still hours of darkness two events occurred that would lose the city to the Greeks finally and irrevocably. The troops with Boniface of Montferrat were disquieted by the proximity of the Greeks to them. They therefore took measures to protect themselves from attack during the night. They lit a fire, with which they hoped to keep off the Greeks. But the fire quickly burned out of control. Although it had buildings of great grandeur set in comparatively open spaces, Constantinople also had more than its share of overcrowded streets where thousands of dwellings, homes to hundreds of thousands of ordinary people, were crammed together like rabbit warrens. Once fire took hold, it proved impossible to stop. Rapidly the flames spread. It was the third great fire to damage the city in the space of a year. Villehardouin, attempting to describe its seriousness, tells us that more houses were consumed in the blaze than existed in entire towns in the West. The fire burned away destructively, consuming with it the defenders' desire to resist.

Around midnight, Murzuphlus led a force out of his quarters, telling his people that he was going to lead an attack on the Franks. He was lying. In an act eerily reminiscent of the flight of Alexius III only months before, he was abandoning his people. Unlike the last Emperor to flee the city, he was leaving when the enemy was in the bowels of the city, not while they were still outside of those formidable walls. Murzuphlus had talked a good fight but, sadly for the Greeks, his actions did not match his bluster. When it came to the crunch, he was as spineless as his predecessors, valuing his own skin far more than the well-being of his subjects. His failings were even greater than those that came before him. Few had expected much of the weak Alexius IV and the blinded Isaac, but Murzuphlus had promised much to his people, assuring them that he would drive the enemy back into the sea. In the end, his words meant little, promises or not. Murzuphlus made his way out of the city through the Golden Gate, away towards safety for the time being. It was an act imbued with the deepest irony – it was through this gate that victorious

Byzantine generals had for centuries made their triumphal return to the city after successful campaigns.

None of this was known to the Franks. They roused themselves early in the morning of Tuesday 13 April 1204 to find the air acrid with the smoke from the charred remains of incinerated buildings. Most of them had slept fully armed, knowing that today they would once again have to risk life and limb if they wished to earn glory. They rubbed the sleep from their eyes, stretched aching limbs and looked purposefully towards the heart of the city. They made their way towards the inner defences, but as they did so they quickly became aware that resistance had disintegrated. Incredulously, they walked on to find that there were 'none to oppose them'.[16]

It was perhaps not to be wondered at. The inhabitants of the city had fallen prey to a succession of Emperors whose incompetence was quite probably unmatched in Byzantine history. Not since the days of Manuel Comnenus some thirty years before had there been anyone on the throne of this great but dying Empire who had been remotely fitted to hold in his hands the governance of such a marvellous heritage. In the space of a year, three regimes had come and gone. The people had no will left to fight because they had been given no leadership from any of the nonentities who had taken it upon themselves to claim the throne of Byzantium. By nature a pessimistic people, the blackest nightmares of the Greeks had assumed a terrible, painful reality that was to them unbearable. The barbarians were in the heart of the city with no possibility of being dislodged. Nine hundred years of history were destroyed in a few days. An invader finally ruled in the unconquerable city.

The incredible truth of the situation slowly dawned on the crusaders. After the effort, the bloodshed and the heartache of the past months the greatest city in Christendom had fallen into their hands. An immense store of wealth was theirs, and the city was defenceless at their feet, incapable of fighting back. A quietness descended on the city as its inhabitants began to think the unthinkable. It was the precursor to a great tension, a calm before the storm pregnant with threat and menace. A tempest was brewing that would shake the city, the Empire and the world to its very foundations. God's army had won at last, God's will had surely been done. Now it was time for the victors to claim their prize.

CHAPTER TWELVE

Aftermath

Early in the morning a delegation of clerics from Constantinople made their way to the camp of the crusaders. They came with the tidings that Murzuphlus had fled, and with him a sizeable proportion of the population of the city. Knowing full well that the city was now wide open to the crusaders, the clerics begged that they might be shown mercy. Constantinople was now home only to the poor and the weak; understandably, the citizens was terrified of what might happen. The rules of Medieval warfare, such as they were, meant that a city that resisted was fair game to be sacked if finally taken by force.

The crusaders were presumably overwhelmed at the news; with wonderful understatement Robert of Clari says that they were 'mightily glad' at the tidings.[1] The leaders of the crusade took stock of the situation and announced that anything valuable in the city should not be arbitrarily looted; rather, anything that was taken of all but nominal value should be brought to certain collection points where a proper distribution of the loot could be made.

They then decided what the reward of the army should be. Effectively, they gave the army *carte blanche* to do with the city as it pleased for the next three days, provided only that the rules concerning the retention of valuable items were observed. The army had been away from home for two years or more. It had suffered much in this time, from conflict, disease and all the other problems that beset a Medieval army on campaign. Further, it should not be assumed that the masses were all pilgrims, motivated by altruistic concepts of spiritual self-sacrifice. One of the by-products of committing oneself to the crusade was that a man could no longer be tried by secular courts for his temporal wrongdoings. Consequently, some criminals saw in the crusade the chance to escape punishment for their crimes, and were not slow to take advantage of the possibilities that this offered.

The entrenched misunderstandings of East and West meant that the crusaders taken as a whole had little regard for the heritage that Byzantium represented. To many of the army, the citizens of the Empire were little more than heretics; had not their own priests told them on so many occasions that Byzantium had wrongly thrown aside the rightful rule of Rome? All of these factors combined meant that the crusaders were hardly likely to be merciful in their treatment of the city. They do nothing, however, to justify what happened next.

Robert of Clari and Villehardouin both say something about the loot that was taken; they are silent as to how it was seized. It is impossible to believe that Villehardouin, with his eye for detail and a good story, did not know of the details of what happened. It is equally difficult to escape the conclusion that he was to an extent embarrassed by what went on. There is no attempt in his chronicle to justify the actions of the victorious army, rather a complete avoidance of the issue altogether. It is left to others to chronicle the fate of the city, and a dreadful fate it was indeed.[2]

The army made its way into the city in search of loot. Quickly, they started to help themselves to the wealth of the city. This included the significant stocks of wine possessed by the citizens. Alcohol inflamed their passions still further, until all control was lost. The mob – for it deserved no better name by now – helped itself to everything that it wanted. Women were thrown to the ground and raped where they were in the streets. Men who tried to intervene and protect wives or daughters were killed on the spot. Even the nuns in their convents were violated – a feature of the sack that was to appal no less a personage than Innocent III when he heard of it – and virgins dedicated to Christ were defiled by the very men who had sworn on holy relics to fight to the death for the faith that they held dear.

In a desperate attempt to squeeze every last drop of wealth from the city, citizens were tortured until they blurted out where they had hidden their treasures. The lust for material reward assumed unbelievable proportions. Statues that had been founded half a millennium before the birth of Christ were melted down for their scrap value. The antique heritage of the city was decimated in the abuse that followed the fall of the city.

There was only one exception to this general rule. Venice was a cultured city – it is no coincidence that within a century or two the city would be at the heart of that amazing outpouring of creativity known to historians as the Renaissance. The Venetians recognised much that was of artistic value in the city, and took it for themselves. Most famous among the objects garnered in this way were the four bronze horses that even now adorn the basilica of St Mark in Venice.[3] Many other priceless objects were taken in this way, ironically preserving some of the heritage of Byzantium for future generations to appreciate (a thought that surely would not have been foremost in the minds of those responsible for the sack of the city).

Perhaps the greatest outrage was that committed against the spiritual heritage of the city. The city was the greatest centre in the world for the holy relics of Christianity. Typical of this was the Church of the Blessed Virgin of the Pharos, described by Robert of Clari.[4] The chronicler details an incredible list of the items held here. There were two pieces of Christ's cross, 'as large as the leg of a man'. There was also the iron of the lance with which the Centurion had pierced the side of Christ and, almost inevitably, two nails that had been driven through His hands and feet. There was a phial containing drops of his blood and the tunic that he wore at his execution. There was also the Crown of Thorns, 'with thorns as sharp as the points of daggers'. In addition, the church also held a part of the robe of the Virgin and the head of John the Baptist. That one church alone could hold such a vast array of relics gives some clue to the size of the industry (for such it surely was) within the walls of Constantinople.

Such relics were both a source of fascination and a strong incentive to loot for many of the Crusaders. Even priests were not above involving themselves in this aspect of the rape of Constantinople. Two days previously, Abbot Martin of Pairis had been salving the consciences of the army at Communion. Presumably, along with the rest of the priests, he also took the oath on holy relics to respect the sanctity of the Christian heritage of Constantinople. Yet, when the time came, his willpower was lacking. As he saw others looting, he resolved that he 'should not remain empty-handed while all the others became rich'. Not wanting to sully his hands with worldly treasures, he instead began to plan how he could obtain some relics. He knew of a church in the city that held the tomb of the Emperor Manuel Comnenus, and made his way there accompanied by two chaplains. The church was already being ransacked by soldiers who were grabbing hold of the silver and gold plate items in the church. Martin, however, 'thinking it unworthy to commit sacrilege except in a holy cause', decided to look for more sacred objects.

He turned on an old man who was there, who was according to the chronicler, 'definitely a priest'. He shouted at him that unless he showed him where the holy relics of the church were hidden, he could 'rest assured that you will be punished at once by the penalty of death'. The old man did not understand the words of the Abbot but he knew well enough what he meant from his demeanour. He took Martin to an iron chest which, when opened, proved to be filled with holy relics. The Abbot picked as much as he could up in the folds of his robe and made his way from the church. On his way back to the ships in the harbour many asked him how he had fared. Smiling, he replied, 'We have done well' to which they responded 'Thanks be to God'.[5]

Given the attitude of this man of God in the aftermath of the fall of Constantinople, it comes as no surprise to find that nothing was sacred.

One of the great churches of the city was that of the Holy Apostles. It was the last resting place of many Byzantine Emperors, including none other than Constantine the Great himself. The bodies of the Emperors were buried, as many well knew, in ornate dressings, liberally sprinkled with precious jewels. Even these mortal remains were not safe from the lusts of the Franks. The tomb of Justinian, one of Byzantium's most renowned Emperors, was torn open and the corpse of the Emperor, over 500 years old but apparently undecayed, was stripped of the jewels that had been buried with it. As one modern historian has said, 'sacrilege could hardly go further'.[6]

The Church of St Sophia was arguably one of the greatest churches in the whole of Christendom. Mules were taken down its aisles and loaded up with plate. A prostitute sat on the throne of the Patriarch and sang ribald songs. The hinges of the doors were made of silver; they were ripped off and melted down. Soldiers drank wine from the chalices used in the service. The catalogue of profanities was endless, and can be only remotely understood even in the context of the longstanding failure to comprehend all things Byzantine burned deep into the psyche of so many from the West.

Nicetas Choniates was beside himself with grief at the outrage: 'Oh, city, city, eye of all cities, subject of narratives over all the world, spectacle above the world . . . you have drunk to the dregs the cup of anger of the Lord.'[7]

It is one thing to try to understand the sack of the city, but quite another even to attempt to justify it. After all, only a matter of days beforehand many of the host had sworn to protect the Christian heritage of the city. But in the blood lust of its capture, such vows became quickly meaningless. If the holy men, those who gave the moral lead to the expedition, could not stop themselves from plundering the city's churches, then what hope did the ordinary soldiers have? When he heard of the fall of Constantinople, Pope Innocent was delighted as he believed (completely erroneously) that it would help to reconcile the Latin and Greek Churches. When details of the sack reached him, however, he appeared to be deeply shocked, sending a furious missive to the leaders of the crusade, reserving his opprobrium particularly for the leading churchmen with the expedition.

Innocent was not naïve. He well knew that the disgraceful actions of the crusade would alienate the Greeks even more from the West. He realised the reality of the situation. The sack of the city was always likely, perhaps even unavoidable, but, even by the standards of the day, he could not admit that it was right. Of all the crimes against humanity committed by this and every other crusade, this was one of the most unacceptable, for it was a crime perpetrated by a Christian army against one of the greatest cities in Christendom. Sadly, the actions of victorious armies against civilian populations in any era is often shameful. The massacre of much of the civilian population in Drogheda by Cromwell, or the destruction of Badajoz in the Peninsular War by Wellington's army are two of many examples that might be quoted in support of this contention. The particular horror of this sack – even at the time – was that it was committed by a Christian army. This should not blind us to the fact that there was much rejoicing in Western Europe at the news of the fall of the city but it is surely more than coincidence that. within the course of the succeeding century, several leading poets of the time (for example, Guy de Provins and Guillaume of Toulouse) were vitriolic about the role of the Church in the crusading movement. The sack did nothing to further the cause of the Catholic Church; combined with other events it would, in time, damage its reputation seriously.

After three days of frenzied behaviour, the leaders of the crusade called a halt to the plundering. They demanded that all the valuables taken by the looters should be brought together to collection points in three churches in the city (the irony seems to have been lost on Villehardouin) where the goods could be valued and divided up among the participants in the ratios agreed beforehand. Many of the looters were reluctant to hand over what they had stolen. Stuffily, Villehardouin recorded that 'not a few kept things back, despite the excommunication of the Pope'.[8] We may be sure that the Venetians, with their ships lying at anchor in harbour, salted much of the wealth of the city away for themselves. Yet the penalty for those who did not comply with the rules was grim indeed. One of the knights of the Count of St-Pol tried to take more than was his due. He was hanged with his shield draped around his neck, a sombre warning to those who chose to ignore the wishes of the leadership.

Indeed, Villehardouin and Robert of Clari are very much at odds in their views on the division of the spoil, undoubtedly reflecting their different positions in the hierarchy of the expedition and how they individually benefited from the rich pickings. Villehardouin castigated those who chose to keep back goods from what he described as 'the common stock', whereas Robert protested bitterly that those who led the expedition were rapacious in their appetite for wealth, and were grossly unfair towards the rank and file. One thing they could agree on, however, was that the prize was a huge one. Robert catalogues the wealth taken in an awe that is obvious even now:

and it [the booty] was so rich, and there were so many rich vessels of gold and silver and cloth of gold and so many rich jewels, that it is a fair marvel, the great wealth that was brought there. Not since the world was made was there ever seen or won so great a treasure or so noble or so rich, not in the time of Alexander nor in the time of Charlemagne nor before nor after. . . . For the Greeks say that two thirds of the wealth of this world is in Constantinople and the other third scattered throughout the world.[9]

Villehardouin was less effusive but no less impressed at the wealth of the city, merely remarking that the loot taken (including his presumably arbitrary estimate of what was stolen and not handed over to the leadership) amounted to a sum in the region of 400,000 marks. Out of this, the Venetians were paid the large amount still owed to them from the debt accrued at the start of the crusade and thereafter, and the balance was divided equally between them and the army.

The next issue requiring resolution was the thorny one of who should rule the Empire. Immediately after the fall of the city, Boniface of Montferrat had placed himself in the Bucoleon Palace. This was one of the two imperial palaces of the city at that time and, along with the Blachernae Palace, it had been identified as the residence of the Frankish Emperor in the city once he had been installed. Consequently, it was difficult to believe that Boniface's actions in occupying the Bucoleon were merely coincidental. It is easy to construe his occupation of the palace as a fairly blatant way of staking his claim for the throne. After all, he had been recognised as the leader of the expedition at the outset. Further, through Renier of Montferrat he had family connections with the Byzantine Empire. He appeared in some respects to be an obvious candidate for the throne.

But Boniface had been inextricably linked with Alexius IV, who had proved such a disappointment to the crusaders although it was they who were responsible for bringing him to power. Once the latter's fortunes changed for the worse, it was inevitable that Boniface's prospects would suffer seriously too. And, in some ways, Boniface had always appeared to be reactive in his actions. He was late to come to the crusade. He did not command the largest element of the army. When the crusade changed direction at Zara, he had not even been present (although he would certainly have known of the plans to attack the city). And in the great land battle outside the walls of Constantinople when Alexius III had attempted to drive away the army, he had not even been given command of the vanguard. This last honour had been awarded to another man, Count Baldwin of Flanders. The Count had been involved in the crusade from the start, and he did command the largest single force in the army. Even now, the Blachernae Palace was held by his brother, Henry.

It was clear – indeed, it had been so for some time – that there were two leading candidates for the throne: Boniface and Baldwin. Some suggested that Dandolo might be a candidate, but he was an old man who probably realised better than most that the position may well be a poisoned chalice. He had no interest in being considered for the role. It would therefore be a straight contest between Boniface and Baldwin.[10]

Both men manoeuvred for position. The key to gaining the throne was the composition of the small electoral caucus that was responsible for adjudicating on the respective claims of the rivals; this would be made up of six Venetian representatives and six from the army. The parliament that was assembled to discuss the position wisely urged both men to respect the rights of the other, cautioning whoever might win the election to be magnanimous and generous towards the loser. Wary of attempts to load the electoral body in favour of one body or the other, the representatives of the army would, it was eventually decided, all be clerics.

On the appointed day, the caucus met at the palace that housed Dandolo. They retired to a chapel, where a holy mass was said so that the representatives might be guided by God to make the correct decision. In this sanctified atmosphere they arrived at their decision. There were, according to Robert of Clari, no dissenters. The electors stepped out of the sanctuary to face the army and inform them of the decision that had been made. Their spokesman was Nivelon, Bishop of Soissons. He quietened the crowd, and announced their decision. 'Lords,' he addressed the crowd, 'we have chosen one whom we ourselves know to be a good man . . . we will name him to you. He is Baldwin of Flanders.'[11]

The crowd roared their assent, with Baldwin's supporters clearly ecstatic. Generously, Boniface of Montferrat stepped forward to offer his congratulations to his rival. However, it was a bitter blow to the hopes of the Marquis who had, at the last hurdle, been robbed of one of the greatest prizes in the world. It was also a significant political decision. It meant that the German Emperor could not rule in both the West and the East – a fact that possibly contributed to the outcome of the election in no small measure. In reality, the composition of the caucus, with so many churchmen involved from regions close to the homelands of Baldwin of Flanders, made the result a formality, and Boniface had probably prepared himself for rejection beforehand. Despite his apparent affability towards Baldwin, it was still a great personal disappointment. Although not exactly sworn enemies from this point on, neither man respected the other. And as events would soon demonstrate, the amiability displayed was cosmetic in the extreme.

Nevertheless, the coronation of the first Emperor of the Latin Kingdom of Byzantium was a splendid affair. On the appointed day,

Baldwin was led by his nobles through the streets of Constantinople to the Holy Church of St Sophia. He was taken into a side chamber, where he was prepared for the ceremony. They dressed him in hose of vermilion samite and shoes that were covered in precious stones. Then they put on a coat and a cloak, and finally a mantle. This latter garment was particularly splendid. It was finished with eagles made of jewels that dazzled in the sunlight, so much so that it seemed to Robert of Clari 'as if the whole mantle were ablaze'. Baldwin was led to the great altar of the church, preceded by Count Hugh of St-Pol carrying the imperial standard and Boniface of Montferrat with the great crown. At the altar, he knelt in front of the bishops. He was disrobed so that he was naked from the waist up and in this suppliant pose he was anointed. Then he was dressed once more. The climax of the ceremony came when the bishops lifted the great crown from the altar and placed it reverently on the head of Baldwin I, Emperor of Byzantium.

Next, they placed on him a jewel that had once belonged to Manuel Comnenus, a jewel of incredible value that Manuel had purchased reputedly for the immense sum of 64,000 marks.[12] Then the newly crowned emperor was led to his throne. No longer suppliant but rather accepting the homage of his new vassals, Baldwin received due reverence from both the crusaders and the Greeks in the church. At the culmination of this dazzling event, Baldwin was escorted in regal procession back to the Bucoleon Palace, where a great feast was held.

Robbed of this marvellous prize, Boniface of Montferrat had not been idle in the interim. The widow of the late Emperor, Isaac, was a woman much renowned for her beauty. Further, as the sister of the King of Hungary, the lady Margaret was an excellent catch indeed. Seeing that she was available, Boniface courted her and it was agreed that they would quickly be married, an event that followed soon after. Boniface then planned to carve out a principality of his own. He had been promised a large amount of land in Asia Minor, but in truth he much preferred the country around Thessalonica. Accordingly, he planned to approach the new Emperor and ask whether he could exchange his lands in Turkey for those on the mainland.

Baldwin could not rest on his laurels. His new Greek subjects needed to be brought to book as quickly as possible. At this moment in time, Baldwin was Emperor only in one city and its immediate environs. If he wished to be Emperor of Byzantium in fact as well as name he needed to go on a progress around his territories and woo his new subjects to him, either by persuasion or, if necessary, by force. He therefore decided that he must lead his army out once more, this time to ensure that the Greeks would accept him as their sovereign.

There were at this time two former Emperors still alive and within four days' of Constantinople. Alexius III was in the city of Messinopolis. When Murzuphlus had left Constantinople, he had also made his way to Messinopolis. He set up camp outside the city. Envoys were sent into Messinopolis to see if Alexius III and Murzuphlus could reach some kind of rapprochement. Alexius III received his approaches sympathetically. Eventually, Murzuphlus was enticed into the city, where he was invited to a feast with Alexius. His own character should have warned Murzuphlus to be wary of a trap, but he was unwisely off his guard when he accepted the invitation. When he was safely locked inside the palace where Alexius was residing, he was overpowered by his guards. Murzuphlus was thrown to the floor and his eyes were ripped out – a traditional conclusion to the story of would-be usurpers in Byzantium. Murzuphlus was far too dangerous to be allowed to remain as a rival to Alexius III.

Murzuphlus and Alexius remained in the city of Messinopolis and it was to this place that Baldwin headed. The inhabitants of the land through which Baldwin progressed paid homage to their new Emperor with little sign of resistance. Seeing that there was little obvious sign of support for him, Alexius III fled once more, this time from Messinopolis. Murzuphlus also managed to make good his escape. Shortly after they left, the city was surrendered to Baldwin who was, naturally, delighted at the way that the situation had been resolved. It was while they were here that Boniface approached Baldwin to ask for the lands around Thessalonica. This, however, proved problematic. Baldwin explained that the lands so coveted by Boniface had been granted to the Venetians and they were therefore not his to give. Boniface took himself off in a great rage.[13]

The breach was a serious one. This was no mere exchange of words. Boniface took himself away from the camp of Baldwin, and he took with him many important men, such as James of Avesnes, William of Champlitte and most of the German knights in the army. While Baldwin headed for Thessalonica, determined to impose his rule there, Boniface rode with his army to the city of Demotica, which was surrendered to him. Worryingly for Baldwin, some of the Greeks appeared quite happy to throw in their lot with the Marquis, swayed by his marriage to their former Empress.

Baldwin successfully progressed to Thessalonica, gaining the submission of several important cities on the way. Boniface, however, was also not idle. With his army he headed for the city of Adrianople, one of the older and more important cities of the Empire. It was garrisoned by a force left there by Baldwin. It soon became apparent that Boniface planned to take the city, by force if necessary. He set up his tents around the perimeter walls and laid siege to it. Open warfare had broken out between the two leaders of the expedition within months of Constantinople being captured.

Frantic at this turn of events, the garrison commander at Adrianople, one Eustace of Saubruic, sent messengers to the leaders who remained in Constantinople. Indeed, a considerable number of important men had stayed behind in the city. They were shocked and infuriated at the enmity that now existed between Baldwin and Boniface. A parliament was held in the Blachernae Palace; among those present were Dandolo and Count Louis of Blois. At the end of the debate, they asked that that experienced negotiator Villehardouin himself should make his way to the siege of Adrianople and see whether he could placate the two men. The marshal replied that he would do so willingly, and that he would take with him Manasses of l'Isle.

When he heard that Villehardouin was approaching his camp, Boniface rode out to meet him. He greeted him warmly – according to Villehardouin the two were 'on very good terms' – but the marshal reproached him sharply for his actions. He pointed out to the Marquis that he should have taken his grievances to those in Constantinople, who would surely have done all that they could to redress the wrongs. Boniface tried to excuse himself by saying that Baldwin had acted in bad faith towards him, but Villehardouin was, of course, right. The crusaders were newcomers in the region. Their grip on the throne of Byzantium was tenuous in the extreme, and if it were ever to be strengthened it meant that they must show a united front to those whom they would rule. Such an open display of division could only encourage those who did not accept the legitimacy of Baldwin's rule to resist even more strongly. Such a public fall-out could do nothing but harm to the future of the Latin Empire, and it reflected extremely badly on both men.

Suitably chastised by Villehardouin, Boniface said that he was content to put his case before the other leaders in Constantinople. He was prepared to accept the judgement of men such as Dandolo, Conon of Bethune, Louis of Blois and Villehardouin himself, pointing out that none of the men were ill-disposed towards him and 'all of whom knew well what was the covenant made between himself and the emperor'.[14] As a result of these negotiations a truce was agreed and the siege was raised, much to the delight of those present. Boniface then returned to his base at Demotica.

Meanwhile, at Thessalonica Baldwin was incensed when he heard that Boniface had laid siege to Adrianople. His temper was not improved by a serious epidemic that hit his camp, taking the lives of forty knights. He resolved to march on Boniface and punish him for his petulance. As he progressed towards Adrianople, he was met by envoys who told him that a truce had been agreed. There were some within his council who advised that Baldwin should reject the plan that Boniface's complaint should be heard by the leaders in Constantinople. However, Baldwin wisely ignored their exhortations that he should teach the Marquis a lesson and agreed to return to Constantinople so that his clash with Boniface could be sorted out amicably. He had been poorly advised by those who advocated a violent rebuff to Boniface. Their policies were driven by machismo rather than wisdom. The fragile new Empire needed cohesion and cooperation if it were to thrive. Further, Baldwin was not, and never could be, an autocrat. He owed his place to many others, particularly to the Doge and his Venetians, and he could not afford the luxury of haughtily ignoring their views. Such a stance would clearly fail to appreciate the political realities of his position.

The Emperor then fell in with the requests of the envoys who had begged him to return with them to Constantinople. On his return, Baldwin was urged by the other leaders to accept their adjudication in the dispute with Boniface. He agreed to do so. Boniface was then summoned from Demotica. There were some in his entourage who encouraged him to resist conciliation, but the Marquis decided that his most fruitful policy would be one of appeasement. Consequently, he made his way to Constantinople accompanied by one hundred knights. This impressive procession was greeted by Dandolo and Count Louis of Blois, and the arbitration then commenced. At the conclusion of their deliberations, they awarded Thessalonica to Boniface. Effectively, the Marquis' complaints were upheld, a worrying indictment of the political judgement of Baldwin in deciding otherwise in the first instance. Boniface dutifully gave up Demotica to the Emperor and made his way to his new territories to establish his rule.

The Latins then renewed their campaign in a systematic attempt to bring other parts of the Byzantine Empire to accept their suzerainty. Many cities were seized, although it quickly became clear that the process of subduing the Greeks would take an exhausting length of time. One day Thierry, brother of the Count of Loos, was riding through the countryside when he came across a group of refugees in a defile. They were extremely well dressed, making it obvious that the party – a sizeable one – was escorting a person of great importance. In their midst was a man who had clearly been brutally blinded, a man whose thick eyebrows hung heavily over his empty eye sockets. It was none other than Murzuphlus. His escort was quickly overpowered and the usurper Emperor was taken back in triumph to Constantinople.

There was enormous contempt among the Latins for the treacherous behaviour of Murzuphlus against their protégé, Alexius IV. Even though he had been cruelly blinded, there was never the remotest chance of any mercy being shown to Murzuphlus now. No ordinary execution would do for this contemptible man; a special fate was required. In the end, it was decided that the blinded Murzuphlus should be forced to climb the spiral staircase of one of the great columns in the city, and then throw himself off, so that his body would be smashed to pieces on the streets below.[15]

The process of conquest continued. In Asia Minor, a rival dynasty headed by the Byzantines attempted to form a kingdom of its own. It was headed by a Greek noble named Theodore Lascaris. An army led by Peter of Bracieux and Payen of Orleans went out to meet the forces of Lascaris. The two armies clashed on the field of battle at a place called Poemaninon. Although the Latins were, according to Villehardouin, heavily outnumbered, they threw themselves into the fray with their customary abandon and their frenetic efforts terrified the Greeks, who quitted the battlefield, leaving the Franks as victors. Theodore, however, would not surrender so meekly. He raised another army, under the command of his brother Constantine. The Franks had taken possession of the city of Adramittium. Rather than face the uncertainties of a siege, the garrison commander, none other then Henry, brother of the Emperor Baldwin, sallied forth from the city walls. Then there was an intense fight with much hand-to-hand conflict, but once again the Franks were the victors. Constantine Lascaris retreated with his defeated army, and the Franks were left in peace to enjoy the hard-won riches they had gained by their conquests in the region. However, it was not the end of the Lascaris dynasty. It would lick its wounds, and set up the capital of a new Empire at Nicaea from where the eventual overthrow of the Latin Empire of Byzantium would emanate.

Other battles took place all around the Empire. In mainland Greece, Boniface of Montferrat continued to expand his territories. The hostilities were particularly intense around Corinth and the city of Napoli, with the Franks by no means having everything their own way. Meanwhile, William of Champlitte and Geoffrey of Villehardouin set off into the Morea, eventually taking the city of Modon after a tremendous victory against the Greeks. The city of Coron was also conquered and given into the hands of Geoffrey of Villehardouin (nephew of the chronicler, although confusingly for historians he bears the same name). The principality that was carved out here proved to be one of the longest lasting parts of the Latin Empire, and certainly provides one of the few positive features of it.

Yet despite these victories, one threat to the Franks remained. A year previously, during the siege of Constantinople, the well-mannered approaches of Ioanittsa the Bulgarian had been rudely rebuffed. Of all the mistakes of the leaders of the Fourth Crusade, this would prove the most disastrous. It was a particularly stupid act on the part of the Franks. That the man was ruthless was not in doubt, but he was an ally of Pope Innocent himself, having recently changed his allegiance from the Orthodox Church to the Roman Catholic Church.[16] He could have made a tremendous ally for the Franks (although he should never have been trusted completely), but their actions had made of him a bitter enemy.

Ioanittsa made an alliance with some of the Greeks who opposed Baldwin. In Demotica an uprising broke out that took the Franks completely by surprise. The garrison of the citadel was overwhelmed and massacred almost in its entirety. Those who escaped fled from the city to Adrianople. Messengers were despatched, panic-stricken, to Baldwin. The Emperor had recently suffered several personal losses. His wife, Mary, had died a few months previously. The Franks had also just lost Count Hugh of St-Pol, a man of great stature whose demise was keenly felt. Baldwin had few men with him, but he raised a small force to go out and meet the Greeks. He caught up with them at the city of Arcadiopolis, which belonged to the Venetians but had not yet been occupied by them.

They arrived there before dawn. Early in the day, battle was joined. The Franks laid about the enemy with great vigour, their strength in open battle once again obvious for all to see. Many of the Greeks were cut down, and a tremendous victory was won. However, there were not enough Franks to hold the city itself. Indeed, their position was serious. The conquest of the Byzantine Empire was a huge task, and there were simply too few of them to accomplish the feat. They were spreading themselves far too thinly. A much more sensible approach would have been to concentrate their efforts on some key strategic targets, although such a policy allows too little for personal ambition and the needs of great men to carve out their own territories. However, the weaknesses of this piecemeal approach to conquest were clearly demonstrated now. Messengers were sent frantically over the Bosphorus to Henry at Adramittium, telling him simply to abandon his conquests and hurry back to the side of Baldwin.

This was a point of great crisis for the fledgling Emperor and his new kingdom. Villehardouin admits that Baldwin, Dandolo and Count Louis of Blois were greatly troubled by the situation, 'for they saw that they were losing the whole land'. Payen of Orleans and Peter of Bracieux received a similar summons, telling them to rush back across the Straits. Others received the same instruction. The conquests so hard won in Asia Minor were largely given up without a fight. Mere survival was a far greater priority than conquest now.

The Greeks in Adrianople had also rebelled, and those Franks who could had fled the city. Baldwin's desperate efforts to raise an army allowed him to despatch a small force led by Villehardouin towards the city, although as the chronicler himself admits 'these were few enough, seeing that all the land was being lost'. Everywhere, the flames of rebellion were fanned by the hatred of the Greeks for their new masters. At the castle of Stanimac, a Frankish knight, Renier of Trit, held out miraculously despite the fact that he had only fifteen knights. In Constantinople itself, where Baldwin had remained pending the arrival of reinforcements, the Emperor was apoplectic at the length of time it was taking for help to arrive.

However, reinforcements did begin to trickle in. Enough men arrived for Baldwin to decide that he could now set off after Villehardouin. The chronicler wisely criticises the Emperor for this, pointing out that he would have been better placed if he had waited for more men to arrive. In all, there were one hundred and forty knights in the force, which duly linked up with Villehardouin at the castle of Neguise. There, the leaders of the army decided to lay siege to Adrianople.

At daybreak, they set out. To their consternation, they saw the flags of Ioanittsa flying from the ramparts, although he himself was not in Adrianople. The city was 'very strong and very rich and very full of people';[17] it presented an enormous challenge to the Franks. They attacked two gates of the city on 29 March 1205. However, there were just too few of them to provide a serious threat to the defenders. The army was soon joined by the redoubtable Dandolo with another force, but it quickly began to run short of supplies. Then, terrifying news reached them. A large army was heading straight for the Franks, led by none other than Ioanittsa himself.

The Franks were by now tightening the siege, building engines and digging mines. They knew for sure that the arrival of Ioanittsa was imminent when they received news, on 13 April, that his troops were only some 10 miles away. The Bulgarian leader sent a raiding party against the camp of the Franks. It was beaten back but many of the lightly armed men in the camp pursued them. These men were castigated for their actions, as they left themselves wide open to a counter-attack from the Bulgarians which could have decimated them, although on this occasion they escaped from the consequences of their foolhardiness. The leaders gave strict orders that the action must not be repeated in future; the army should stand where it was until told otherwise.[18]

On the morning of 14 April, one year to the day after the final attack on Constantinople, the camp woke early to hear Mass and eat breakfast. Their repast was disturbed by the wild war cries of the Bulgarians charging down on them. They were driven back, and Count Louis of Blois, a man of great experience but apparently little wisdom, charged after them. Many followed him. Inevitably, the Bulgarians counter-attacked, shooting clouds of arrows into the ranks of the crusaders. Count Louis was badly wounded and the fragile confidence of the Franks quickly began to evaporate. His men urged Louis to escape from what was rapidly degenerating into a catastrophe. The proud lord reproached them, stating that 'the Lord God forbid that ever I shall be reproached with flying from the field, and abandoning the emperor'.[19]

Louis paid with his life for his imprudence in charging at the enemy. It is easy to admire the courage of such men, but, unfortunately, it is equally as easy to see the inevitable results of their naïvety. Whether through overconfidence or plain arrogance, the battle was lost. The mêlée soon became a rout. Many of the Franks, totally outnumbered and outmanoeuvred, fled from the field. Their Emperor was not among them. He could have escaped but felt that it was his place to set the example. Thus gloriously did Baldwin hold his ground. The men around him were overwhelmed and he himself was finally captured. He was taken from the battlefield to a distant castle owned by Ioanittsa. He would never taste freedom again.

Within a year the Latin Empire had plunged from the euphoria of victory to a situation in which it appeared to be on the point of premature collapse. The Franks were brave men, but they were not wise. They had done little to win over the Greeks to their side, and without their support the Empire was doomed to fail. They had exacerbated their political naïvety with tactical incompetence. Completely ignoring their plan of battle, which would have ensured a fighting chance of beating back the attacks of Ioanittsa, they had consigned themselves to defeat through an immaturity in conflict of breathtaking proportions. Without an Emperor and with little in the way of an army to call on for its defence, it appeared that the Latin Empire was on the brink of complete destruction.

CHAPTER THIRTEEN

A Kingdom without a King

The flower of Western chivalry lay crushed in the fields outside Adrianople. The forces of Ioanittsa had blown the army away as if it were chaff in the path of a whirlwind. Those that had survived by refusing to be drawn into the trap so neatly laid by the Bulgarians, and so naïvely accepted by the Westerners, in desperation looked for their next move. Not for the first time, they turned for advice to Dandolo. In every sense, the Doge was the elder statesman of the expedition. Time and again, they had turned to him for counsel when they were unsure of their best course of action. No one could deny that the Doge was a proud man, but he was also a sensible individual with a sharp and pragmatic mind. Not for him the futile gesture of glorious defeat on the field of battle. He was no coward and he would not shirk a fight given reasonable odds. Here, however, the odds were so heavily stacked against the crusaders that their chance of survival in open battle would now be incalculably small. Dandolo realised that there was only one way out of the predicament in which they now found themselves. The unthinkable had to be faced. The siege must be raised and what was left of the army must flee towards safety as quickly as possible.

Dandolo, however, was no weak military strategist. If the army were to fly openly from the Bulgarians, then they in turn would seize on what they may well perceive as a sign of panic and turn the reverse into a rout. To run openly was to invite a massive attack from the Bulgarian horsemen, who would find it impossible to resist. The army would be cut to pieces in the process. It was therefore necessary to hide the retreat of the crusaders from them for as long as possible. They made careful plans. There was one other major leader in the camp at the time; once again, it was a stroke of incredible good fortune for all future historians that Geoffrey of Villehardouin, upon whose chronicle so much of our knowledge of these events relies, was right in the middle of crucial events.

Villehardouin and Dandolo decided that Villehardouin would remain in full view of the Bulgarians, his men drawn up in battle array prominently in front of the camp. Meanwhile, Dandolo would return to the camp 'and put heart into the people'.[1] He would tell those there to stay quiet but to be prepared to move as soon as it was dark. Then the army would move as quietly but as quickly as it could, back towards

Constantinople. Effectively, Dandolo hoped to give the army a head start in a race in which the ultimate prize would be survival. Villehardouin would form the rearguard. He would be in for a fraught journey.

Villehardouin acted out his part to perfection, and the aggressive posture of his men served to discourage further attacks on the camp. As soon as the shadows of night fell over Adrianople, the crusaders ran for all they were worth. In their wake, they left most of their possessions. Survival was now all that mattered. The last thing that the army needed was to be impeded by their baggage train. It was a panic-stricken force. One group, led by a knight from Lombardy named Gerard, was so terrified that it moved ahead of the rest of the army and made their way to Constantinople, normally a five-day journey, in two days. When they reached the city, they broke the news of their defeat to the Papal legate, Peter of Capuano. The result was pandemonium. Those who had been left in Constantinople had visions of their city being ransacked once more, this time by the ferocious, barbarian Bulgarian hordes.

Baldwin's imprudence in setting out to face Ioanittsa was amply demonstrated by the fact that there were now 7,000 armed men present in Constantinople. A force of this size, composed of well-armed Western troops, might have proved decisive in battle against the Bulgarians. Now, however, when they heard of the disaster at Adrianople, the fighting spirit of those in Constantinople evaporated. There were five Venetian ships in port at the time. As many as possible of the 7,000 made their way to them, resolved to place as much distance as they could between themselves and the city. Peter of Capuano and Conon of Bethune, who had been left in command of the city, made their way out to the ships, pleading with those on board not to desert the crusade. Their efforts were futile. The ships made sail out of the harbour, setting their course homeward to the West.

Meanwhile, Dandolo's ruse had worked well. The army had managed to dupe the Bulgarians enough to make some progress before their departure was discovered. The Bulgarians attacked the fleeing crusaders but Villehardouin did his job admirably, managing to beat back their frenetic attacks. In the course of their withdrawal, the Franks had been met by reinforcements. Peter of Bracieux and Payen of Orleans had brought their men over from Asia Minor and made their way towards Adrianople, expecting to fortify the Crusaders in their siege of the city. They were horrified when they heard of the loss of Baldwin and so many others. Nevertheless, they quickly made themselves useful. Villehardouin and his troops were exhausted from their efforts to keep the enemy at bay and the additional troops took their place in the rearguard. The impetus this gave to the army proved decisive. With the help of these extra allies, the crusaders at last made their way safely back to the city of Rodosto, where they were admitted by the Greek residents who were obviously intimidated enough even by this decimated force to let them in without resistance.

According to Villehardouin, the force decided that it was safer here than it would be in Constantinople. They sent messengers by sea to those left in the great city, advising them 'not to be anxious about them, for they had escaped, and would repair to the city as soon as they could'.[2] One suspects that the words were for effect only. Reading between the lines in Villehardouin's chronicle, it seems as if many of the crusaders accepted that the city was lost.

The port of Rodosto is not far from Constantinople. Ironically, while the crusaders were seeking respite there, the refugees making their way homeward from Constantinople sailed into the harbour. The delight of those in Rodosto at the arrival of these fresh troops was quickly turned to despair when they heard of their plans to sail back to the West. Once again, there was much pleading with them to change their minds. The Empire was on the point of collapse and the men on board could play a vital role in its future. Without them, all might well be lost. The pleas of Villehardouin and the others fell on deaf ears. At dawn the following day, the fleet upped anchor without those on board even going ashore to tell those in the port that they were determined to go. Understandably, a great deal of criticism was directed at them for their perceived desertion.

Those who remained were soon joined by Henry, the brother of the captured Emperor. He had made all speed to bring as many men as he could over from Asia Minor. He arrived too late to influence the battle at Adrianople. On his way to the city, he had heard from some of the Greeks in the area of the defeat and capture of his brother. Finding out that the army had repaired to Rodosto, he had made his way to the port with great haste. In fact, Henry had with him many Armenians, who had accompanied him from Asia Minor. Nervous of their fate at the hands of vengeful Greeks in the region, who resented the support they had given to the Western troops, they had decided to cross over the Straits and take their chance with Henry. It was a fatal error. In his hurry to reach Rodosto, Henry had left many of them in his wake; unable to keep up, a large number, including many women and children, trailed far behind. Many of these stragglers fell victim to Greeks in the area, who picked them off at will.

On his arrival at Rodosto, Henry was met with a great outpouring of grief, Villehardouin describing how there were 'many tears shed for sorrow by those who had lost their friends'. However, difficult as it was to pick up the pieces from this disastrous turn of events, it was imperative

9. A thirteenth-century siege scene, with a mangonel at the top left (from the Maciejowski Bible).

10. *A twelfth-century illustration of a Mediterranean galley.*

under heavy attack. They had to erect strong palisades to keep out the enemy, and the besiegers quickly became the besieged. Although they had ladders and siege engines with them, they could make little impression on the well-fortified city. At the height of the siege, Peter of Bracieux was hit by a rock from a mangonel and lingered close to death for some time. Fortunately, he recovered, and was carried away on a litter. After some days of the siege, Henry could see that little would be accomplished by prolonging it longer. He therefore brought it to an end and instead started to raid the surrounding countryside.

Meanwhile, Ioanittsa pushed on towards Thessalonica. Boniface was despondent inside the city, ruing the loss of Baldwin, of so many of his friends and indeed of his city of Ceres. However, although the Bulgarians wasted much of the land, the defences of the city intimidated them and dissuaded them from attacking the city. Instead, they pushed on to Phillipopolis. The city had once been the residence of Renier of Trit. It was also home to a strange Christian sect known as the Paulicians. They were not ill disposed to Ioanittsa and had approached him, suggesting that he should take possession of the city. When he did so, Renier had too few men to resist them. He was forced to abandon Phillipopolis, and made his headquarters in the castle of Stanimac instead. Now Ioanittsa took possession of the city, which was meekly surrendered by the residents. Little good did their passivity do them. As soon as he had taken control of the city – which Villehardouin insists was only after a promise to protect the lives of the inhabitants – Ioanittsa sacked it. The archbishop of the city was killed, and some of the leading inhabitants were flayed alive. Others were decapitated and many of those remaining were taken off in chains to live out their lives in slavery. Phillipopolis, described by Villehardouin as 'one of the three finest cities in the empire of Constantinople', was levelled. Its palaces and houses were set aflame, and the towers and walls pulled to the ground; a sad end to a fine city.

The position of the Latin Empire was now perilous indeed. It was not to be improved by another crushing defeat at the hands of Ioanittsa. The Franks had installed a garrison in the city of Rusium, located in the middle of a rich and fertile land. Command of the garrison was given to Thierry of Loos, assisted by Thierry of Tenremonde as Constable. On the night of 30 January 1206 Thierry of Tenremonde set out on a raid accompanied by 120 knights. At first, everything went splendidly. A party of Bulgarians were taken by surprise in a nearby village and many of them were slaughtered. Well satisfied at its success, and the large number of horses it had captured, the raiding party made its way back towards Rusium.

Unbeknown to the raiders, however, the timing of the raid could not have been worse. In a tragic coincidence, on the very night that the raiding party set out, a large Bulgarian force was making its way towards Rusium. This was no mere skirmishing force; it consisted of 7,000 men. They approached the walls of the city but, finding their access barred, turned back. Only 3 miles or so from the city they rode headlong into the returning raiding party. The Franks drew themselves up in tight formation, aiming to avoid the Bulgarians and make their way into the city. As they did so, the Bulgarians fell on the rearguard. The fighting was fierce and the noise deafening, with the shouts of the combatants mingling with the frantic neighing of the horses, many of whom were quickly injured in the battle. The sheer size of the Bulgarian force meant that the rearguard was all too soon swept aside and forced back onto the next squadron of Frankish horse. This squadron in its turn was forced back. The losses of the Franks rapidly escalated.

A well-armed Frankish knight was more than a match for one, or indeed several Bulgarian warriors. In this battle, however, the numerical difference between the two forces was decisive. There was just too great a disparity for the superior fighting skills of the Franks to be made to count. Further, the mêlée rapidly developed into a confused, close-quarters battle in which the Franks could not organise thier cavalry in such a way that they could deploy a charge against the enemy. The Bulgarians pressed home their advantage with vigour, driving great wedges into the Frankish squadrons. The fight between the Franks and the Bulgarians proved to be a horrible mis-match for, as Villehardouin remarks, 'the latter began to slaughter them'.[4] At the conclusion of this massacre, only ten knights managed to fight their way back into Rusium; the rest were either dragged in chains into captivity or lay still, where they had fallen, their life-blood drained from them. Panic-stricken by this reverse, those left in Rusium crept away that very night and made a run across country to the city of Rodosto, abandoning Rusium to its fate.

When new of the disaster at Rusium reached the ears of those in Constantinople they were distraught because, as Villehardouin remarks, 'they thought of a truth that the land was lost'. For his part, Ioanittsa was naturally enough delighted at the progress of his forces. It must have seemed to him that his ambitions to rule in Constantinople were on the very brink of being brought to a glorious reality. Nor was the massacre at Rusium the last of the disasters to befall the Latins. Not only did the Bulgarian tribes support Ioanittsa, but large numbers of Greeks flocked to his side. He had assembled a huge force and most of the country now belonged to him. His very reputation struck fear into the hearts of his enemies. When he moved to attack the city of Arcadiopolis, the

Venetians – who had claimed the city in the division of the Empire – abandoned it without a fight.

Ioanittsa also attacked the important city of Napoli, which was part of the fief of Vernas, a Latin baron who had married Agnes, the sister of the King of France and the former wife of the late Greek Emperor, Alexius II.[5] The garrison was led by a knight named Begue of Fransures. The city was captured; once again, wholesale massacre followed. Begue was seized alive, taken before Ioanittsa and killed on the spot. Vast numbers of the inhabitants were sent into slavery and the city was destroyed. Soon after, Rodosto was brought down, to be sacked with horrific savagery. Yet more towns fell to Ioanittsa: Heraclea, Daonium, Tzurulum. Behind the mighty walls of Constantinople, the Franks looked on in furious frustration, too few to intervene and obstruct the advance of Ioanittsa. Thousands of those captured in this blitzkrieg, Latin and Greek,[6] were massacred or taken in chains to a life of subservience in Bulgaria.

Nothing it seemed could defeat the ambitions of Ioanittsa but history is littered with examples of tyrants whose violent excesses have paved the way to ultimate self-destruction. Ioanittsa's greatest enemy was himself. Large numbers of Greeks had initially given him their support, but when they saw the way that their cities were handled by the Bulgarian king, they quickly perceived that a future empire led by Ioanittsa was a bleak prospect indeed. They had no love whatsoever for the Latins and were by nature inimical to a Western ruler such as Baldwin of Flanders. Yet the situation was so grave that many now decided to bear the unbearable and opted to side with the Latins.

The Greeks made secret approaches to Vernas, whom they hoped would prove sensitive to their advances given his marriage to their former empress. Ambassadors were sent to Vernas offering to make concessions if Henry of Flanders would aid the Greeks. The cities of Demotica and Adrianople, the only Greek cities of note now left in independent hands, would be handed over to the Latins. The Greeks were so desperate that they would even submit themselves to Latin rule. After much discussion and debate, the Latins decided to accept these terms; it would indeed have been an act of the grossest folly if they had done other, as alliance with the Greeks was the only way that they could hope to rule in Byzantium.

It is not known if Ioanittsa was aware of these negotiations. If he was not, the reality of his situation soon began to show itself. He advanced towards Adrianople and Demotica, hoping to lay claim to the cities. As he did so, the Greeks in his army started to slip away, firstly in ones and twos, then by the score as the trickle became a flood. If he was in any doubt as to the way in which the wind was now blowing, it was cruelly shattered by his arrival in front of Adrianople. He asked the Greeks inside the city to surrender it to him. Polite as their response was, it brooked no equivocation. In reply to his demands, they responded civilly but negatively:

> Sir, when we surrendered to you and rebelled against the Franks you promised to protect us in all good faith and keep us in safety. You have not done so but you have rather utterly destroyed Byzantium; and we know full well that you will do to us what you have done to others.[7]

Incensed by their rebuff, Ioanittsa laid siege to the nearby city of Demotica, wasting the countryside around and constructing siege engines in an attempt to batter the recalcitrant Greeks into submission. Frantic messages were despatched to Constantinople, begging the Franks to come to their aid. In truth, there was little that the Latins could be expected to do and there were some in their ranks who urged caution. However, desperate times call for desperate measures and it was decided that Henry of Flanders would assemble such as an army as he could with the depleted numbers available to him and set out to the relief of the Greeks.

While there were assuredly many men in that army who believed that they were embarking on a suicide mission, they were inspired and emboldened by the preaching of the Papal legate, who granted an indulgence to all those who took part in the expedition.[8] The army marched to the city of Selymbria, one of the few cities still in their hands, and stayed there for over a week. Daily, more messages were received urging the Franks to push on to the relief of Adrianople and Demotica. They moved on to the city of Bizye, but no further until even more desperate tidings were received from Demotica. The city walls had been breached in four places, and twice Ioanittsa's men had actually taken portions of the walls before being driven back. If help did not arrive quickly, the city must fall.

For the Franks, it was a question of now or never if they wished to relieve the cities under attack. Common sense dictated that they would have no chance in battle against Ioanittsa's vast numerical superiority but, in truth, desperate measures needed to be adopted if the Franks were to have a future of any sort in Byzantium. There was great debate as to what the Franks should do next. The final decision rested with Henry of Flanders. No doubt praying fervently that he was not about to make the greatest mistake of his life, he announced his plan to the army. They would push on to the relief of Demotica. Henry epitomised the Frankish spirit when he said simply but sincerely: 'Lords, we have come so far that we will be forever shamed if we do not relieve Demotica. Let every man confess and receive communion, and then let us put our army in battle order'.

Only 400 knights remained in the army. They asked the messengers from Adrianople how many men were with Ioanittsa, and received the unwelcome answer that his army consisted of 40,000 men. Undaunted by this disparity, the Franks arrayed themselves in eight battalions and a rearguard and set out for Demotica. Their mission appeared to be hopeless, leading Villehardouin to exclaim that 'no army ever advanced seeking battle so perilously'. Not only were they massively outnumbered, there were also many in their ranks who mistrusted the sincerity of the Greeks' conversion to the Latin cause. Despite their serious reservations, they pushed on.

As they neared Demotica, news reached Ioanittsa of their imminent arrival. He deliberated on his next move. His decision, when he made it, was an incredible one, which at the time seemed to Villehardouin to be nothing less than a miracle. Rather than face the advancing troops, Ioanittsa decided to raise the siege and move away from them. Even today, his decision is bewildering. Perhaps his intelligence was faulty, and he overestimated the size of the force on its way to face him. Possibly, the reputation of the Franks as fighting men still intimidated potential opponents, although this is hard to believe given the constant reverses that Western armies had suffered in the region during the past year. More probably, Ioanittsa's men were itching to return home, having already been absent for some time. It is also likely that Ioanittsa was unnerved by the desertion of the Greeks, which made him unsure of whom he could really trust.

Whatever the reason, there was no doubting that Ioanittsa was gone. As Henry of Flanders approached Adrianople a few days later, the population flocked out to meet him, bearing crosses in a moving procession that made its way through the city gates to welcome him. In a supremely ironic turn of events, the Franks were greeted as liberators. Having received their adulation cordially, Henry resumed the chase after Ioanittsa. They moved on for a while until they reached a castle at Fraim. Incredibly, a bitter dispute broke out among the Franks, the cause of which is unknown but the result of which was the desertion of a sizeable number of men. Fifty knights left the army in this quarrel. In the space of a few days, all that was best and worst in the temperament of the Franks had been displayed. Their bravery in pushing on against Ioanittsa when heavily outnumbered is obvious for all to see; so, sadly, is the myopia of the same knights when petty infighting took precedence over the strategic imperatives of the desperately frail new Empire. As a result of this short-sighted bickering, the pursuit was called off.

Henry then considered his next move. Renier of Trit was still holding out heroically after a siege of thirteen months in the castle of Stanimac, during which time his garrison had been forced to eat its horses to survive. It was therefore decided that a force would be sent to relieve him. Their mission was still perilous as they were forced to cross hostile territory for three days before reaching Stanimac. For his part, Renier of Trit was deeply concerned to see a large force approaching his castle, believing it to be the enemy. Great was his rejoicing then when he saw that it was in fact a relieving force.

They took up residence in a town at the foot of the castle. The discussion quickly moved on to an exchange of news on the war. Rumours had apparently already been circulating in the army that Baldwin of Flanders was now dead. Sadly, Renier of Trit told the troops that he knew for a fact (although Villehardouin does not explain how) that these stories were true. Convinced by his arguments, and with heavy hearts, the barons accepted that their Emperor had died at the hands of Ioanittsa. Shortly after, the relieving force, accompanied by the unconquerable Renier of Trit and his few gallant followers, left Stanimac and rode back to the camp of Henry. Thus, after its glorious defence, the castle of Stanimac was abandoned to the enemy.

The tales of the demise of Baldwin were, it transpired, all too true. According to the Greek chronicler Nicetas Choniates, Ioanittsa was outraged by what he regarded as the treachery of the Greeks. In a fit of pique, he had Baldwin dragged from his prison and had his arms cut off at the elbows and his legs at the knees. Then he was thrown outside to die. It was an unworthy end to a gallant, if unsuccessful Emperor. The story may of course be exaggerated but it fits well enough with what else is known of Ioanittsa. In his rage, Ioanittsa at once demonstrated both the ferocity that made him a conqueror and the inadequacies that would have made him a disaster as an Emperor. The Greeks had seen the error of their ways just in time; however bad Latin rule might be, they would be little more than slaves if Ioanittsa was Emperor.

Thus the first short chapter of the Latin Empire was brought to a close. It was an episode characterised by one disaster after another. It was a miracle that it had survived its first year. Yet the Franks had clung on tenaciously, more by instinct than by design. The future, however, was far from promising. Much hard work and even more luck would be required if the Empire were to live much longer. A new Emperor would soon be crowned, the sixth in three years, an inauspicious record even by Byzantine standards. Many a passionate prayer must have been offered up that God would look on the new incumbent of the throne with greater favour than He had shown his predecessor.

CHAPTER FOURTEEN

The End of the Dream

Henry of Flanders returned to Constantinople as Regent of the Empire. He would soon become more than that. The barons agreed among themselves that he should be crowned the next Emperor. It was the logical choice; Henry had in practice been the head of state for some months. He had been with the crusade from early on, and was a participant in most of the key events that had taken place. He had shown himself to be a strong leader in battle, and had also proved to be adept in affairs of diplomacy and politics. Although Robert of Clari referred to some objections from the Venetians to his election, which were soon overcome,[1] there was no logical alternative to Henry as Emperor. Accordingly, he was confirmed as the new ruler of Byzantium.

He was crowned in St Sophia on 20 August 1206. Villehardouin declaims that he was crowned 'with great joy and great honour', but the novelty of such coronations must surely by now have been wearing a little thin. And the parlous state of the Franks' hold of the Empire was clear for all to see. The only substantial force of Western troops left outside Constantinople and the Frankish territories around Thessalonica was commanded by Vernas, and he had with him only forty knights.

The Franks desperately needed a change in fortunes if they were to survive. So far, after the initial conquest of Constantinople, they had not been blessed with good luck. However, with the appointment of Henry as Emperor, providence was to smile on them. Without a doubt, Henry would prove to be the outstanding Frankish Emperor of the short-lived Latin state of Byzantium. Not only would he be a capable leader in times of war, but he would also show himself to be a true statesman. Of all the Frankish leaders, he understood the realities of survival in the region. He knew that to bully the Greeks would only alienate them. Rather he sought to understand them, and to be sympathetic to their grievances. In so doing, he earned their respect and they were by and large prepared to support him, even though he was a Westerner.

All this, of course, was not foreseen at the time of his coronation. At first, it seemed like business as usual. Hardly had the celebratory cheers of the crowds in Constantinople died down when news came that Ioanittsa had once more invaded the Empire. His target, not for the first time, was Demotica. The city was ill prepared to deny him entry.

Although he avoids outright criticism, Villehardouin hints that Vernas had been lax in his responsibilities. The damage caused by the artillery of Ioanittsa during the previous siege had not been repaired, and the garrison was weak.[2] Consequently, when the Bulgarian king appeared before the city he virtually only had to walk in and take possession. Having captured it easily, he levelled the walls, looted its treasures and took thousands of its citizens into captivity.

Understandably, the people of Adrianople were terrified that a similar fate awaited them. They sent messengers post haste to Henry, begging him to come to their aid. The new Emperor gathered together the strongest army that he could and set off to the relief of the city. Ioanittsa's scouts heard of his coming and reported back to their master. Rather than engage in open battle, the Bulgarian king decided to hold on to what he had already won and retreated before the Emperor.

But he was dilatory in withdrawing. When Henry reached Adrianople, the Greeks there told him that Ioanittsa was only a day's march away. Probably, he was slowed down by the vast array of captives with him. For four days, the Franks chased after them. They came to a city called Veroi, which they took possession of. The surrounding country was well endowed with livestock, and the Franks took their fill. While here, they received information that Ioanittsa was encamped in a valley about 10 miles away. Henry despatched a force composed of some Greeks from Adrianople and Demotica who had accompanied him, bolstered by two battalions of knights, one led by the Emperor's brother, Eustace, and the other by a knight named Macaire of Sainte-Menehould. When the two armies clashed, there was a fierce fight and the Bulgarians were finally routed from the field.

The aftermath of the battle provided a tremendous fillip, both to the Greeks and to the fortunes of Henry. According to Villehardouin, 20,000 captives were freed, men, women and children. Also recovered was a great amount of booty. Apparently, the line of prisoners released stretched for more than 5 miles. Further, when the captives reached Veroi, their rights were punctiliously respected. The freed prisoners were kept apart from the rest of the army, and their possessions were properly guarded.

The recovery of the captives and their treatment afterwards must have provided Henry with a tremendous public relations success. According to Villehardouin, 'not one penny's worth' of the captives' possessions was stolen by the Franks.[3] The next day, Henry returned to Adrianople, well satisfied with his work. He then made his way to Demotica to see if the defences of the city could be patched up. Ioanittsa, however, had made too thorough a job of the destruction. The walls were beyond repair.

While he was here, Henry received a delegation from Boniface of Montferrat in Thessalonica. Boniface had sent a messenger to discuss a proposal with the Emperor. Boniface had a daughter, Agnes, back home in Lombardy – would it not be an excellent idea for Henry to take her as a wife? There were indeed excellent strategic reasons for the match, which would unite the two most powerful Frankish families in Byzantium. Baldwin of Flanders, Henry's late brother, had, of course, not always seen eye to eye with Boniface and, although there was no evidence of any continuing bitterness between the two families, such a marriage alliance would certainly bring their interests closer together. The Emperor thought it an excellent idea, and agreed to the plan. Then, after spending a few more days in the area, he returned to his capital.

But Henry still had many other problems to distract him. Now he had to despatch a force under Peter of Bracieux across to Asia Minor to deal with more attacks from Theodore Lascaris. The truce between the Franks and the Greeks based in Nicaea had broken down. There were frequent battles between the two in the conflict that followed, with both sides suffering losses. However, although the situation was, in Villehardouin's words, 'perilous', the Franks managed to hold their own. Thierry of Loos, who had been given the city of Nicomedia as part of his fief, even made his way into Greek territory and conquered the city (it was still in Greek hands even though it was theoretically 'owned' by Thierry) although it was only a day's march away from Nicaea.

Neither was Boniface of Montferrat idle, rebuilding the devastated city of Seres, the destruction of which by Ioanittsa had caused him so much grief. Soon after Christmas, messengers arrived in Constantinople from the court of Boniface to say that Agnes had now arrived. Accordingly, arrangements were made by Henry to receive her in appropriate style. Geoffrey of Villehardouin and Miles the Brabant were tasked with going out to Abydos to meet her. This they did, finding the lady to be 'very good and fair'. They escorted her into Constantinople in a manner befitting the arrival of a queen.

The couple were married in a splendid ceremony in St Sophia on 4 February 1207. Both wore a crown for the occasion, a very visible statement of their regal status. A great wedding feast was then held in the Palace of Bucoleon at which, no doubt, much wine was consumed and many boisterous oaths of loyalty were sworn. Sadly, after this splendid start the marriage would not be an auspicious one. Agnes soon succumbed to an illness, leaving Henry a widower after a very short married life.

But Henry's domestic difficulties were overshadowed by yet more attacks on his Empire. For some time, the thing most feared by the

Franks was that their meagre resources would be overstretched by having to fight on too many fronts at the same time. Now this became a frightening reality as Ioanittsa entered into an alliance with Theodore Lascaris, meaning that the Franks could look forward to having to deal with attacks both from the north and from across the Bosphorus in Asia Minor. The first attack came from Ioanittsa, who had gathered together another very large force. They overran the country right up to the gates of Constantinople and then turned their attentions once more to Adrianople. Ioanittsa erected thirty-three petraries to batter down the walls. The situation of the defenders was parlous. Apart from the Greeks in the city, there were only ten Frankish knights in situ, led by one Peter of Radinghem.

More frantic messages were despatched to the capital begging for help. It was a terrible situation for Henry. He did not have enough men to intervene effectively. However, it was against his nature to stand idly by and leave the city to what would undoubtedly be an awful fate. He therefore patched together as sizeable a force as he could from his much-depleted resources and prepared to set out towards Adrianople. He also sent word across the Straits to his brother, Eustace, urging him to bring over as many men as possible to assist in the rescue attempt.

Such news was, of course, music to the ears of Theodore Lascaris. As soon as he discovered that the Franks had withdrawn a large part of their forces from Asia Minor he renewed his attacks with great vigour. He set out with a large body of men to lay siege to the castle of Cibotos. It was held by only forty knights and the castle was in a poor state of repair. As such, it would be unable to resist a prolonged siege. At the end of the first day of bitter hand-to-hand fighting only five Frankish knights were unhurt and one, Giles, the nephew of Miles the Brabant, had been killed.

Despite these events, the defenders somehow managed to send a messenger on the short sea crossing to Constantinople. It did not take him long to make his way to the city. Henry had not yet left Constantinople, and the messenger found him eating in the Palace of Blachernae. His story was soon told. The castle of Cibotos was surrounded and the men inside were hugely outnumbered; unless a force was sent out to rescue the garrison at once then there was no hope for them. The Emperor took counsel with the few men left around him, including Conon of Bethune and Villehardouin. The talking was short and to the point. Quickly they agreed that they must attempt to rescue their men at Cibotos. Word spread rapidly throughout the harbour area that as many men as possible were to make their way across the Straits to extricate their trapped colleagues. The docks burst into life, with Venetians and Pisans manning their ships and making them ready for departure as quickly as they could.

There was no time for a proper marshalling of forces. Each leader just laid hold of the first ship that he could and set sail at once with as many men as he had been able to assemble. They rowed through the night, and as the early morning sun warmed the earth the Emperor hove into view of Cibotos. It was a wonderful sight for the garrison, who had not slept a second, fearing at any moment one last effort from the Greek enemy. Henry, however, was still in a perilous position. His full force had not yet caught up with him. He had with him sixteen ships; facing him were sixty Greek galleys.

Henry reasoned inwardly for a few moments. The odds against him were great, but if he delayed then he felt sure that the castle would be lost. To a man of his character, there was no decision to make. Regardless of the consequences, he would attack, saving the castle or perishing in the process. His boldness paid off. The Greeks onshore drew up their men on the beach to resist any attempt at a landing but their fleet, despite their great numerical superiority, backed away from the enemy; once again, the decline in Byzantine naval fortunes in the past few decades was apparent for all to see. They missed their moment. More ships now arrived to support Henry, and as night fell the Western fleet prepared for battle on the morrow. Their preparations were unnecessary. During the night, the Greeks dragged their fleet ashore and burned their ships. They then withdrew from Cibotos.

It was a heroic effort from the Emperor, yet he could see that the castle was completely indefensible. Accordingly, he took the garrison on board ship, and abandoned Cibotos to the Greeks. He returned to Constantinople and considered whether to push on to Adrianople. His presence was desperately needed. Yet he was torn two ways, conscious that as soon as he left to aid the city more attacks would be launched in Asia Minor. Against his better instincts, he did not move towards Adrianople, where the situation was now critical. Several breaches had been made in the walls of the city, Bulgarian sappers were at work undermining more of the defences, and the persistent bombardment of the petraries added to the damage. The fighting was fierce, with the defenders not giving an inch despite the frenzied attacks of Ioanittsa.

It seemed that the city could not hold out, but the defenders were saved by an unexpected turn of events. Despite the fact that Adrianople appeared to be on the verge of collapse, Ioanittsa raised the siege. The citizens thanked God. Providence had saved them from ruin, or so they believed. The truth was more prosaic. Many of Ioanittsa's army wished to return to their homes – they had been campaigning long enough, they reasoned. Large numbers therefore simply upped camp and went. Simply because of his inability to hold an army together, yet another great prize had been wrenched from the hands of Ioanittsa when he was on the brink of victory.

But such elation that was felt when this news reached Constantinople quickly evaporated. Again, Theodore Lascaris took advantage of the distraction caused by the attack on Adrianople to launch another raid, this time against the city of Skiza. It was garrisoned by Peter of Bracieux, who was forced to defend against both a land attack by Lascaris and an assault from the sea. To add to his problems, the local Greeks had also risen against him, massacring every Latin they could lay hands on. Fourteen ships set out from Constantinople to raise the siege. As they approached the city, astonishingly the enemy fleet once more meekly turned tail and fled. They hurried after the Greek galleys but could not catch them, and after two days of futile pursuit called off the chase and returned to Skiza, having driven the enemy off and saved the city.

From Skiza, the fleet made its way back to Constantinople. Henry now intended to relieve Adrianople at last, but his plans were again thwarted by news that Theodore Lascaris had renewed his attacks in Asia Minor. His target was Nicomedia. Henry was forced, albeit reluctantly, to abandon his plans to march to Adrianople and instead shipped his army over the Bosphorus to the aid of Nicomedia. When Lascaris heard that he was on his way, he abandoned the attack and returned to Nicaea. The city was left in the hands of Thierry of Loos and Henry returned to his capital. But Thierry was careless. Soon after, he was out foraging with a small number of men. He did not exercise due caution. Lascaris was in the area with a much greater force, which fell upon the unsuspecting Franks. Although the Franks fought bravely, they were too few in number and were overwhelmed. Thierry was twice wounded. Unable to fight his way out, he was taken, badly injured in the face and with his very life in the balance.

The small number of Franks who managed to fight their way clear rushed back to Nicomedia with the grave tidings. They placed themselves in the Church of St Sophia, which they had fortified as best they could. Messengers were sent immediately to Henry begging that he send help. The Franks who were in the city had provisions for five days or so, and time was therefore of the essence. Henry, again in the process of preparing to march on Adrianople, was forced to amend his plans and rush troops over to Nicomedia. Lascaris again withdrew when Henry's army was at hand. The Emperor made the most of his time in the region by punishing the local inhabitants who had rebelled against the rule of the Franks. A large number of cattle and many prisoners were taken.

While Henry was encamped in the meadows by Nicomedia, a delegation came to him from Lascaris, offering a truce for two years if, in return, Henry would destroy the fortifications at Skiza and also those erected at the Church of St Sophia in Nicomedia. If he consented to do this, Lascaris would return all the prisoners he held, of whom there were a goodly number after the recent battle. Henry took counsel with his advisors, but, in reality, there was little option. The Franks were short of men. They would be hard-pushed to fight successfully on one front; to do so on two was quite beyond their resources. However heavily it weighed on them, the Franks had no real choice but to avail themselves of the offer. The deal was struck accordingly and the fortifications were duly destroyed and the Frankish prisoners returned.

This at last gave Henry the chance to renew his attempts to march to Adrianople. He reached the city without incident. The inhabitants were delighted to see him, as the city walls were still in an appalling state after their recent battering from the artillery of Ioanittsa. The Emperor and his army camped in the fields around the city. Foraging parties were sent out to find food, of which there was plenty. Many of those who accompanied the Franks in their foraging were poorer inhabitants of Adrianople and eagerly helped themselves to corn, which they loaded onto carts and started to ship back to the city. However, some were careless. The countryside was hilly and wooded, in short a perfect setting for hit and run attacks from Ioanittsa's men. Many were lost partly, it is true, because of the poor guard placed over them, but partly because of their own recklessness.

To counter these attacks, Henry sent out more troops to guard the foragers. Even then, the troops found many of the passes back to Adrianople guarded and had to fight their way through. The foragers eventually arrived back at Adrianople – where large amounts of provisions were handed over to the grateful citizens – but they had paid for these supplies with much bloodshed and not insignificant losses.

Meanwhile, Boniface of Montferrat was making some progress in conquering more land for the empire in his kingdom around Thessalonica. Boniface had not seen Henry for some time, and he now sent word that he considered an audience expedient. The land was teeming with enemies, who, up until now, had prevented the two men from meeting. However, Boniface managed to make his way to Messinopolis, and he suggested that the Emperor do likewise. Henry readily agreed and, leaving the army at Adrianople in the reliable hands of his trusted advisor, Conon of Bethune, he set out with a strong guard towards Messinopolis. The two men were delighted to see each other again. Boniface offered the city to Geoffrey of Villehardouin, the chronicler, who was happy to accept. He also offered homage to his Emperor, and the meeting broke up cordially after two days, with the two leaders agreeing to convene again at Adrianople in October, when they planned to launch a joint attack on Ioanittsa.

The reunion would never take place. By the time the appointed date was reached, Boniface of Montferrat was dead. Only a few days after the meeting with Henry, the Marquis had set out on a raid with a small group of men. He rode into the lands of the Bulgarians. When the natives saw how small his force was, they attacked the rearguard. When the cries of battle reached him, Boniface leapt into action. However, he was careless. He did not have his full armour on. He charged headlong into the mêlée around the troops at his rear, driving the enemy back with his lance. But a freak arrow struck him under the armpit. The wound was a deep one, and bled profusely. Attempts to stem the flow were futile, and it soon became clear that the Marquis had not long left for this world. He soon expired, surrounded by his small group of men, who had formed an impromptu bodyguard around their dying baron. These brave men were overwhelmed and killed.

The Bulgarians were ecstatic at their success. The head of the Marquis was removed and sent to Ioanittsa in triumph. Villehardouin was fulsome in his epitaph for the Marquis describing him, as 'one of the best barons and most liberal, and one of the best knights in the world!'[4] Certainly, although the supreme prize for which he had longed eluded him to the end, he had nevertheless carved out a kingdom for himself in the East to match his lands in Lombardy and the West. His had been a successful and rewarding life, although it never quite attained the heights of glory and achievement that he had wished for himself. He could not be accused of being an underachiever, but, for Boniface, the ultimate accolades of greatness, while so close to hand, had always remained tantalisingly out of reach.

There is reason to surmise that the death of the Marquis was followed not long after by that of another prominent figure in the crusade. Shortly after this incident is related, Geoffrey of Villehardouin's chronicle stops abruptly and without a logical conclusion. The chronicler had been faithful in his recording of these great events and we can only assume that the sudden end to his tale is evidence that Villehardouin himself expired. The debt owed to the chronicler cannot be exaggerated. Through his work, great events that took place centuries ago are brought to life again. It is the fortune of historians that he left as his legacy eye-witness accounts of those events, in which he was so intimately involved. Villehardouin always told his story well and most of what he relates can be viewed as objective and reliable, although on occasion his own personal bias breaks through. His language is not overly elaborate, for he was a practical man, a man of action rather than a thinker. But Villehardouin was an important individual for reasons other than his chronicle. He was a leader of men, a vital figure in the hierarchy of the Frankish Empire, and his loss would leave a gap that would be hard to fill.

It is left to that other chronicler, the man of the rank and file, Robert of Clari, to finish off the story of the early days of the Latin Empire of Byzantium. After the death of Boniface, Ioanittsa marched on Thessalonica. He laid siege to the city. Before long, however, the sweetest of news reached the ears of the Franks defending the city. Ioanittsa was dead. According to Robert of Clari, supernatural influences were at work in his demise. Thessalonica was home to the mortal remains of St Demetrius. According to Robert, the saint would never allow the city to be taken by force, although as the Franks themselves had won it by such means the saint was presumably not impartial in his loyalties. Accordingly, the Saint made his way to the tent of Ioanittsa, where he ran the Bulgarian king through with a spear. It is an attractive story, although a natural death is the more probable reason for the demise of Ioanittsa.[5]

Ioanittsa's death was a great boost to the Franks. Although he was a powerful man, he was ruthless and cruel. To the Franks, he seemed a terrifying barbarian, and indeed to modern eyes he appears little better. He was spiteful and knew or cared little about winning the hearts of the men he hoped to rule. As such, he was doomed to fail in his attempts to take the Empire, although in truth he had at one stage been mightily close to achieving his ambition of sitting on the Imperial throne in Constantinople.

Ioanittsa's nephew, Boris, now took his place. Henry enquired of his advisors as to how he should deal with the new king. He was surprised and at first resistant when they suggest that he ask for the hand of Ioanittsa's daughter in marriage.[6] She was by all accounts beautiful, but she was also, in the eyes of the Emperor, of barbarian stock and therefore quite unsuitable as a consort for the ruler of Byzantium. The barons urged him to reconsider. They were obviously deeply concerned at the state of the Empire. They were proud men, who ordinarily would have shared the prejudices of the Emperor and would have been equally dismissive of marriage to a barbarian. But these were desperate times. If the Empire was to outlive its infancy, convention had to be ignored.

Within a few short years, then, the Latins had started to adopt the ways of the Greeks, the ways of diplomacy and strategic positioning. The hotheads who had set out at the start of the crusade were either dead, in the minority or, by now, painfully aware that martial prowess alone would not suffice. There were indeed more weapons available than spear or sword. If they could not conquer by force of arms, they had to find other ways of co-existing with their immediate neighbours. The arguments of his advisors eventually convinced Henry to fall in with their scheme. A delegation was sent to the Bulgarian king to seek terms for the marriage. Robert tells us that the people wished to kill them when they arrived, but they survived to present their case to Boris.

Boris was pleased to fall in with the plan. Indeed, it was a great feather in his cap to have a cousin as Empress of Byzantium. He sent her to Constantinople, arrayed in great finery and accompanied by many riches, as befitted one who was about to sit on the Imperial throne. Even the horses were draped in vermilion samite, which was so long that it trailed eight feet behind each animal. The Emperor came out to meet his bride, and to welcome her to her city. It is difficult to believe that the inhabitants of the vast metropolis took kindly to having a Bulgarian princess as their new Empress, although they themselves had suffered so much in the past few years that perhaps they were prepared to accept the unthinkable.

Robert's account ends at this point, although in his case it is a structured conclusion which tells us only that he had nothing else that he wished to say. Henry would, it transpired, be a fine Emperor. Under his leadership, the Latin Empire survived and even, to a moderate extent, prospered. There were perhaps two major reasons for this. Firstly, there were the qualities of Henry himself. He proved to be a good Emperor, possessed of the greatest quality required for success in the East, that of tact. Bombastic gestures and autocratic rule would, he knew, be his death warrant. Therefore, he opted for a style of leadership exemplified by sympathetic diplomacy. Nowhere was this more apparent than in his religious policies. There were undoubtedly quite a few Latin zealots who wished to impose the rites and dogma of the Roman Catholic Church on the Greeks. Henry, however, would have none of this, knowing full well that such an imposition of Western mores would ignite a conflagration in his Empire. Henry therefore rebuffed such attempts. Because of this, above all else, the Greek population accepted him as Emperor, which was in itself no mean feat for a Latin.

Secondly, Henry's position was assuredly made more secure by the disunity of those parts of Byzantium that remained outside of Latin rule. The regime of Theodore Lascaris based in Nicaea has already been touched upon, but there was also a Byzantine state set up around Epirus, in north-western Greece. This was founded by Michael Angelus Ducas, a relative of the same Alexius III who had played such an inglorious part in the events of the Fourth Crusade. This state was a constant menace to the Frankish territories that had been established in Greece. A third state was established around Trebizond on the north coast of Asia Minor. Surviving relatives of the Comnenus dynasty set it up. Its geographical isolation made it appear peripheral to the affairs of Constantinople, but ironically there was in this a real advantage for the dynasty. Because it was remote from the centre of affairs, it managed to outlive even Constantinople, not falling to the Ottoman Turks until some years after the city itself did.

The lack of one recognised leader among those Greeks who opposed Latin rule (of whom there were many) meant that, despite having enemies surrounding its borders, the Latin Empire was not threatened with imminent catastrophe. However, matters did take a turn for the worse when the Latin Emperor, Henry of Flanders died prematurely at the age of forty in 1216. His successors were not of the same stamp, and the Latin Empire gradually but inevitably declined. It lived on for a few decades, largely because its Greek opponents could still not unite behind one leader. However, all this changed when Theodore Lascaris' successor, John III Vatatzes, defeated the ruler of Epirus, Theodore Ducas, in battle. Constantinople was encircled by the Greeks who, crucially, were led by one man. The Latin Empire did not immediately fall even then. Vatatzes died in 1254, with Constantinople still in the hands of the Franks. His son, Theodore II Lascaris, reigned for only four years and was then replaced by a child, John IV. The regency of the kingdom was assumed by Michael Paleologus, who soon took the throne on a permanent basis.

To Paleologus fell the crowning glory of the Byzantine revival. He headed the army that entered the ancient capital of the Empire in triumph. The city of Constantine returned to Byzantine hands once more, and a Greek again sat on the Imperial throne. But he succeeded to an empire that was in a state of abject poverty. Deprivation was apparent everywhere in Constantinople. The Imperial treasury was empty, denuded of its resources by the Franks' ever more desperate attempts to stave off imminent catastrophe. The last Latin Emperor, Baldwin II, fled ignominiously to Italy. Soon after the city's fall, Michael Paleologus was crowned as Emperor. With him were his Genoese allies. Relationships between Genoa and Venice had been frosty for some time. Among many other things, the two states had argued and fought bitterly over the island of Crete, which had been handed to the Venetians after the sack of Constantinople. They were still fighting bitterly in the increasingly irrelevant rump Christian state of Outremer. It was a sweet moment of triumph and revenge for the Genoese over their despised Venetian enemies. Not long after the coronation of Paleologus as the Emperor Michael VIII, the deposed Emperor, John IV, still a boy, had his eyes torn out. Some things in Byzantium never seemed to change.

The Greek Empire, however, was living on borrowed time. After nearly a thousand years as the protector of Greek and Roman heritage, it was exhausted. While it declined, new enemies appeared, vital, strong and acquisitive. For another two hundred years the Empire staggered on from one crisis to the next, its lands swallowed up by the advancing, irrepressible tide of Ottoman conquest. Soon the Empire had disintegrated almost completely, until Constantinople itself was all that remained, a tiny island surrounded by territory wrenched from the Greeks by the Turks. Then, on 29 May 1453, Ottoman cannons reduced the fortifications of Constantinople to rubble. Hordes of ferocious Turks, hungry for plunder, poured through the breaches and overwhelmed the defenders. The last Greek Emperor, Constantine XI, died a hero, struck down by Turkish scimitars as he fought to the last on the streets of his city, an example that his much less valiant predecessors, Alexius III and Murzuphlus, would have done well to follow. With the passing of the city, antiquity came to an end. Already, in Italy, the full flowering of the Renaissance was not far away. A new classicism was about to be born.

To what extent can the events of the Fourth Crusade be held responsible for the demise of the Byzantine Empire? In truth, probably not greatly. The very fact that the Fourth Crusade succeeded in taking the impregnable city of Constantinople speaks volumes for the decline in the condition of Byzantium that was already existent at the beginning of the thirteenth century. The health of the ancient Empire had been deteriorating for some time. The disastrous outcome of the Battle of Manzikert laid the foundations for the ultimate destruction of Byzantium, as it opened up Asia Minor to the invasions of the Turks. The loss of Asia Minor, its vast reserves of manpower and richness of agricultural produce (not for nothing was the region known as 'the granary of the Empire'), was a blow from which Byzantium never recovered. Reverses such as that suffered at Myriocephalum only reinforced the perception that Byzantium was terminally ill.

Of course, the Greeks added to their troubles by their incessant internal infighting, as well as the increasing autonomy of many of the provinces, so well evidenced by the fact that the Byzantine Empire managed to live on even when Constantinople fell to the Franks. A succession of weak Emperors at the close of the twelfth century completed the process of accelerating the decline of Byzantine power, and set the tone for the conditions which were so conducive to a Western victory in the Fourth Crusade.

Nevertheless, the Franks vision was faulty. The Byzantine Empire should have been supported by the West, not torn apart by it. Byzantium was the bulwark that protected the West against increasing incursions from the East, from hostile elements such as the Mongols and, ultimately, the Ottoman Turks. It is, of course, the gift of hindsight that enables us to see this. At the time of the Fourth Crusade, the Ottoman Turks were not perceived as a force so powerful that their invasion of Europe would only be arrested at the gates of Vienna. We should not therefore judge the Franks too harshly for lacking the vision to see that the Greeks, a people who they had often been told were a heretic race, were fundamental to the future defence of Christendom. Rather, we should reflect on the demise of a great civilisation, the timeless Empire of Byzantium that stretched back two thousand years to the birth of Ancient Greece and its glories, and ponder deeply that nothing, however permanent it might seem at the time, lasts forever.

CHAPTER FIFTEEN

The Diversion Debate

No sooner had the Fourth Crusade taken Constantinople than a great debate commenced about how it had arrived there in the first instance. At the time, there was widespread satisfaction in Western Europe at the outcome of the crusade, although there were some murmurings at the manner of the sack of Constantinople. Within a few short years however apologists for Pope Innocent III were blaming Boniface of Montferrat and the Venetians for the diversion of the expedition, obviously nervous at some aspects, at least, of the outcome. But these debates were nothing compared to what happened much later. In the nineteenth century particularly, historians started to expound a variety of views on the diversion. At times, the debate was as intense, as divided and as heated as virtually anything that happened to the crusade. Historians took sides, often on nationalistic grounds, blaming one party or another, or offering the view that what happened at Constantinople was nobody's 'fault' but was merely the result of a number of accidents and coincidences.

So heated did the arguments become, with so many permutations and theories offered, that some leading historians threw up their hands in horror and did their utmost to dissuade others from lending their own particular perspective to the debate. One of them, Achille Luchaire, was blunt in his opinion, stating that 'historical science has something better to do than to discuss indefinitely an insoluble problem'. Luchaire was an outstanding historian but perhaps less of a judge of human nature. The curiosity of humanity demands that we seek for answers to great events. Above all else, mankind is irresistibly attracted to a conspiracy theory.

And it is just as well for an understanding of history that this is the case. In our search for answers, we find a greater understanding of events. We do not find truth – that is too much to ask for incidents that happened so long ago, and more often than not there are too many conflicting factors involved to allow the luxury of simplistic black and white views of what happened. But we do find elucidation.

To understand more adequately what happened to the Fourth Crusade, we need to look at the key players in its tumultuous events, individually and collectively. It is my contention that many individuals and parties contributed in part to the diversion. To identify individuals as being solely responsible is to miss the essential point; that the Church, the

Venetians, Boniface of Montferrat and Philip of Swabia, the Byzantines and, of course, the body of the crusade itself, all took a hand in the course of events. To blame one party in isolation of the others is to ignore a regular lesson of history; that events are shaped by a variety of contingencies, and do not take place in isolation of other great events or, indeed, historical trends.

People were not slow to blame the Church and, more specifically, Pope Innocent III for the diversion. The Greeks were particularly quick to point the finger at the pontiff. To them, the diversion was nothing more than a not very subtle attempt to enforce the reunion of the Latin and Orthodox Churches. It is a known fact that the young Alexius did in fact visit Pope Innocent III in an attempt to persuade the pontiff to support him in his claim for the throne before the crusade set out. Indeed, Innocent wrote to Alexius III, telling him of the young man's visit. The letter is a classic example of political language; diplomatic and non-committal but with subtle undercurrents. The tone of Innocent is punctiliously neutral, but it is possible to read some veiled threats behind the pretty phrases. Innocent says that the young Alexius presented 'a serious complaint' to the Papal court. Worryingly for the current incumbent of the Byzantine throne, Alexius III, Innocent does not say that he found those complaints to be unjustified. Rather he points out that Philip of Swabia offered his support and mentions that the young Alexius 'wished to honour the sacrosanct Roman Church in every way within his power'.[1]

The timing of this letter is important. It was written as part of an ongoing correspondence between Alexius III and Innocent during which the pontiff had been trying his utmost to bring the two Churches back together. It is possible to construe a hidden meaning behind the words of Innocent; that, if the young Alexius is prepared to accept the suzerainty of the Latin Church, then Alexius III should do likewise. It is reading too much into the letter to draw the conclusion that Innocent has tacitly offered his support to the young Alexius, but it does evidence something that is well enough accepted generally – that Innocent was a skilled political manipulator who would not hesitate to employ any tools at his disposal to bring about his political objectives.

Certainly rumours abounded soon after the fall of Constantinople that the Pope had actively sanctioned the diversion. So fierce did this debate become that the anonymous supporter of Innocent III who wrote the *Gesta Innocentii* was quick to implicate the Germans in the plot and exonerate his patron from the events that took place at Constantinople. However, that could not entirely explain away the ambiguous attitude of Innocent towards the taking of Constantinople. He was quick to praise the capture when he first heard of it, only becoming critical of the attack when he heard of the excesses that accompanied the triumph of the Latins. The response of Innocent III to the attack is a good barometer to his thinking on the subject. He initially congratulated the leaders of the crusade because he believed that the events at Constantinople might bring about a reconciliation between the two Churches. However, this naïve notion was disabused when he heard of the manner of the city's capture. It might be difficult to accept that Innocent, who became such a master intriguer during his time as Pope, could so badly miscalculate the effect of the Latin conquest on the already distant possibility of a reconciliation of the Churches of East and West. Yet we should remember that he was, for a pontiff, a young man, in the early years of his reign, and it is easily conceivable that he completely misread the situation. The reality, of course, was that such excesses as accompanied the sack made any such reconciliation, always a remote contingency, an impossibility.

Innocent, of course, remained in the wings of the great events of the Fourth Crusade once the expedition set out. Not so the clerics who accompanied the armies. They played an important role in many of the events. As one example – there are several others – the armies had asked for the guidance of the Papal legates after the unsuccessful attack on Constantinople at the beginning of April 1204. They had received the assurance that the diversion was a legitimate Christian act. In the context of the crusade, such an affirmation has huge significance. Crusaders were not just warriors; they were armed pilgrims. Our concerns at the excesses of the Fourth Crusade should not blind us to the fact that a large proportion of the army had accompanied the expedition because of the spiritual benefits they would receive as a result. Innocent III had promised an extremely generous Papal Indulgence as part of the rewards offered to the crusaders. This was no symbolic gesture. To the Christian warrior, it was a deeply sought-after objective to earn the right to benefit fully from these rewards. A lead from the legates that the crusade was exceeding its authority in attacking Constantinople must have called the enterprise into grave doubt. Villehardouin particularly tells us on plenty of occasions that there was much division in the army; a firm stand from the clerics against continuing the attack might have been decisive.

However, they legitimised the diversion. Indeed, in Villehardouin's account they not only offered tacit support, they actively encouraged the attack. As far as the role of Innocent III is concerned, the Pope was quick to publicly condemn his legate, Peter of Capuano, when he heard of his actions, particularly when he removed from the crusaders the obligation to continue to Jerusalem before they could benefit from the Indulgence offered by the Pope. To the world at large, at least, Innocent was scathing in his attacks.

It is, of course, possible to argue that Innocent's stance was for public posturing only, and that he was willing to sacrifice the reputation of his legate for the objectives of his pontificate by benefiting from the capture of Constantinople while refusing to sanction it too openly. And his record does give some cause for concern. He had already sanctioned a crusade against other Christians on a previous occasion. And he would use it as a crushing weapon against the Cathar heretics in the south of France only a few years later. But he had stated often enough that the only legitimate aim of the crusade was the recovery of Jerusalem. He had been openly campaigning for a crusade for years before Alexius, the young pretender to the throne of Byzantium, had escaped. A great deal of the credibility of his still infant pontificate rested on the success of the crusade. One is forced to ask whether Innocent would invest so much time and effort to call a crusade for the recapture of Jerusalem – and it had been one of the central themes of his pontificate since its beginning – only to legitimise its diversion to Constantinople.

The nature of Innocent the man gives a clue as to what may have happened. From early on, there was an awareness that the crusade might go off course. The diversion to Zara was discussed with Innocent before the crusade even left harbour at Venice. Innocent was quick to stamp his authority on the crusaders by condemning this plan, and stated that it must not be carried out. Yet a few weeks later, his legate meekly acquiesced to the diversion to Zara. This means that either the legate was a weak man, and as such a poor choice on Innocent's part, or that he had been briefed by his master that the paramount concern of the Pope was to keep the expedition together. Villehardouin himself says often enough that this was the foremost priority of the leaders of the crusade, and it may be that Innocent shared this view. In order to maintain the unity of the crusade, it might be necessary to allow the secular leaders of the expedition some leeway in their actions – but absolutely only on the proviso that the expedition treated Constantinople as a stopping-off point on the way to Jerusalem.

Innocent was a pragmatic man. He had expended much effort in assembling the crusade in the first instance. The lustre of crusading had been tarnished somewhat since the heady euphoria of the First Crusade. Bitter reverses and the consumption of massive resources for minimal gain during the Second and Third Crusades – as well as the many minor expeditions that had taken place – meant that it was difficult to rekindle the enthusiasm of men for the crusading ideal. Recruitment had not been easy – the huge over-estimation of the numbers expected to arrive at Venice was evidence enough of that. The temperament of the expedition was not robust. Therefore it might be necessary to give the crusade some latitude in its actions in order to retain a semblance of unity.

Therefore, at the end of it all, we find Innocent expressing his anger towards his legate, Peter of Capuano, in one thing above all others. The pontiff was furious that his legate had absolved his Crusaders from the obligation to complete the journey to Jerusalem. Innocent might have been willing to tolerate the diversion; in some respects he might even have welcomed it. But it was clear that for him it was a means to an end – it was not an end in itself.

Innocent may have believed that the capture of Constantinople would help to unite the Greek and Latin Churches, but in this he was clearly wrong. His view of events has to be seen for what it was – the perspective of a man hundreds of miles and weeks of travelling away from events. From his distant viewpoint, it was easy enough to believe that the conquest had been welcomed by some of the inhabitants of the city, furious at the treatment of their Greek Emperor, Alexius IV, at the hands of Murzuphlus. When he heard of the full details of the sack, Innocent was intelligent enough to know what it meant. It was a dagger thrust deep in the heart of Innocent's reunification plans. The pontiff knew well enough that a forced reunification, without a degree of consensus from the Greeks, was doomed to perish. From the horrific events of the sack, Innocent knew that the seeds of hatred for the West – which in reality had been always present – would grow into a greater loathing of the Latins than had ever before been present. With the gift of hindsight, we can see that the reunification, which was never likely to happen anyway, was now completely unattainable.

Innocent's role, then, was a reactive one. There is no evidence, other than the accusations of his natural enemies, that he plotted the diversion of the crusade. All his public pronouncements were against it, and we do not have any convincing evidence that his private motives were any different than his declared priorities. It is too much of a leap to move from a position where it is argued that Innocent accepted the diversion as an event over which he had little control to one that he actively connived in. And there is one fact above all others that we should bear in mind. For a century and a half there had been an ongoing struggle between the religious and secular authorities over who should have supremacy. The Fourth Crusade is evidence in its own right that the Pope was now losing this battle. The pontiff was still a key player but the great men of the secular world were not prepared meekly to do his bidding and were becoming ever more difficult to lead in the direction that the Pope wanted them to go. Time and again in the accounts of Villehardouin and Robert of Clari we find the Church retrospectively approving of events, rather than being in the vanguard of their inception. Innocent could not have made the crusade move on Constantinople even if he had wanted to.

That said, the religious aspects of the attack on Constantinople cannot be ignored. It was a city that was, as we have seen, awash with relics. The adoration of relics, and the desire to own them, was at the core of Medieval Christianity, which was in its turn at the core of Medieval life. Many men held a genuine and deeply felt awe of such relics. Why go to Jerusalem when so much of the Holy City's heritage was now in Constantinople? Thus we can read of the enthusiasm with which men like Abbot Martin of Pairis threw themselves into the pillaging of the city, fired up with the prospect of gaining so much religious booty to take back with them to the West. And the relics taken as prizes formed an immense haul, adding enormously to the stock and prestige of places such as Venice or Halberstadt. There were certainly enough men who also believed that the Greeks were schismatics, little more than heretics, and that the city was therefore fair game for an attack by a Christian army.

If we can criticise the Church it is for its inability to offer strong opposition to the diversion. The legate certainly was asked for his view on enough occasions to allow him to speak out against the attack on Constantinople. There was enough dissension within what was after all a Christian expedition assembled ostensibly for religious motives to suggest that a public stand against the diversion might have proved decisive. Therefore, the greatest accusation we can make against the Church with any confidence is that, apart from questioning the moral validity of its stance (and however morally reprehensible it might appear to us, we should remember that the paradigms of the world were vastly different in the thirteenth century than they are now), it sanctioned the progress of the crusade as it headed down a path that would inevitably lead to the final destruction of the ideal of unity of Eastern and Western Christendom. Its inaction brought about the very thing it desired less than any other – the final, irreversible breakdown of relationships between the Greek and Roman Churches.

Early on in the debate, the Papacy's supporters tried to cast the blame elsewhere. The anonymous writer of the *Gesta Innocentii* specifically attributes the diversion to an agreement between the young pretender Alexius, Philip of Swabia and Boniface of Montferrat. Much of the debate has centred on the timing of Alexius' visit to the court of Philip of Swabia. Villehardouin and Robert of Clari occasionally vary on the details of the events; in this case, they are a world apart. Villehardouin has Alexius arriving in Italy only a short while before the crusade diverted to Zara. The pretender to the throne was then summoned by the leaders of the crusaders to Zara to present his case to the army. The decision to ask Alexius to come to meet the crusaders was therefore made while the army was at Zara; the diversion thus began there.

On the other hand, Robert of Clari says that during the discussions of the army at Zara about whether Alexius should be asked to come to them or not, Boniface of Montferrat mentioned that he had seen the pretender 'last Christmas' while he was at the court of Philip of Swabia. This of course gave him much greater opportunity to hatch a plot with Alexius. Unfortunately, with such a substantial difference in timing, we need corroborating evidence to lend credence to one date or the other, and it is in short supply. There is a mention in some records of the time, *The Annals of Cologne*, which appears to suggest that Alexius arrived in Germany some time late in 1201, which would fit in better with Robert of Clari's account. We also have the benefit of the letter that Innocent wrote to Alexius III, describing his visit from the pretender. One of the modern commentators on Byzantine history, Henri Gregoire, builds his case on the fact that in the account Innocent says that Alexius visited him 'formerly' when he could have used the adverb 'recently', implying that the audience with the Pope took place some time before the letter was written, again lending support to Robert's account.

In the debate about the date of Alexius' visit to Philip of Swabia's court there is a great danger that historians have missed the wood for the trees. Much energy has been expended in arguing about the precise timing of this visit, yet the date of this is only half the story. It is one thing to say and even to prove that Alexius arrived in Germany in 1201 (and for every historian who agrees that Robert's account is right, there is another to disagree), but quite another to prove that such a plot took place involving Philip of Swabia and Boniface of Montferrat.

We therefore need to stand back from events a little and examine whatever evidence we have to give us a better insight. Firstly, there is no serious suggestion that the visit to the court of Philip of Swabia did not take place at all. That much is agreed. There is also no doubt that Philip of Swabia, through his connection to Alexius by marriage, was a natural supporter of his claim to the throne. However, Philip had too many problems of his own to lend anything other than nominal support to Alexius. He was involved in a bitter dispute with Otto of Brunswick over his claims to be German Emperor. He could not afford to support Alexius too openly. He was already at odds with Pope Innocent – a dangerous position to be in for an insecure claimant to the throne. Open support for Alexius would alienate him still further. If he had any judgement at all, this is not a situation in which Philip would want to be involved.

Conversely, the Germans had a recent history with the Byzantines that, to say the least, was difficult. Frederick Barbarossa had been on the verge of attacking Constantinople during the journey to the Third Crusade, and relations during the Second Crusade had also been strained for a while. Further, confrontations in Italy and, more recently still, the involvement of the Germans in the affairs of Cyprus – traditionally and, until recently, practically in the Byzantine sphere of influence – had increased the tension. And Boniface of Montferrat was no friend of Byzantium either. His brother, Renier, had died at the hands of the Byzantines. And another brother, Conrad of Montferrat, had, according to the chroniclers, been shabbily treated by them. Therefore, he was a natural enemy of the Greeks.

All this is true. The replacement of the current regime in Byzantium with Alexius would certainly be welcomed by Philip of Swabia, provided that it did not put him on a collision course with Innocent. And Boniface would be very supportive of this venture. However, there is one more factor that must be considered, and that is the position of Boniface as the leader of the crusade. That he came from a family with a prestigious crusading background is beyond dispute. Yet we must not forget that he was not the first choice leader of the expedition, and that when Tibald of Champagne died, he was not even a second or third choice. Further, although he provided significant manpower resources to the crusade, his men were outnumbered by those from Flanders and France. He did not naturally command the support of the majority of the army. Although not exactly a leader in name only, he could not dictate the course of events to the army. In the decisive battle outside Constantinople that resulted in the eventual flight of Alexius III from the city, Boniface was not given command of the vanguard in the battle. That honourable role was given to Baldwin of Flanders. After the demise of Boniface's protégé, Alexius IV, his stock declined. Of course, it must be agreed that this was partly as a result of the close association of his interests with those of Alexius. The failure of Alexius to deliver on the promises made to the crusaders must have weighed heavily against Boniface. Yet the rapid decline of his fortunes at this time demonstrates that his command over the army was never strong.

It would be wrong to speak of the army as one coherent entity. Many different interests were represented within its ranks. The men from Flanders would naturally gravitate towards support of Baldwin. Many men were there because they genuinely desired the spiritual rewards promised from the crusade. As such, they had no particulatr affiliation to Boniface. However, Nicetas Choniates, the Byzantine chronicler, in his interpretation of events is unequivocal – the diversion was the result of a plot with Philip of Swabia. Philip was the liege lord of Boniface, and

Boniface was a loyal subject. Both Robert of Clari and Villehardouin nominate Boniface of Montferrat as the major reason for the diversion. But he was not in a position to dictate to men that they would go where they did not wish to go. In an expedition such as this, no one man can single-handedly change the objectives of the expedition. And it is demonstrably the case that the authority of Boniface was insufficient on its own to force the army to head for Constantinople. The army would not be led where it did not want to be led.

Who, if anybody, was in control of the expedition? When what happened to the Fourth Crusade is closely examined with an objective eye, it is impossible to avoid the conclusion that the party most in control of events were the Venetians. It was they who provided the transportation and, from the moment that the crusaders were completely unable to fulfil their financial obligations to the city, it was they who held the upper hand. However, it requires a substantial leap of faith to go from baldly stating this to asserting that the diversion was entirely the Venetians' responsibility. That they were best placed to direct the course of the crusaders away from the Muslim Levant does not actually prove that they did so.

This has not prevented some historians from maintaining that this was the case. In the nineteenth century, a German historian, Carl Hopf, triumphantly announced to the world that he had come across a treaty that proved decisively that the Venetians had entered into an alliance with the Egyptians. The terms of this treaty stipulated that the Egyptians would offer trading concessions to the Venetians in return for their friendship. Hopf dated the treaty to 13 May 1202. The implication was clear. If this date was genuine, then the Venetians were in league with the Egyptians and never had any intention of taking the crusade to Egypt. Other contemporary historians were quick to seize on Hopf's treatise and for a time it was widely accepted that the diversion of the crusade was a clever Venetian plot. Then, in 1877, a work was published that demolished the contention of Hopf. In an absolutely stunning example of scholarship, drawing on literary sources from all over the Middle East, a French historian, Gabriel Hanatoux, demonstrated that the treaty almost certainly dated to a time around March 1208 – that is to say four years *after* the crusade took Constantinople. Hanatoux's use of his sources still stands as one of the greatest examples of historical detective work on record, and it is absolutely convincing.

However, the treaty should not be completely ignored, even though it clearly post-dates the diversion to Constantinople. It is evidence of something that has always been widely known and accepted by most historians – that is, that relations between Egypt and Venice at this period in history were good. The Venetians had significant trading interests in the country, which would have been seriously jeopardised had they transported the crusade to the country. In all probability, the interests of their nationals in the country would have been badly damaged if they had acted as the agent by which the Christian army descended on Egypt. It is untenable to argue that the Venetians' interests would be advanced by an attack on the country.

There must be serious doubt then that the Venetians would have nominated Egypt as a target for the crusade if they were given a choice. However, they were not given that choice. Villehardouin and the other ambassadors of the crusaders' leaders approached them with a request for the provision of a huge fleet. The Venetians demanded a high price for this, and that price was settled. As far as the Venetians were concerned, the crusade was a commercial transaction. I cannot see that, when the deal was struck, the Venetians had any intention other than fulfilling their part of the bargain to take the crusade to the East. It may not have been agreed that they would take the fleet to Egypt (the view that this was the eventual destination rests anyway primarily on the account of Villehardouin, without too much corroborative evidence), but that they expected to have to take the crusade to the Muslim East when the deal was made is a conclusion that is very difficult to avoid. Otherwise, we are faced with the hypothesis that the Venetians virtually abandoned all other commercial business for a period of over a year on the off-chance that they would subsequently be able to manipulate the crusaders to their own advantage. The Venetians were merchants, probably the most successful mercantile power in the West at that time; that they would risk so much on a hunch that they would subsequently be able to dictate the course of the crusade is a premise which will not stand up to closer analysis.

The Venetians accepted, then, that they would have to transport the crusade to the Muslim East at the outset. Egypt would certainly not be their preferred choice, but they were renowned at playing 'double bluff' with their trading partners. They had quite happily been involved in helping the Christian cause in previous crusades while at the same time providing materials for armaments to the crusaders' Muslim enemies. They were past masters at this particular ploy. If no alternative course of action presented itself they would probably have fulfilled their part of the deal, and shipped the crusade to Egypt, albeit without a great deal of enthusiasm.

They did not need to do so. At a crucial point in time, the young pretender to the Byzantine throne escaped to the West. He had friends in the region. Boniface of Montferrat particularly espoused his cause. And the Venetians were very happy to fall in with the scheme to install him as

Emperor of Byzantium. Recent relations with Byzantium had been poor. Their citizens had been massacred in Constantinople on several occasions in the past twenty years. For centuries a traditional ally of the Greeks, in recent times they had seen their influence decline to the profit of states such as Pisa and Genoa. To this extent, both Boniface and the Venetians were guilty of playing a prominent role in the diversion. Their willingness to divert the crusade was made all too easy by the nature of the treaty between the Venetians and the crusaders.

Everything comes back to the terms of that treaty, and the over-optimistic assumptions that were made when it was entered in to. From the moment that the crusaders committed themselves to paying for a fleet that was far bigger than it needed to be, they were in difficulties. The planning of the leaders of the crusades must have been sketchy in the extreme. Possibly they overestimated from the outset the interest that there was likely to be in the expedition. Certainly they were completely unprepared for the challenges involved in coordinating the journey of so many men so that they were all filtered through Venice. Many men chose to make their own way to the East. For a large number of crusaders, of course, the crusade was a deeply personal experience. It did not require obedience to the whims and dictates of earthly leaders. Their allegiance in this particular quest was to a far higher authority.

When the crusaders gathered at Venice, it was quickly apparent that there was a massive shortfall in numbers. This put the crusaders in a difficult position, but it was also a dreadful situation for the city of Venice, and particularly its octogenarian Doge, Enrico Dandolo, who had invested so much personal credibility in the provision of the fleet for the crusade. We should not forget that the position of Dandolo at this stage must have been a precarious one. For over a year, virtually all the commercial efforts of his city had been directed towards providing the fleet required under the terms of this treaty. Now he was faced with a situation that looked like one of the greatest commercial disasters of all time. If something could not be done to recover something from the débâcle, then the future of the Doge was black indeed. Faced with the awful warning of the fate of Vitale Michiel some thirty years before, Dandolo had to act quickly to protect his own interests, and those of his citizens.

In this respect, the diversion to Zara provided an opportunity to pay off at least part of the debt that the crusaders owed to the Venetians. It might be enough to save Dandolo for now, although his position was still tenuous as he was still gambling – as indeed he was forced to do – on the crusaders making further conquests that would enable them to pay off more of the outstanding sum. I do not think that we will ever prove that at this stage a diversion to Constantinople was planned. Certainly, both

Villehardouin and Robert of Clari, as well as Nicetas Choniates and the letters of Pope Innocent, agree that the young Alexius had made contact with at least some of the crusaders before the expedition sailed. The germ of the idea of a diversion had therefore certainly be planted. How deeply rooted it was must, sadly, remain conjectural.

It was events at Zara, and shortly thereafter, that were crucial to the diversion. Even if the leaders of the expedition wished to move it on to Constantinople, they were not in a position to enforce such a stance on the army. Alexius was introduced to the main leaders of the army following the attack on Zara and, for a time, the discussions that ensued were so complex that the whole expedition threatened to fall apart. It is difficult to underestimate the symbolic significance of the city of Jerusalem to the Medieval Christian mind. The city – the 'navel of the world', as the eleventh-century chronicler Henry the Monk described it – was always placed at the centre of the maps of the world that were produced at the time. The inference is clear; to the Christian, the city was at the heart of everything. Some commentators[2] have argued that, at the time, people were beginning to think differently of the city. The act of pilgrimage was as much about visiting relics as it was about visiting the holy places themselves. As so many relics were now held in Constantinople, then the city was not without religious attractions to the pilgrims.

There is an element of truth in this. Relics indeed played a critical part in Medieval religion. However, care should be taken in taking this theory to extremes, certainly in the context of the early thirteenth century. Many of the pilgrims were still set on making their way to the Holy Sepulchre, and they would not consider their journey complete until they arrived there. Jerusalem was still a place with a mystical aura that could inspire the pilgrim like no other, the place where Christ Himself had suffered and died and founded the faith that had inspired so many to make the journey.[3] That Constantinople was an unacceptable second choice to many is evidenced by Villehardouin, more or less explicitly. The chronicler tells us that many of the rank and file were not told that the original destination was Egypt because of the adverse reaction that would ensue. If this is true, how much more unacceptable would be a diversion to a country that was not even peopled by the Muslim enemy? For many of the crusaders, the only acceptable conclusion would be when they arrived at the Holy City itself, and redeemed explicitly the terms of their religious vows, and thereby qualified for the full benefits of Innocent's Indulgence.

The critical period of the crusade occurred when Alexius was introduced to the other leaders after the fall of Zara. Indeed, Villehardouin frankly admits that the arguments at this time were great. Some even deserted, such as Simon de Montfort. Others had made their way straight to Syria. Much debate took place but the ultimate result was that the destination of the crusade was changed to Constantinople.

Even then, this would only be a stopping-off point on the way to the Muslim Levant. Once Alexius had been installed, then the journey could resume. The diversion was made because it suited the interests of both Venice and Boniface of Montferrat for it to be made. Frankly, it also suited the ambitions of some of the leaders of the army. It would help to pay off the enormous debt still owed to Venice. It would additionally provide considerable wealth to the leaders, to whom Alexius in his turn would owe a great debt.

But the crusaders had made two major miscalculations. Firstly, they had assumed that Alexius, as the legitimate heir to the throne, would be welcomed by the people. He was not, partly because he came accompanied by a great number of Franks. And second, the Franks had assumed that the wealth of the city was inexhaustible. In this, too, they were grossly mistaken. Years of misrule had emptied the Treasury disastrously. The agreement that Alexius had entered into with the crusaders was undeliverable. Worse followed when Alexius was deposed and murdered. Now any legitimate claim that the crusaders might have to an interest in the rule of Byzantium was gone. They were faced with a terrible dilemma. Either they meekly gave up everything they had sacrificed so much for so far, or they attempted to enforce their claims by power of arms. The rest, to use a cliché, is history.

Some historians subscribe to the view that the Fourth Crusade veered so wildly off course because of a series of accidents. Certainly, when the Crusade first set out no one expected Baldwin of Flanders to be Emperor of Byzantium. However, this view is too generous. It implies that man has no ability to judge for himself whether a certain course of action in a given set of circumstances is right or wrong. That there was great concern over the diversion within the ranks of the crusade itself is beyond doubt. Too many crusaders went their own way and refused to fall in with the schemes of the leadership. The diversion came about because of a unique series of events that no one could have foreseen at the outset but the end could have been different if men had acted differently. The sack of Constantinople was not an accident. It happened through opportunism. The difference is profound.

Of course, historians tend to talk only of the attack and capture of Constantinople when they talk of the Fourth Crusade. Many crusaders did in fact make their way to the Holy Land. Ironically, their help was not especially needed. The rump Kingdom of Outremer had been living in relative peace with its neighbours for some years and was anxious that this state of affairs continued. There would be no great battles fought against the Saracen enemy, and no glorious reconquest of Jerusalem. The pilgrims that made their way to the Kingdom had nevertheless done their utmost to fulfil their vows.

In the long run, Outremer was anyway doomed. There were simply too few Franks in the Kingdom for it to be viable. A strong enemy could demolish the remnants of the Kingdom at will. Outremer was only surviving on sufferance. The diversion to Constantinople caused nothing but harm for Outremer. Men who might have made their way to the Kingdom in future now made their way to the Latin Empire of Byzantium, depriving Outremer of much needed supplies of manpower. The Crusade therefore worked against virtually objective that it had started out with. It brought the end of Outremer nearer. Rather than bringing the Churches of Rome and Constantinople together, it drove them further apart. And it further weakened a Byzantine Empire that was already terminally sick.

More than a city fell when Constantinople was captured. It was symptomatic of the great confusion in crusading ideals that followed the failure of the Third Crusade. Men no longer knew what to believe. The crusading impetus would live on, long past the end of Outremer itself. But its aims would become ever more confused and less capable of acting as an impetus to men in the future. The great fires that decimated this ancient and venerable city, 'the eye of the world', during the Fourth Crusade summed it up well enough. An Empire was consumed in flames, the conflagration sparked by the very people whose own long term interests would have been best served by supporting the tottering edifice of Byzantium. The idealism of crusading perished along with Constantinople.

The story of the diversion is a complex one. Man is a complicated creature, and history is shaped by a variety of factors, acting in conjunction one with another to create a certain outcome. The sack of Constantinople was not the 'fault' of one single party or another. It happened because an opportunity existed and men were flawed enough to take advantage of it. The tale of the fall of Constantinople is a story of greed, of ambition, of misguided motives, misinterpreted circumstances and the frailties of human nature. As such, it is far from unique in the annals of history.

Notes

INTRODUCTION

1. Sidney R. Packard, *Twelfth Century Europe: an interpretive essay.*

CHAPTER 1

1. His name says it all; translated it means Robert 'the cunning'.
2. As described by William of Apulia, a Norman chronicler of the time, and quoted in E. Hallam (ed.), *Chronicles of the Crusades.*

CHAPTER 2

1. It was the swan-song of the Byzantines in Italy. No further attempt would be made to reconquer lost lands in the Peninsula. Far more pressing problems closer to home would distract their attention.
2. In fact, Frederick Barbarossa would be involved in an extended period of hostility with the Papacy as he sought to recover what he saw as the rights of the German Emperor in Italy.
3. This was not just on xenophobic grounds. Many of the leading families of Byzantium had secured their fortunes by opportunistic marriage treaties. Manuel's

dealings with the West removed a traditional source of profit from them.

CHAPTER 3

1. Alain Decullier in *The Cambridge Illustrated History of the Middle Ages,* ed. R. Fossier, p. 510.
2. Robert of Clari, *The Conquest of Constantinople.*
3. See page 31 of the present work.
4. Letter from Frederick Barbarossa to his son, Henry, dated 16 November 1189.
5. Amalric, King of Cyprus and Jerusalem, would a few years later seek the help of the German Emperor, Henry VI, and become his vassal, firmly placing the island in the German sphere of influence; a move hardly likely to endear the Germans to the Byzantines.

CHAPTER 4

1. From the *Gesta Innocent III* (*The Life of Innocent III*), written anonymously in or around the year 1208.
2. This Frederick might not have been welcomed so much by Innocent if he knew what the

future held for the young child. He would one day lead an expedition to the East and would in fact be crowned Emperor in the Church of the Holy Sepulchre in Jerusalem. Unfortunately, when this event took place, Frederick had been excommunicated by the Pope of the day, Gregory IX – only one violent disagreement among many in the history of Frederick and the Papacy. However, all this was nearly thirty years into the future at this stage in our story.

3. Letter of Innocent III written at Rieti, dated 15 August 1198.

4. This was a very real benefit to the crusader. There are many reported instances of a man's property, and even his family, being abused while he was away on crusade. The protection of the Papacy was a not insignificant consideration.

5. Even during the course of previous crusades, such confused interpretations of Papal policy had occurred, as for example with Peter the Hermit and many other less renowned itinerant preachers during the preaching of the First Crusade. The opportunity for such misunderstandings to occur was, of course, much greater now that more local responsibility was assumed for preaching the Cross. For a good account of the preaching of the Fourth Crusade, see P.J. Cole, *The Preaching of the Crusades*, Chapter 4.

6. It was the first time that such a universal tax had been applied to the Church. Innocent implied that it was a one-off expedient but inevitably it set a precedent that would be frequently followed in the future.

7. It would be entirely wrong to think of the knightly class as one unified whole. There was a huge range of incomes represented within this slightly artificial caste system.

8. The use of ships to transport crusaders was a more expensive, though much safer way of travelling than the land routes. This effectively debarred participation in the crusade to many of the poor who had accompanied earlier crusades.

9. That is not to say that if the opportunity for booty were to present itself men would scrupulously avoid the chance to benefit from it; the events of the Fourth Crusade provide the clearest evidence possible that many of the crusaders were quick to seize opportunities for profit that might come their way.

10. From Innocent III, *Register*, ed. O. Hageneder and A. Haidacher, and quoted in J. and L. Riley-Smith, *The Crusades: Ideal and Reality*, p. 121.

11. Robert of Clari, who also composed a detailed narrative of the crusade, was a knight accompanyinhg the expedition, although he was not a leading figure in the same way as Villehardouin was. He was a vassal of Pierre of Amiens, in the north of France.

12. There were some elements of democracy in Venetian society.

The Doge, who was elected, relied on his Council to give advice. His position was not always secure, as we have already noted with the assassination of Vitale Michiel some years earlier, and he would be well advised to keep the people of Venice on his side.

13. Villehardouin, p. 5.
14. Interestingly, Robert of Clari – who was not present – states that the Venetians originally wanted 100,000 marks for this but Villehardouin, who was of course part of the team of envoys, does not mention this.
15. D. Queller, *The Fourth Crusade.*
16. It would be a mistake to assume that the only pilgrims journeying to the East were those involved in the major crusades that have, rather pretentiously, been given numbers by historians. In between these main expeditions, bands of pilgrims, or even individuals, made their way to the East regularly.
17. Queller estimates that some 450 transports would be needed for an army of the size projected.
18. Villehardouin, p. 7.
19. This was presumably a courtesy only. Given the huge number of ships hired from Venice, it was inconceivable that more transport should be needed.
20. He was never crowned, being assassinated before his coronation took place.
21. We should perhaps be cautious in reading too much into their delight. Subsequent events revolved around flaws in the treaty. As one of its authors,

Villehardouin would be hardly likely, writing in retrospect, to criticize it, although as I have contended earlier he must have been briefed by his masters as to some parameters within which he could negotiate, and he should not take the sole blame for its errors of judgement.

22. His son, Count Tibald V of Champagne, would play a prominent part in later crusades and would also become a poet of some note.
23. Conrad journeyed on to Outremer, where he led the defence of Tyre in the aftermath to the disaster at the Battle of Hattin. The port was one of the few Frankish possessions left, and was the springboard from which a recovery of sorts was launched. As such, he was something of a heroic figure.

CHAPTER 5

1. This is the version given by Nicetas Choniates, a contemporary Byzantine chronicler. His writing is a useful counterbalance to the western view promulgated by Villehardouin and Robert of Clari. He was an important citizen of Constantinople, and his narrative covers a range of events, spanning many years of Byzantine history.
2. This version is given in the *Chronicle of Novgorod*, a Russian account supportive of the Byzantines.

3. Robert of Clari, p. 47.
4. Extracted from the *Gesta Innocentii*, translated by Queller and quoted in his work *The Latin Conquest of Constantinople*, p. 32.
5. Villehardouin, p. 15.
6. Count Hugh of St-Pol, from Picardy in northern France, who was an experienced crusader.
7. There is a small discrepancy between Villehardouin (p. 17), who states that 34,000 marks were outstanding, and Robert of Clari (p. 41), who states that the amount was 36,000 marks. As Villehardouin was closer to the leadership of the expedition, I have assumed that Villehardouin quotes the correct figure.
8. Even with royalty, however, this was far from complete. There were many Englishmen who set out on the Third Crusade, for example, before Richard the Lionheart sailed for the East.
9. Villehardouin writes that half of the men of Venice had been conscripted to join the fleet, the participants being chosen by lot – see p. 39.
10. Even in modern times, with the benefits of improvements in agricultural techniques and control of the Nile by the Aswan dam, over 95 per cent of the population lives in a small band of land a few miles either side of the great river.
11. A strategy that was indeed to be followed by both the Fifth and Sixth Crusades, which both made Egypt their target.

12. Bernard of Clairvaux, as quoted in *Chronicles of the Crusades*, p. 22.
13. Indeed, some historians have asserted that news of the diversion to Egypt had leaked out before the crusaders reached Venice and, as a result, many chose to bypass the army in Venice, thereby partly explaining why there was such a great shortfall in the number of men arriving in the city. However, this must remain speculative.
14. Robert of Clari, p. 43.

CHAPTER 6

1. Robert of Clari, p. 43.
2. For an excellent and comprehensive account of Medieval siege weapons, see J. Bradbury, *The Medieval Siege*, Chapter 9. The job of the two types of machine were similar, but a mangonel hurled large stones while a petrary threw smaller rocks.
3. Mining was one of the most feared assault weapons in this period. The only effective counter-measure was for the defenders to dig their own mines in an attempt to locate the enemy and drive them out. Once a mine had been dug, the roof of the mine was shored up with timbers that were then set alight. As these timbers burnt, the roof of the mine would collapse, bringing down the wall above it.
4. Sadly, Fulk of Neuilly had died before the crusade had even left Venice. Therefore, he did not see the fruits of his exertions.

5. Villehardouin, p. 26.
6. Ironically, the subsequent exploits of Simon, and indeed the other crusaders who went to Syria, helped to prove the point of those who wished to attack Constantinople. The crusaders who arrived in Syria achieved virtually nothing from their exertions.
7. Robert of Clari, p. 59.
8. Villehardouin provides a long list, including Odo of Champlitte, James of Avesnes and Peter of Amiens, as well as many others – see p. 29 of his Chronicle.
9. The reference to the numbers that had left already is a very strong clue as to how worrying and well-established this trend was.
10. Villehardouin, p. 29.
11. Robert of Clari, p. 60.

CHAPTER 7

1. Villehardouin, p. 30.
2. This was the start of a long Western occupation of the island. The Franks were to divide it into three territories, and build many towers and fortresses on the island, many of which still dot the landscape. One hundred and fifty years later, the island – which would become known as Negroponte – would pass to Venetian rule.
3. Villehardouin, p. 30.
4. The island had a thriving silk industry during Byzantine times, and therefore was not without wealth.

5. Guy was an important man, described as a 'great lord of the host' by Villehardouin. Even today, his massive castle – although much damaged during the First World War – still retains an awesome presence that dominates the surrounding land, and gives a clue to the power of its castellan.
6. Villehardouin, p. 31.
7. Ibid.
8. The Bosphorus is very narrow, separating Europe from Asia with a stretch of water less than a mile wide in places.
9. It was generally believed in the West that the Byzantine fleet was a major threat to the expedition. In fact, it had been allowed to decline through the weak rule and myopia of the sub-standard Emperors of the past thirty years. The fleet was a shadow of what it had once been, and would make virtually no contribution to the forthcoming events whatsoever.
10. Significantly, Villehardouin makes no mention of a counter-attack from the Byzantine fleet. It could, of course, have been caught by surprise, although this is hardly credible given the proximity of the crusaders to the city in the days leading up to the passage through the Bosphorus. It is far more likely that the Byzantines were afraid to attack the ships – a revealing insight into the state of the Byzantine navy at this time.
11. Shipbuilding was at an interesting stage of development. Many ships were propelled both by oars and

sail (it should be noted that the galleys oars were not, at this stage, rowed by slaves). However, the steering of the ship relied on steering-oars to control their direction. These worked well if the wind was in a favourable direction, but were much more difficult to use if the wind were adverse. It was not until the development of the stern-rudder later in the thirteenth century that this problem was overcome. At this stage, adverse winds could pose major problems.

12. Muslim reports from the Battle of Arsuf some twenty-five years earlier speak of apparently unharmed crusader knights riding on oblivious, with vast numbers of arrows stuck in their armour which had failed to penetrate.
13. Villehardouin, p. 35.
14. Ibid., p. 37.
15. Knights from Southern Europe typically wore slightly less cumbersome helmets to reflect the difference in climate that could make heavy helmets unbearably uncomfortable. See D. Nicolle, *The Medieval Warfare Source Book*, pp. 134–5.
16. Villehardouin, p. 38.

CHAPTER 8

1. The Medieval day was marked off into three-hourly intervals. The first of them, called prime, was at six o'clock in the morning, with tierce following at nine o'clock.
2. Villehardouin, p. 39.

3. One should not underestimate the advantage given to the crusade by the local knowledge that the Venetians had gained by having a presence in the city for centuries.
4. Robert of Clari describes the Venetians preparations in some detail – see p. 71.
5. Villehardouin, p. 39.
6. So called because Bohemond had stayed there during the First Crusade.
7. Villehardouin, p. 43.
8. Robert of Clari, p. 71.
9. Ibid., p. 75.
10. In fact, relations with his wife – who had frequently been suspected of infidelity – were not good.

CHAPTER 9

1. Villehardouin, p. 45.
2. Once again, one is reminded how close Villehardouin was to the centre of events and how fortunate it is for historians that he chose to commit his memoirs to paper; he was uniquely placed to give a view on many of the key events of the crusade.
3. Villehardouin, p. 46.
4. Ibid., p. 47.
5. Robert of Clari states categorically that the Franks moved out of the city because the Greeks 'were traitors' (p. 80). They took the precaution of leaving one of their number, Pierre of Bracheux, as a resident in the Palace of Blachernae.

6. The Emperor had anyway understandably lost much of what little vitality he had while in captivity. He showed more interest in the predictions of his astrologers than he did in affairs of state.
7. She had enjoyed, if that is the right word, a traumatic married life. She had been married first to the Emperor Alexius II, and then, while little more than a child in her early teens, had been forcibly wed and raped by Andronicus Comnenus after he had killed her husband. It was after he in turn had been savagely executed that she had finally married Branas, who was subsequently bested by Conrad of Montferrat during his time in Constantinople.
8. Villehardouin, p. 50.
9. In fairness to both Isaac and his son, Alexius, there was never any chance that this reunification could take place, and neither attempted to make it happen.
10. There is conflicting evidence as to when this happened. Villehardouin (p. 51) places the event after the great fire that Nicetas Choniates suggests post-dated the pogrom against the Westerners.
11. Such complaints were a constant source of tension between raw crusaders from the West and Christians who had spent some time in the East. The Christian community in Outremer itself lived by and large in peace with the Muslims and traded peacefully with them. They would have dreaded the arrival of new crusaders from the West, who could not accept such tolerance.
12. Villehardouin, p. 53.
13. A choice that was not, I believe, without significance. Conon was renowned for his fiery oratory, not his diplomatic skills. There seems little likelihood that the crusaders were planning to employ subtle persuasion to convince the Emperor to pay off his debts; this was an attempt to bully him to do so.

CHAPTER 10

1. 'Murzuphlus' is a nickname, which approximately translates as 'bushy eyebrows'. This was a reference to his extensive eyebrows, which apparently almost joined over the bridge of his nose. Presumably, the characteristic did nothing to improve his attractiveness.
2. It is said that he never wore the same clothes twice and that he bathed everyday – something of a novelty at the time.
3. Ioanittsa's original reticence in swearing allegiance to Alexius had now led to an open outbreak of hostilities against him.
4. Robert of Clari, p. 82.
5. Ibid., p. 84.
6. Villehardouin (p. 55) says that 'so many of the Greeks had come down to the shore that they were without end and innumerable, and their cries were so great that at seemed as if earth and sea would melt together'.

7. The chroniclers tell conflicting tales of the end of Isaac. Some ascribe his death to natural causes, while others believe that he was murdered by Murzuphlus. The former view seems to me the most likely, simply because Isaac was so peripheral to the affairs of the Empire by this stage anyway; all that an assassin would do would lend some sympathy to this pathetic figure, while if he were left to live his impact on affairs of state would be non-existent.

8. The events of the previous few days had been so haphazard that it is unlikely that Murzuphlus' succession was part of a wider conspiracy, though given his power and personality and the vulnerability of Alexius IV it was surely only a matter of time before one was hatched. Rather, it appears from the evidence that he saw an opportunity from the tumultuous events that were taking place and proceeded to grab it with alacrity.

9. Villehardouin, p. 56.

10. Ibid.

11. Six o'clock in the evening.

12. Robert of Clari, p. 89.

13. Robert of Clari was elated at the loss of the icon, which he ascribed to divine intervention. He reasoned that the Emperor had no right to hold the throne of Constantinople, and therefore no right to take the icon into battle. Its loss was God's judgement on the legitimacy of his reign.

14. This is an interesting insight into the intelligence-gathering resources of the crusaders. It intimates that by no means all those inside the city were opposed to them.

CHAPTER 11

1. In reality, the Venetians were still owed a significant sum by the army, so they would receive a higher proportion than this in practice.

2. The latter palace was in the south of the city, close to St Sophia.

3. Villehardouin, p. 59.

4. The confusion in theological thinking, and the weakness of the clerics with the expedition, becomes more marked as the crusade evolves. The fact that many of the crusaders would not complete the pilgrimage to Jerusalem meant that there must be much doubt whether the conditions required to earn the Papal Indulgence had been fully complied with. No doubt the clerics, driven by expediency, reassured the consciences of any of their flock who asked the question of them.

5. The strong moralistic tone adopted by some critics of the crusade needs to be balanced by a recognition that both parties were capable of employing methods that seem, by modern standards, to be barbaric in the extreme. Any moral judgements made need to take account of the violent times in which these events took place.

6. The name is ironic in the light of this attack by those sworn to

defend Christianity launched on other Christians; it means 'Christ the All-Seeing'.

7. The phrase concerning the extent of the assault comes from Villehardouin (p. 60), who describes the attack as covering an area so wide that it involved 'more than a hundred different places'.

8. Three o'clock in the afternoon.

9. Villehardouin, p. 60.

10. Robert of Clari, p. 94.

11. As one example, the crusaders marched in solemn procession around the walls of Jerusalem during the course of the First Crusade when the initial attack on the city had failed. They were led by the priests, carrying their religious regalia and praying fervently to God. Many other such examples could be quoted.

12. These men were named individually by Robert of Clari. Undoubtedly, there must have been many other unnamed priests who also participated.

13. Robert of Clari, p. 94.

14. Villehardouin, p. 61.

15. One wonders whether even at this stage Baldwin was staking a claim to be elected Emperor by the army by occupying Murzuphlus' tents.

16. Villehardouin, p. 64.

CHAPTER 12

1. Robert of Clari, p. 100.

2. The principal chroniclers who describe the rape of the city are Nicetas Choniates and the Russian chronicler who assembled the *Chronicle of Novgorod.*

3. The four horses overlooking St Mark's Square are copies of the originals, which are now housed inside the basilica.

4. See Robert of Clari, p. 103.

5. The story was related by Gunther of Pairis, in his *Historia,* and is quoted in D. Queller, *The Crusades: Idea and Reality* (pp. 172–3). The actions of Abbot Martin are bizarre, given the fact that at the siege of Zara he had been so horrified at the turn of events that he actually asked to be released from his crusading vows.

6. J. Godfrey, *The Unholy Crusade,* p. 128.

7. Nicetas Choniates, as quoted in A.S. Atiya, *Crusade, Commerce and Culture.*

8. Villehardouin, p. 66. The chronicler is, of course, not strictly accurate in his assertion. The threat of excommunication if the crusaders did not comply with the rules on the division of the booty came from the Pope's representatives and not Innocent himself. The distinction is a subtle one, and would certainly have been lost on most of the crusaders, but the pontiff was furious at the actions of his envoys during the final days leading up to the fall of the city and appears – at least superficially – to have been very embarrassed by their stance.

9. Robert of Clari, p. 101.

10. The Venetians would appoint Thomas Morisini as Patriarch in

line with the terms of the
agreement.

11. Robert of Clari, p. 115.

12. To put the value of the jewel in
context, it is worth recalling that
this amount was three-quarters of
the sum that it cost the crusaders
to hire the entire Venetian fleet
for one year.

13. There are some discrepancies
between the accounts of
Villehardouin and Robert of Clari
at this juncture. Villehardouin
mentions that Boniface had
already previously approached
Baldwin while in Constantinople
and had won his agreement to his
request to take Thessalonica, only
for the Emperor to change his
mind at Messinopolis. No such
prior agreement is mentioned by
Robert – who as he was not a
leader of the expedition would
not, of course, necessarily have
known about it – who has the two
men falling out as soon as
Boniface broached the subject.

14. Villehardouin, p. 75. This
reference to the covenant
between Boniface and Baldwin
further suggests that there was a
prior agreement between the two
to give Thessalonica to Boniface.

15. The fate of Alexius III, who was
also captured, was less grim. He
was sent back to Montferrat.

16. In fact, he was crowned by a Papal
legate.

17. Villehardouin, p. 91.

18. This advice was totally correct.
The history of the crusades is
littered with tales of defeat for the
Franks when their forces had lost
their discipline and charged
wildly at the enemy.

19. Villehardouin, p. 94.

CHAPTER 13

1. Villehardouin, p. 96.

2. Ibid., p. 98.

3. It proved to be an unfortunate
choice of burial place for
Dandolo. So reviled was he by his
Greek enemies that when, half a
century later, a Greek dynasty
recaptured Constantinople, his
bones were disinterred and
thrown to the dogs roaming the
streets of the city.

4. Villehardouin, p. 108.

5. Alexius II was the tragic child
emperor who was displaced and
subsequently murdered by the
much-reviled Andronicus
Comnenus.

6. By definition the Greeks suffered
by far the greatest losses as the
Franks were relatively few in
number, although we should not
forget that significant Latin
populations existed in Byzantium
long before the Fourth Crusade
set out.

7. Villehardouin, p. 113.

8. In itself, this is an interesting
pointer as to the confusion
inherent in the thinking of the
Church, as the legate was
legitimising an attack on a king
who had, only a few years
previously, offered his
subservience to Innocent III, who
for his part was only too eager to
accept it.

CHAPTER 14

1. Robert of Clari, p. 126.
2. Villehardouin, p. 117.
   Villehardouin appears to be a trifle harsh in his implied criticism. It is unclear how Vernas was supposed to garrison both Adrianople and Demotica adequately when he had only forty knights with him.
3. Ibid., p. 119.
4. Ibid., p. 133.
5. This should not imply that the story was doubted by Robert of Clari. He was a true man of his time: such stories of supernatural intervention in the affairs of this world were far from exceptional, and were widely believed.
6. By this time the Emperor was a widower.

CHAPTER 15

1. From Innocent's *Epistolae*, as quoted by Queller in *The Latin Conquest of Constantinople*, p. 31.
2. See, for example, the theories of A. Frolow, a brief synopsis of which is given in Queller, *The Latin Conquest of Constantinople*, pp. 97–100.
3. The counter view to Frolow's arguments was made principally by Paul Alphandery; see Queller, *The Latin Conquest of Constantinople*, p. 101.

Select Bibliography

Primary Sources

The two major works referred to extensively in are those of Villehardouin and Robert of Clari. Page numbers given refer to these editions:

Marzials, F. *Villehardouin and de Joinville: Memoirs of the Crusades*, J.M. Dent & Sons Ltd, London, 1908, repr. 1957

McNeal, E.H. *The Conquest of Constantinople, by Robert of Clari*, Octagon books, repr. 1966

These books are quite old, and the general reader may find the following more accessible, which uses both Robert of Clari's and Villehardouin's texts to relate some of the incidents in the Fourth Crusade:

Hallam, E. (ed.). *Chronicles of the Crusades*, Bramley Books, Godalming, 1996

Brief extracts are also quoted in:

Brundage, J.A. *The Crusades: A Documentary Survey*, Marquette University Press, Milwaukee, repr. 1976

For the acccount of Nicetas Choniates refer to:

Van Dieten, A. *'Historia' of Nicetas Choniates*, 2 vols, Berlin and New York, 1975

The *Chronicle of Novgorod* can be found in:

Mitchell, R., and Forbes, N. *The Chronicle of Novgorod (1016–1471)* in Camden Third Series, London, 1914

The account of Gunther of Pairis can be found in:

Andrea, A.J. (ed.). *The Capture of Constantinople: the 'Hystoria Constantinopolitana' of Gunther of Pairis*, University of Pennsylvania, 1997

More detailed bibliography of the primary sources can be found in Queller's *The Fourth Crusade* (details below).

SECONDARY SOURCES

Several modern works are available that analyse the events of the Fourth Crusade. See especially:

Godfrey, J. *The Unholy Crusade*, Oxford University Press, 1980
Queller, D. *The Fourth Crusade*, Leicester University Press, 1978

There are, of course, a number of broader histories of the crusades. The following selection may be useful to the general reader:

Atiya, A.S. *Crusade, Commerce and Culture*, Oxford University Press, 1962
Bartlett, W.B. *God Wills It!*, Sutton Publishing, Stroud, 1999
Boase, T.S.R. *Kingdoms and Strongholds of the Crusaders*, Thames & Hudson, London, 1971
Erbstosser, M. *The Crusades*, David & Charles, Newton Abbot, 1978
Mayer, H. *The Crusades*, trans. J. Gillingham, Oxford University Press, 1972
Riley-Smith, J. *The Crusades: A Short History*, Athlone Press, London, 1987
Runciman, S. *A History of the Crusades*, Vol. 3, Cambridge University Press, 1954. Reissued by Pelican 1971; this also has an extensive bibliography of primary sources.
Setton, K. (ed.). *A History of the Crusades*, Vol. 2, University of Wisconsin Press, Madison, Milwaukee and London, 1969

There are a large number of books on the diversion theory, although many of them are very old and difficult to find. The following has a synopsis of many of the major theories, as well as a detailed bibliography:

Queller, D. *The Latin Conquest of Constantinople*, John Wiley & Sons, New York, London, Sydney, Toronto, 1971

There is also a useful article by Queller entitled 'A Century of Controversy on the Fourth Crusade' in *Studies in Medieval and Renaissance History*, VI, 1969.

For the military background to the period, the reader could refer to:

Bradbury, J. *The Medieval Siege*, Boydell, Woodbridge, repr. 1998
France, J. *Western Warfare in the Age of the Crusades, 1000–1300*, UCL Press, London, 1999

Kennedy, H. *Crusader Castles*, Cambridge University Press, 1994

Koch, H.W. *Medieval Warfare*, Bison Books, London, 1978

Nicolle, D. *The Medieval Warfare Source Book*, Vol. 1., Arms & Armour Press, London, 1995

For the vital subject of spiritual and philosophical motivations for the crusading movement, all of the following are invaluable:

Brundage, J.A. *Medieval Canon Law and the Crusader*, Madison, Milwaukee and London, 1969

Cole P.J. *The Preaching of the Crusades*, Medieval Academy of America, Cambridge, Mass., 1991

Riley-Smith, J. *What were the Crusades?*, McMillan., London and Basingstoke, 1977

——. 'Crusading as an Act of Love' in *History*, 65, 1980

——, J. and L. *The Crusades: Ideal and Reality*, Edward Arnold, London, 1981

For developments in the Papacy at this time, the following is appropriate:

Tierney, B. *The Crises of Church and State 1050–1300*, University of Toronto Press, 1988

Chivalric developments played a part in the crusade. Useful references may be found in:

Barber, R. *The Knight and Chivalry*, Boydell, Woodbridge, 1974

Keen, M. *Chivalry*, Yale University Press, New Haven and London, 1984

For a general history of Byzantium, a very readable account is found in:

Norwich, J.J. *Byzantium: The Decline and Fall*, 3 vols, London, 1995

There is an edited edition of the above in:

Norwich, J.J. *A Short History of Byzantium*, Viking, London, 1997

For the early wars between Byzantium and the Normans, see:

Norwich, J.J. *The Normans in the South, 1016–1130*, Longmans, London, 1967

Good general background studies of the period may be found in:

Barraclough, G. *Eastern and Western Europe in the Middle Ages*, Thames & Hudson, London, 1970

Bartlett, R. *The Making of Europe*, Allen Lane, The Penguin Press, London, 1993

Fossier, R. (ed.). *The Cambridge Illustrated History of the Middle Ages*, vol. 2, Cambridge University Press, 1997

Holmes, G. *The Oxford Illustrated History of Medieval Europe*, Oxford University Press, repr. 1991

Packard, Sidney R. *Twelfth Century Europe: an interpretative essay*, University of Massachusetts Press, 1973

Southern, R. *The Making of the Middle Ages*, Pimlico, London, republished 1993

For the Eastern Mediterranean at this time, the reader could refer to:

Holt, P.M. *The Age of the Crusades: the Near East from the Eleventh Century to 1517*, Longman, London, 1986

Some discussion on developments in Bulgaria at the time of the crusade may be found in:

Sedlar, J.W. *East Central Europe in the Middle Ages, 1000–1500*, University of Washington Press, Seattle and London, 1994

Finally, economic influences affected the environment of the Eastern Mediterranean significantly during the twelfth and thirteenth centuries, and were also a major factor in the evolution of the crusade. Useful references may be found in:

Goodrich, M. et al. (eds). *Cross-cultural Convergences in the Crusader Period*, see especially chapter 7, Peter Lang, New York and Washington, 1995

Hodgett, G.A.J. *A Social and Economic History of Medieval Europe*, Methuen & Co., London, 1972

Postan, M.M. *Medieval Trade and Finance*, Cambridge University Press, 1973

Index